FAMILY, SELF, AND SOCIETY

Emerging Issues,
Alternatives, and
Interventions,
Second Edition

Edited by

Douglas B. Gutknecht
Edgar W. Butler

UNIVERSITY
PRESS OF
AMERICA

LANHAM • NEW YORK • LONDON

Copyright © 1985 by

University Press of America,® Inc.

4720 Boston Way
Lanham, MD 20706

3 Henrietta Street
London WC2E 8LU England

Printed in the United States of America

British Cataloging in Publication Information Available

Library of Congress Cataloging-in-Publication Data

Main entry under title

Family, self, and society.

  Includes bibliographies.
  1. Family—Addresses, essays, lectures. 2. Family—
United States—Addresses, essays, lectures. 3. Life
style—Addresses, essays, lectures. 4. Family social
work—Addresses, essays, lectures. 5. Family social
work—United States—Addresses, essays, lectures.
I. Gutknecht, Douglas B. II Butler, Edgar W.
HQ734.F24185   1985   306.8'5   85-22784
ISBN: 0-8191-5048-7 (alk. paper)
ISBN: 0-8191-5049-5 (pbk. : alk. paper)

All University Press of America books are produced on acid-free
paper which exceeds the minimum standards set by the National
Historical Publication and Records Commission.

Dedicated to our students, families, and a peaceful world for future generations, and to Cindy and Patty.

ACKNOWLEDGEMENTS

We are indebted to many selfless people who have assisted us in the preparation of this second edition: our colleagues who shared their time, perspective and research with us; our students in courses such as Marriage and the Family, Sociology of the Family, Alternative Lifestyles, Human Sexuality, Family Dynamics and Crisis Counseling, Family and Marital Counseling, who served as our inspiration and critics; all who assisted in research, typing, and manuscript preparation, Joan Noguera, Laurie Mc Laughlin, and Barbara West, Chapman College, Orange; Wanda Clark, Marjorie Souder, Marilyn Dick, and Nancy Rettig, University of California, Riverside. We would like to underscore our appreciation to two excellent journals which deserve our support: <u>Society</u> and <u>Family Coordinator</u> (now <u>Family Relations</u>). Finally, a special thanks to our families and loved ones for their constant encouragement and love.

TABLE OF CONTENTS

ACKNOWLEDGEMENTS   v

PREFACE   xi

SECTION I   1

FAMILY, SELF, AND SOCIETY: MANAGING CHANGE
AND TRANSITIONS - EDGAR W. BUTLER
AND DOUGLAS B. GUTKNECHT

CHAPTER 1   27

MARRIAGE: THE DREAM AND THE REALITY - LUCIANO
L'ABATE AND BESS L. L'ABATE

CHAPTER 2   41

THE GROWTH PERSPECTIVE OF INTERPERSONAL
RELATIONSHIPS: A NEW VISTA - HERBERT A. OTTO

CHAPTER 3   49

INDIVIDUAL AND FAMILY WELL-BEING OVER THE LIFE
COURSE: PRIVATE AND PUBLIC DIMENSIONS -
DOUGLAS B. GUTKNECHT

CHAPTER 4   69

EDUCATION FOR CHOICE: IMPLICATIONS OF
ALTERNATIVES IN LIFESTYLES FOR FAMILY LIFE
EDUCATION - ELEANOR D. MACKLIN

SECTION II   97

PROBLEMS AND ISSUES FACING INDIVIDUALS
AND FAMILIES - DOUGLAS B. GUTKNECHT AND
EDGAR W. BUTLER

CHAPTER 5   109

VIEWING LOVE AND SEXUALITY TODAY AND
TOMORROW - DOUGLAS B. GUTKNECHT AND
EDGAR W. BUTLER

CHAPTER 6   139

SEX AND GENDER ROLES: TOWARD EQUALITY? -
EDGAR W. BUTLER AND DOUGLAS B. GUTKNECHT

CHAPTER 7   155

VOLUNTARY CHILDLESSNESS: SOME NOTES
ON THE DECISION MAKING PROCESS -
PATRICIA THOMAS CRANE

CHAPTER 8   167

THE ONE-CHILD FAMILY: A NEW LIFE-STYLE -
SHARRYL HAWKE AND DAVID KNOX

CHAPTER 9   179

FACT AND FICTION IN MODERN DIVORCE: DIMENSIONS
AND ISSUES - DOUGLAS B. GUTKNECHT AND
BARBARA L. WEST

CHAPTER 10   205

ALCOHOL ABUSE AND THE FAMILY STRUCTURE -
PETER M. NARDI

SECTION III   217

WORK, STRESS AND PERSONAL LIFE:
MANAGING BOUNDARIES AND COORDINATING ROLES -
DOUGLAS B. GUTKNECHT

CHAPTER 11   233

EXPLORING THE IMPACT OF TELEVISION UPON
YOUTH AND FAMILY LIFE: CHALLENGES AND
OPPORTUNITIES - DOUGLAS B. GUTKNECHT

CHAPTER 12   249

HOME COMPUTERS AND THE FAMILY -
KARL P. REITZ

CHAPTER 13   265

THE FAMILY AND THE FIRM: A COEVOLUTIONARY
PERSPECTIVE - ELAINE KEPNER

CHAPTER 14   287

WORK ROLES AS STRESSORS IN CORPORATE
FAMILIES - PATRICIA VOYDANOFF

CHAPTER 15   303

DUAL-CAREER FAMILY STRESS AND COPING:
A LITERATURE REVIEW - DENISE A. SKINNER

SECTION IV   323

COPING WITH FAMILY PROBLEMS AND
CONFLICTS - RICHARD NYBERG AND
DOUGLAS B. GUTKNECHT

CHAPTER 16   327

A FAMILY INTERVENTION: THREE PERSPECTIVES -
JAMES BUCHHOLZ AND RICHARD NYBERG

CHAPTER 17   355

SEEKING FAMILY THERAPY: THE PROCESS
OF ASKING FOR HELP - JANE TOTMAN

PREFACE

Seldom can any work serve all the needs, interests, and intellectual predilections of its intended and eventual readers. Our coverage in the second edition is weighted in the direction of topics of current interest and relevance such as family wellness, the relationship between work and family, computers, and media, etc. Hopefully, we have provided a sense of the complexity, diversity, controversy, and vitality of emerging interests in the field. We believe our book can be used as either a core or supplemental reader in a number of courses including marriage and the family. Many of the articles were written to offer insight into therapeutic and problem solving strategies of use to counselors, community workers, clinicial sociologists, social workers, students, human resource and relations specialists.

OVERVIEW

The second edition of Family, Self and Society has been completely restructured and rewritten to cover emerging issues and trends impacting the modern family, while continuing to cover important traditional topics. The new edition highlights five themes; 1) family prevention and wellness, 2) family stress, work and personal life, 3) the growing influence of media, computers and high technology, 4) the need for all family members to acquire family resource skills, and 5) the process of seeking professional help and therapy.
Section I is devoted to managing change and transitions with the role of wellness or well-being, through traditional and alternative lifestyles. Section II is concerned with family problems and trends including those effecting sexuality, sex roles, childlessness, one child families, divorce and alcohol abuse. Section III explores the topic of the stresses, pressures, and technological trends that mediate work and personal life. Section IV explores information, strategies, and therapeutic assistance that families can learn to utilize in a complex and changing world. An appendix of review, discussion and reflective questions has been added to assist the student to facilitate family problem solving and a more lively, relevant and participative learning experience.

SECTION I

FAMILY, SELF, AND SOCIETY: MANAGING
CHANGE AND TRANSITIONS

Douglas B. Gutknecht, Ph.D.* and
Edgar W. Butler, Ph.D.*

I. INTRODUCTORY ISSUES

Profound changes are occurring in the way Americans view the institutions of marriage and family. One
of the most crucial areas of concern for the viability
of American Society and Democracy concern how we interpret and adapt to the increasingly difficult social
changes that are buffeting our basic social institutions, both public and private. Interpretations of
how different types of families are coping with and
managing changes, stresses, problems and social trends
is the focus of this book. Only by unraveling the
threads of these complex and changing relationships and
their impacts upon the changing family, can we hope to
build healthy individuals and families. No one can
deny that today both the family and the larger socioeconomic system are under extreme pressure to perform
and both require more comprehensive understanding about
their interrelationships and functioning.

Two current, partially accurate, portraits emerge
from the vast number of articles and books on marital
and family life. The first view considers the family
as in a state of crisis, decline, or collapse. The
second view paints the family as merely going through a
natural, inevitable, and historically recurrent set of
changes and transitions. The former view often ignores
the strengths of families and highlights features that
indicate breakdown, whether divorce statistics, family
violence, or alternative lifestyles. The latter view
sometimes mythifies the past and romanticizes the pres-
sent, while ignoring the tremendous pressures that families labor under. The inevitability of change and more
positive view of the role of social conflict in social
life, mixed with both patience and a sense of activism
regarding the possibilities of coping with and managing
change, may still allow a more flexible, humanistic,
and fulfilling family life in the long run. Although
not tied to a nostalgia or a selective historical view
of old fashioned family virtues, we also are not wedded
to a simplistic view of domestic crises. Our view of

1

the need for a resilient family and marital life requires us to enlarge our understanding of how the
public structures impact the family. In addition, we
must focus on strategies and intervention techniques
for anticipating issues and reducing the stresses accompanying rapid social and technological changes in
our modern world. But first, let's review.

II. MARRIAGE AND FAMILY: DEFINITIONS AND CROSS-CULTURAL COMPARISONS

Marriage is a socially legitimate sexual union,
begun with a public announcement, undertaken with some
idea of permanence, and assuming a more or less explicit contract that spells out reciprocal rights and
obligations between spouses and between spouses and any
children they may have (Stephens, 1963:5). From this
perspective, a socially legitimate sexual union means
that the married couple will not come into conflict
with some social or legal norms or be punished for
having sexual intercourse. Thus, a married couple does
not have to be discrete about the fact that they are
having sexual intercourse. Another condition is a
public announcement ranging from a simple announcement
to an elaborate ceremony that includes feasting, fancy
dress, processionals, religious observances, and so
forth. This also implies some idea of permanence; that
is, it is not a one-night or short-term contract and it
will last "til death or divorce do us part." With the
marriage contract, there is an assumption of obligations, which may or may not be specific and formalized.
The marriage contract, whether very formal or only an
assumed understanding between couples, varies among
societies. It spells out reciprocal obligations between spouses and between spouses and children.

The areas associated with this definition are as
follows:

1. Socially Legitimate Sexual Union. Appropriate
   times of socially approved sexual intercourse
   within marriage. In almost every society
   there are certain taboo periods during which
   marital sexual intercourse is not permitted,
   such as during the menstrual cycle and the
   postpartum period. Of course, in our society
   the overtly stated values and norms are that
   sexual intercourse is only permissible when it
   occurs within marriage. In many other societies
   this is not necessarily true and extramarital

sex in some form or another is permitted (Ford and Beach, 1951:113-118).

2. Public Announcement. Virtually all societies have elaborate marriage cermonials which qualify as a public announcement that marriage is about to commence or has commenced.

3. Some Idea of Permanence. The idea of permanence is, of course, a relative one. Stephens cites the Navaho Indians, where only about one woman out of three and one man out of four reach old age with the same spouse; some men had six or seven different wives in succession. Such serial marriage occurs throughout the United States.

4. The Marriage Contract. This is, perhaps, the vaguest of the measures, although generally applicable in our society, overtly or covertly such contracts exist in every society.

The family is here defined as follows:

...a social arrangement based on marriage and the marriage contract, including recognition of the rights and duties of parenthood, common residence for husband, wife, and children, and reciprocal economic obligations between husband and wife (Stephens, 1963:8).

However, there are problems with any definition of the family that attempts to apply to all cultures and situations:

1. Economic Obligations. One of the attributes defining the family is marriage, which we discussed above. A second is reciprocal economic obligations between husband and wife. This is a substantial problem because reciprocal economic obligations are difficult to measure. There are many societies in which husband and wife belong to different economic units. Also there are some societies in which husband and wife do not own property in common. Similarly, at times the nuclear family is often not a separate economic unit, but, instead, a subsidiary of a larger economic unit, most commonly an extended family --multiple generations. Also, the nuclear family may be "split" by having unilineal kin groups; that is, allegiance to parents on each side of the nuclear family. Because of this or other

3

customs, the husband and wife may have little or
no property in common. Finally, in many societies, wives must also do subsistence work and
are partially or wholly self-supporting. Thus,
reciprocal economic obligations in a universal
definition of the family appears to be a questionable criterion.

2. Common Residence. A second defining attribute
   of the family is common residence for husband,
   wife, and children. This also poses problems
   since an earlier study by Murdock (1949) of 125
   societies showed that about one-fourth of them
   were characterized by mother-child households,
   with the father, for at least a good part of the
   time, living in another residence.

3. Rights and Duties of Parenthood. This third
   definitional element has the same problems as
   reciprocal economic obligations since in many instances children live with the father separately
   or with the father in a unilineal fashion; also
   there are substantial numbers of matrilineal
   societies in which father and children belong to
   different kin groups.

There is no known society that clearly and unequivo-
cally does not have a family by his definition. However,
he says that while some come very close to qualifying as
such, there are others that are doubtful, for example,
the Nayars, a Hindu cast group living in southern India.
According to his survey of ethnographic materials in
relationship to the Nayar, they do have a socially
legitimate sexual union, although there is some doubt
whether the marriage begins with a public announcement.
Similarly, the union is not undertaken with some idea
of permanence, and it is doubtful that there is a
marriage contract. Apparently there is no reciprocal
economic obligation between husband and wife, and
similarly, no common residence for husband, wife and
children. The rights and duties of parenthood evidently
do not apply to the father. Similarly, the kibbutzim
of Israel also possess problems insofar as the universal
definition of family is concerned. In the kibbutzim,
marriage is a socially legitimate sexual union, begins
with a public announcement, and is undertaken with some
idea of permanence. However, there is some question
of whether or not there is a definite marriage contract
and there is some question of whether or not there are
economic obligatioans between husband and wife. A common
residence for husband and wife exists separate from the

4

kibbutzim community, but not for children. Similarly, there are few formal rights and duties of parenthood. Thus, there is some question of whether parents and children actually form a family according to the definition outlined by Stephens.

Another doubtful case is Jamaica, where common-law marriage exists as a variant form of mateship. Since it is extremely expensive for a person to get married - a "proper" marriage involves church, wedding fees, special clothes, and other expenses - there are a substantial number of illegal, common-law unions. Some of these are relatively permanent or at least undertaken with the intention of being permanent. Another type of common-law marriage, temporary concubinage, is a result of the itinerant sugar-cane workers and others that move from town to town striking up sexual liaisons. A third common-law pattern is the fatherless family. A woman lives with her children and has a succession of lovers. Sometimes they stay with her for a while in her home, and sometimes they don't even do that. Thus, it appears that there are some exceptions to the criteria that Stephens uses to define marriage and the family. These exceptions are few, although undoubtedly as more ethnographic evidence becomes available, other societies will fall into the doubtful category.

One contemporary approach to the definition of marriage and the family is related to perceptions of the participants (Constantine and Constantine, 1973: 17). From this point of view, marriage is a relationship in which one person sees himself or herself as committed or bonded to another or others in significant ways involving intimacy and assumptions of continuance. Thus, two or more people are married if they perceive themselves as married; that is, to be committed to the relationship. This, of course, is a phenomenological (McLain and Weigert, 1979) approach to marriage. From this point of view, a marriage license, in a legal sense, codifies in some instances what several people already perceive as being a marriage. In other instances, this allows the notion of a family and/or marriage to exist even though according to our current legal code no such family exists. That is, it may exist perceptually, in the minds of individuals who consider themselves involved in a "marriage" or "family." This, according to the Constantines, might enable one to discern whether a son and his girlfriend are "married" or "just living together."

5

There are a number of cross-cultural regularities regarding marriage and the family; among them are the following (Stephens, 1963):

1. Mothers in the same house with young children.

2. There is an almost universal menstrual cycle sexual taboo.

3. Societies with a fairly high percentage of mother-child households require a change of residence for all adolescents or prepubertal boys - that is, the boy does not sleep under the same roof with his mother.

4. Mothers are expected to be married.

5. Marriage is not undertaken beyond the nuclear family.

6. There is recognition of kin ties beyond the nuclear family.

It also appears that women are very rarely more privileged or more powerful than men. Almost universally, tasks such as hunting are done by men, while tasks such as grain grinding and housekeeping are done by women. Men rarely give deference to women unless it is a common man and a noble woman.

II. FAMILY ROLES AND INTERACTION

Within the types of structures of families and households, there are always a variety of positions or statuses. Positions or statuses in the nuclear family consist of wife, husband, and offspring. Of course, in other cultures and societies, both past and present, there are different designations, but in each instance positions and statuses within a kinship or family network existed. Each position or status has a role or roles assigned to it. In the position of wife there are a variety of roles such as maid, cook, mother, housekeeper, sex partner, and so on. "Expectations" and "behavior" are two separate facets of family roles. It is important to make the distinction between role expectations and role behavior, because they may be substantially different. Role expectations can guide behavior, but role behavior may contradict expectations.

6

Positions and roles require interactions or transactions with other persons. Interaction may result in
cooperation or it may result in conflict or other types
of behavior, depending on the fit between expectations
and behavior. That is, persons interacting with each
other, perhaps a wife and husband, may have similar
kinds of expectations for each other, but the behavior
may or may not match the expectations and vice versa.
New roles are constantly added to a given family over
time; some have fallen away or been downplayed. It's
always interesting to try to label various roles that
spouses and family members occupy:

> After a review of family literature, eight roles
> in the positon of spouse, parent, or both were
> identifed: These are: provider, housekeeper,
> child care, child socialization, sexual, recrea-
> tional, therapeutic, and kinship. Traditionally,
> housekeeper, child care and sexual roles have
> been assigned...to the wife...and kinship and
> child socialization roles to both...part of the
> research task is to determine to what extent
> spouses feel that roles should be shared and to
> what extent they are, in practice, shared...(Nye
> and Gecas, 1976: 13).

Members thus define themselves and their places in the
family by their role interactions. It is possible to
see how a family functions by watching these interactions. The members' actions and transactions with one
another tell how they accommodate to one another, the
degree to which they are assimilated into the family,
whether the family operates as an open or closed
system, what boundaries and subsystems exist, and lots
more. For example, questions asked include: Who is
the family spokesman? Are roles established by age,
sex, power, or some other factors? Is what is being
said during public activities supported or contradicted by the family's private behavior? What interactional patterns and boundaries exist and how are they
set up? Are these patterns functional or dysfunctional?

Roles are negotiated and allow family members to
interact by following some standards or rules, both
overt and covert. However, every family member brings
his own unique personality into interaction situations. We each interpret or filter our roles through
our own life experiences. Although the psychologist's
idea of personality indicates we each possess a
domain of recognizable and predictable patterns of
responding to our world, sociologists prefer the word

self because it indicates the importance of flexibility and change in our individualized interactional
patterns. Role analysis allows family members to
reflect about role responsibilities and role performance:

> Along with the normative dimension (what should
> be done or who should do it) and the behavioral
> dimension...we will also consider the degree to
> which individuals are committed to the roles
> (role commitment), the evaluation of their own
> and spouse's role performances (role competence),
> the extent to which they worry about their role
> performance (role strain), the amount of conflict
> which occurs over these roles (role conflict)
> and the outcome of role conflict (role power).
> (Nye and Gecas, 1976:14)

There may be a conflict between the norms of
society, family, and individuals regarding expectations. Thus, there is a need to distinguish between
generalized norms of society and individualized expectations by members within a family. All of the
above, that is, positions, roles, role expectations,
and role behavior, are influenced by social values.
Social values are generally learned orientations
toward life, the specific aspects of which are related to family, children, consumerism, career, security, lifestyle. Values are abstract moral and
ethical ends or purposes worth working towards.

Sociologists, as family researchers and practitioners, are always sensitive to the relationship
between individuals, families, and the larger social
environment which sets the context for learning and
modifying role expectations.

Sociologists define culture as a set of symbols
and ideas such as language, values, beliefs, standards,
and expectations that are both created and transmitted
by societal members. Culture, social roles and institutions like the family, would not be possible without
the ability to use symbols. Culture is the sharing of
common meanings through language. Individuals shape
and reshape cultural values and roles which guide the
ongoing direction of society, social interaction, and
the self.

8

Family Systems

Family members create enduring patterns, assumptions, rules, and expectations through interaction
rituals and ceremonies of communication. Each family
possesses their own unique configuration or system of
assumptions and rules about how to interact within
their own world and how to negotiate with the world
outside the family. Enduring family patterns of
interaction, rules, roles and assumption become identifiable as boundaries for interpretation and interaction, both internally and externally. Each family
system adapts and transacts with other systems. Each
family is a microcosm of the larger society, yet it
is also very, very unique. Families are systems that
make up the larger systems of society. Families,
thus, mirror the strains and contradictions displayed
in the larger social context, while also fighting to
construct a meaningful family identity.

A system, like the family, is a complex network
of interactional patterns between role units and a
specific environmental context. Family role boundaries
separate and define what belongs inside and what
belongs outside the family unit by regulating the
flow of information and activities.

Systems theory addresses inputs and outputs as a
basic part of the framework from which comes many
processes of transformations, depending on family
rules at different levels. The hierarchy of family
rules can change from circular (simple feedback where
members react without higher goals or policies) to
cybernatic control (feedback based upon family rules
rather than any individual decisions, goals or policies) to morphogenesis (which begins to innovatively
or therapeutically question the whole approach to the
system) to reorientation or conversion (which is
fundamental change of the family rule system) (Broderick and Smith, 1979: 115-123).

Kantor and Lehr (1975:116-117) define open or
healthy family systems using such dimensions as family
spaces, rules, alliances and boundaries which frame
family interaction:

> open family boundaries...maximize the potential
> for a joint negotiation of distance.

Clear boundaries, whether rules or role expectations,
allow for optimal patterns of feedback and communica-

9

tion depending upon the changing family situation. Clear boundaries let family members know where they stand and what is expected. Minuchin (1974:54) argues that boundaries "must be defined well enough to allow subsystem members to carry out their functions without undue interference."

Key boundaries exist between each member of the family (self) and between family subsystems (marital, sibling, parental). Healthy families have fluid and adaptable systems, dynamic interaction, and clear boundaries based upon mutual respect, closeness and open communication. Freedom and flexibility to adapt to changing internal and external circumstances is the key.

A family is always subject to inner pressures brought about by changes in its members and subsystems, as well as external pressures to accommodate to significant social institutions. Some families, under stress to change, become increasingly rigid in their transactional patterns and boundaries, resisting any exploration of alternative ways of interacting. Such families become either enmeshed (Minuchin, 1974)--they are too involved and intertwined with one another, and overintrusive on the personal boundaries of other family members or systems--or disengaged--they are too loosely fit together.

Boundaries are the delineations between a family's subsystems and thus need to be clear for proper family functioning. Members of one subsystem (for example, parents) must be allowed to carry out their functions without too much interference (say, from a grandparent); but contact between members of the subsystem and others must be maintained. A parental subsystem may even include a grandparent, so long as the lines of authority and responsibility are clearly drawn in the family. If boundaries become too blurred and the family communicates only within itself, then we can label the situation enmeshed. Enmeshed or rigid boundaries leave no room for creative, flexible and adaptive responses.

Adaptive, family responses by each family are required as members experience their own idiosyncratic growth pains or inevitable conflicts (acquisition of in-laws, new offspring and separation of children or spouses by school, work, divorce, death) (Boss, 1980: 20). At the other extreme, if boundaries become overly rigid and communication across subsystems be-

10

comes difficult, then the family becomes disengaged (Minuchin, 1974). Members of disengaged families are apt to lack a feeling of family loyalty and belonging; they find it difficult to depend on other members or to request help from them when needed. Members of enmeshed families achieve their heightened sense of belonging by yielding their ability to act independently; in disengaged families they overemphasize their autonomy.

Disengaged or diffuse boundaries are often found in families that display isolation, lack of caring contact, and failure to assist other family members. Love and trust are often missing; pain and rejection seem to be the only thing holding people together as everyone escapes into their own lives. In addition cross-generational alliances can disturb family interaction by creating unclear or ambiguous role definitions. For example, when grandparents become parents and control the children, or when the parents become so close to their children that they are unable to exert control or discipline.

Systems theory lends itself well to working with family problems like alcoholism, anorexia nervosa, bronchial asthma, diabetes. It adopts a model that suggests the activities and functions of the family are a clue about how the family is organized or structured. The focus in systems theory is upon the content of transactions which reveal how the family organizes itself.

The reason the systems model works effectively with problem families is because it rejects strictly personalistic or micro frameworks for understanding human behavior. A micro approach zeros in on the individual and his or her intrapsychic problems (the psychodynamic view) or learned maladaptive behavior (the behavioral view) in attempting to understand and then treat that particular individual's symptom. A systems approach goes beyond the individual to look at the context. That is, the systems model analyzes the individual's psychological and behavioral makeup by focusing upon the influences family members have on one another. Although systems theory recognizes that the person's social life experiences do transcend the family system, it believes that patterns of interaction within the family limit the range of each family member's behavior. The systems approach thus operates with a wider lens than does the psychological.

11

Family Conflict Theory

Family systems theory doesn't work for all family situations, problems, or life stages. Family growth and change is an area where systems theory is perhaps not as well qualified. Because family growth requires many adaptations as the family changes and develops, it seems to require a more dynamic and process focus--that of conflict theory and in particular, the principle of conflict management (Sprey: 130-159). In conflict theory, there are various levels of conflict; surface level conflicts, which involve verbal communication, and latent level conflicts, which involve structures or boundaries. As families grow and change, equilibrium is disrupted as the family is faced with alterations regarding the balance of power, authority, and autonomy.

Conflict management is a strategy preferable to the belief in the possibility of total conflict resolution, because it focuses upon manageable and realistic assumptions. Included in the conflict management framework are techniques and strategies for self-awareness, which require family members to be honest with themselves, to seek feedback from others, and to observe how others respond. Other techniques include awareness of relationship traps, the ability to examine assumptions about the world through accurate reality testing, and learning to anticipate "pinch-points", so one can be prepared to renegotiate, if necessary, and strengthen the relationship bonds (Roberts, 1982). Conflict theory and conflict management recognize the inevitability of conflict and the need to find ongoing processes to manage disagreements over those inevitable problems of authority and autonomy.

Exchange and Conflict Theories Compared

Many relationships are based on the premise that those relationships which are maintained offer the most enjoyable rewards for the least cost. This premise is most evident in exchange theory. Relationships continue, or dissolve, based upon some equilibrium of exchanges which each individual is able to achieve. Families work on the same principle. We engage in "give" and "take" as we interact with one another. Therefore, within a marital relationship social behavior is maintained by a perceived satisfactory level of rewards relative to costs. Continuation of the relationship is also affected by

12

the participants' perception of alternative relationships and their comparative rewards and costs.

Over time the interaction of a particular couple
becomes governed by a set of norms reflecting a balance between rewards and costs. In the event that
these norms are violated, for example, by one member
of the couple withholding rewards, the other member
will attempt to reestablish the equilibrium by, for
example, trying to increase rewards or decrease costs.
At the point where rewards and costs are again in
some perceived balance, the relationship is again
viewed as satisfactory.

Marital discord can be described as a function
of the low rate of positive reinforcers exchanged by
spouses. The outcome of this low rate of positive
reinforcement is that each spouse becomes less
"attracted" to the other, and the relationship is
experienced as less attractive.

The exchange or bargaining can take place through
what is called the "marital quid pro quo" (literally
"something for something"). Quid pro quo refers to a
relationship based on the recognition and acceptance
of differences between the partners and a clear
division of labor defining the contribution made by
each. For example: he handles intellectual matters
more capably but is less practical; she is a more
realistic planner and also more sensitive to others
and more social. Or as a second example: he actually
prefers marketing and cooking but is too casual about
finances; she prefers working to home chores, hates
cooking, enjoys arranging and sticking to a budget.
The point is that in functioning relationships an
exchange is made, a kind of contract is formulated,
not based on sterotyped sex roles but on abilities
and interests. However, this theory does not directly discuss the issue of promiting high-quality family interaction and well-being.

Case Studies

To demonstrate the importance of using theory to
diagnose family life, consider the issue of coping
with marital boredom. In a changing marital relationship where there is failure to adjust to new demands and expectations, marital boredom can and does
set in. One adheres to a rigid set of roles and
interaction strategies and shortly thereafter there
is marital boredom. For example, Hal and Jan have

13

been married for fourteen years. They are fifty- and forty-fiveyears old respectively, they have one child; they have conflicts about managing dual careers and overcoming differences in leisure activities. Hal has had several affairs and Paula has gained twenty-five pounds. They both feel lonely and angry. Their home has little furniture, they sit alone together without friends and/or club membership. She feels if he can't buy furniture then she won't entertain. He feels because she is overweight and sexually aloof why bother. Neither is interested in the way the other spends leisure time: "if she won't ski, he won't play tennis." The marriage appears lifeless but enmeshed, "If we weren't together, I would be a hermit without her," he thinks, and she thinks, "since I am losing interest in sex and gaining weight who else would want me." When the couple does communicate it concerns their 13-year-old adolescent daughter who appears to be having problems in school.

Taking a system's approach and going through the levels mentioned earlier, the first step in coping with Hal and Jan in marital boredom will have to be circular: simple feedback, converting them from being two individuals to being a team. Self-boundaries would have to be enlarged, choices, exchanges, conflicts would all come into play. As they got to level two Jan and Hal would look more like a unit, exchanging daily trivia for intimacy which might get them to level three: a change in their whole approach to their marriage, making choices about mechanisms for resolving or restructuring conflict so together they enter new activities and share new goals. The positive feelings from trying new activities, perhaps jogging, which helps her to lose weight and sets his mind on new activities like jogging, not extra-marital affairs, might lead them to level four where a total reorientation takes place. Hal and Jan must learn to focus upon their mutual system needs and not only the needs of their daughter.

If we used the systems or exchange theories in dealing with a troubled couple and/or family, the focus would be upon their faulty exchanges or strategies for controlling rewards and costs. For example, a woman insisted her husband be home every night because she suffered anxiety attacks if left alone. However, she refused to acknowledge her behavior as trying to control his behavior. She instead blamed her behavior on anxiety attacks, over which she had no control. The husband faced a dilemma: he could

14

not acknowledge that she was controlling his behavior but he also could not refuse to let her control his behavior. He was in a double-bind situation. As an interested friend, you might try to help them see the nature of their ways of negotiating rewards and costs. Using a conflict theory, you might explore the deeper obstacles regarding autonomy and authority that the couple doesn't recognize. Neither party recognizes the desire to renegotiate areas of independence and control. And using a systems framework you might explore the role of communication and feedback and the need to monitor and establish more innovative mechanisms, policies, and goals for exchanging information. Developing a theoretical focus, however, is not enough to allow us to cope and manage family problems, we also need competencies and skills.

Family Management Skills

Family management is a relatively new idea in the field of family sociology and family studies. The fundamental idea becomes how to apply human relations and behavior management skills to improve family interaction and functioning. Buehler and Hogan (1980:93) define family management "as a goal-directed behavior using decision making, valuing, planning and organizing processes to guide resource use." Their strategy is to facilitate better management of family resources, to reduce stress and relationship problems following any changes in resource availabilty, as a result of a divorce or other changes in family structure. Such changes require families to adopt an essentially open systems model, recognizing the effects of available resources and skills. This ecosystem model suggests that changes in resource availability, allocation or skill utilization, will impact the entire family systems network. Such a review requires families to utilize anticipatory and adaptive response, including the following questions:

How does the family reorganize routine and non-routine task performance such as day - to - day childcare and income tax preparation? What input does the ex-spouse, extended family, friends, or others in the environment provide to the system? How do female-headed families adjust their expenditure patterns to accommodate diminished financial resources? If they increase their market work time, how do they adjust the family systems time? Which standards and goals are adjusted as system resources are changed?

15

Shan Martin (1983) offers an interesting model for possible use in building family management skills because it focuses upon managerial skills which may be learned by any worker or individual. Organizational workers, particularly in the public sector, can guide the management of physical and human resources through the acquisition of human management skills. Mintzberg (1973:189-193) documents such skills as managing relationships, information-processing, introspection, leadership, decision-making under ambiguity, resource allocation, and promoting innovation.

The idea is for each worker or family system member to learn skills which will increase their family involvement and contribution. Shan (1983:98) suggests that in our modern information economy the worker must become more "a source of information for the management of technology, and so in fact is a part of management by becoming primarily fact finder, interpreter, diagnostician, judge, adjuster, and change agent." Learning process or competency skills, not just imposed roles, is the key to democratic participation and involvement in either work or family system (see Section III).

Parents themselves must learn and teach self-management skills to other family members for the maximum utilization of personal and societal resources. This is our definition of family management skills.

This text will explore some of the family management skills essential for understanding, coping with, and strategically monitoring our rapidly changing and complex technological world. Such skills include problem solving, motivation, communication, time and stress management, studying the future family, interpersonal relating, knowledge of new technologies and computers. Understanding new strategies for managing work and personal life in our rapidly changing world can teach us needed lessons about promoting holistic family wellness.

Family Prevention and Wellness

Mace (1983) has posed a challenge for those family studies experts who have focused only upon family problems, crisis, dysfunctions, and disorders, at the expense of positive family functioning, wellness and wholeness. We believe that both perspectives are needed but the reasons for studying problem fami-

16

lies and marital failure should always lead us to more innovative thinking about what is really needed for good family life.

It is important today that individuals begin thinking at an early age about what a blueprint for a healthy family looks like. We will use the following words interchangeably--health, wellness,completeness, actualization, nourishing, and holistic. The promotion of family wellness is closely tied with our strategy of family management, where family members are encouraged and empowered to cultivate their talents and skills. Thus, individual self esteem and personal growth are linked to marital and family goals-- tasks which give meaning and zest to life. Individual and family interests, wishes and goals, should stimulate self-esteem, while building a sense of morality, solidarity, and continuity.

Mace (1983:18-19) suggests that family life should focus on prevention of family difficulties before they cause major problems and breakdowns:

Primary prevention... it means using positive early intervention to enable the family to avoid the kinds of trouble that might otherwise be very damaging.

Secondary prevention... it means a situation in which it is too late for primary prevention. The family members are already in trouble. As a result of poor communication, misunderstandings are causing prejudiced judgments and alienation, and tensions are building up. However, the situation has not yet reached crisis proportions... catching trouble early, so that it doesn't reach serious proportions.

Tertiary prevention...it means a situation where the family is already in serious trouble... providing reeducation to ensure if possible that the family will not again suffer a major crisis based on ineffective communication.

Although these preventive strategies overlap, any hope for the future is based on education, and planning for primary prevention (See Otto, Chapter 2). Preventative approaches include information, skills training with experiencial and behavioral components, and social-environmental change (Mace, 1983:20-21).

17

L'Abate (1983:53-) identifies the three stages of prevention as 1) before it happens (primary) 2) before it gets worse (secondary) 3) before it is too late (tertiary).

Stinnett (1983:30-35) identifies six qualities of strong, well, and healthy families. First is authentic and spontaneous appreciation of family members for each other. Learning to give positive feedback and to perceive the strong points of other family members must be cultivated and practiced. Second, spending enjoyable or genuine time together. Thus families must explore activities they can enjoy together. Third, is commitment to each other's happiness and welfare. Fourth, is good communication patterns. Fifth, is a high degree of religious or ethical orientation. Sixth, is the ability to deal with crisis in a positive manner.

Bowman (1983:44-47), in reviewing general studies documenting family wellness indicators, identifies several trends: 1) many indicators are skill-related; 2) many include spiritual or religious components; 3) one finds comprehensive use of wellness information which becomes useful for a "family check-up", opening up conversation and explanation; 4) interdependence between families and outside resources; 5) identification of causes of wellness outside an ideological framework.

Mace (1983:104-105 defines three essentials for success in close relationships, including marriage and family life. First is commitment by both partners to continued growth. This is the task of reconciling his and her dream that L'Abate discusses in Chapter 1. The dream must include personal growth dimensions but also couple and family goals. Couples must also move from attitude to behavior as a result of the supports family members provide to each other. Second, successful relationships need an effective communication system which allows each partner to accept each other as they are. Third, the succesful relationship is based upon the ability to use conflict and anger as raw materials for growth.

Fishman and Fishman (1983:110) speak of the "enriched marriage as a reciprocally resonant relationship":

Characterized by an ongoing pulsation between the shared experience of an 'US' and the individual experiences of participating selves. The US should not be viewed as an entity but as a process which slowly evolves as the couple moves through family life. The emphasis is upon an organic process of exploratory growth, self-respect and long term commitment. While living in a highly mobile, disposable or throw-away society, couples need a commitment to bonding; the time to unfold, respect for uniqueness and mutual trust. Such bonding allows the ebb and flow of strength and vulnerability, of love and anger and joy and sorrow.

Condon (1983:144-146) identifies six antecedents of family wellness: 1) the opportunity to meet one's own basic needs; 2) the necessity of self-esteem; 3) building problem-solving competence; 4) fate control or the ability to develop self-control and assume responsibilities; 5) freedom from fear; 6) freedom from hostility and resentment.

The Family In the Future

In our assessment, some form of the family will remain the primary unit of our society. The traditional structure, which consists of a homemaker-mother, breadwinner father, children, and grandparents, is now far in the minority however. The modern family now takes on a variety of structural characteristics, and diverse living arrangements. A number of important causal factors created by societal shifts are bringing about these major effects on the family.

Diversity in living arrangements, both in experience of men and women over their life courses and in the makeup of households at given points in time, will continue to mark the next decade. The once typical household--two parents, and children, with a husband-breadwinner and wife-homemaker--has faded in prominence. Although many Americans still live in conventional nuclear families sometime during their lives, traditional families are a minority of all households at any given time. Other types of households--two worker families, families whose children have moved away, retired couples, single-parent families, and men and women living alone--are proliferating and are becoming an increasing proportion of households overall.

The phenomenon of more and more individuals spending less and less time in traditional family

19

living arrangement, has provoked a good deal of social anxiety. First, families and family relationships in our society have long been considered major elements of a meaningful life. If fewer and fewer people live in traditional families, this source of meaning and satisfaction may be lost, leaving many people disoriented and alienated. Second, families have long sheltered and cared for society's dependent members: children, the elderly, the sick, the disabled, and the poor. Changes in the family lead to questions about who will take care of these dependents (Masnick and Bane, 1980).

However, not all family researchers and practitioners view these emerging trends in a negative light. Macklin (Chapter 4) argues for family life education that emphasizes choice and knowledge about diverse lifestyle alternatives. Macklin reviews the contemporary alternatives to the traditional family, notes some of the skills and knowledge required by these alternatives, and suggests a format for preparing students to make appropriate lifestyle choices. Chapter 4 reviews the following lifestyle options and their implications for family life education: to marry or not to marry, to parent or not to parent, to co-parent or single-parent, to make a lifelong or open-ended commitment, degree of androgyny, to be sexually exclusive or non-exclusive, gender of partner, and to live alone or with others. An educational approach is proposed, based on a humanistic perspective and designed to foster knowledge about available alternatives, increased awareness of individual values, and the development of decision-making and conflict-negotiation skills.

The Family and Politics

Here we raise the issue of the importance of the public dimension in viewing family life. The family can no longer sustain the myths of privacy, isolation, self-sufficiency, haven from a heartless world, and emotional sanctuary. In fact, conservative and liberal groups now march behind the banner of protecting and nurturing families.

What has changed is the content and nature of family life. Families were never as self-sufficient or as self-contained as the myth made them out to be...they are extraordinarily dependent on 'outside forces' and influences, ranging from the nature of parents' work to the content of television programing, from the structure of local schools to the organization of health care. All families today need and use support in raising children; to define the 'needy' family as the exception is to deny the simplest facts of contemporary life (Kenniston, 1977:22).

We believe the family must become more activistic and involved with the political world. This means pressuring those making public, employment, or governmental policy decision makers to recognize the impact of their decisions on marital and family life, both traditional and alternative.

Skolnick (1981:42), in a symposium issue of <u>Trans-action</u> on future families, discussed what she calls the 'new domesticity':

> In part, the new mood reflects the movement of the 1960's generation into the next stage of the life cycle - marriage, or at least cohabitation, and childbearing... Faced with job scarcity, a declining standard of living, and uncertain ideas about the future, many people are turning inward to home, family, and private life.

The new emphasis on the importance of families seems to confound old stereotypes regarding conservative - liberal domains of interest.

For example, the Oakland based Friends of Families was begun by Michael Lerner with Oakland City Councilman Wilson Riles, Jr., to address the fact that conservatives have made political points by emphasizing traditional family values. Lerner emphasizes the impact of stress in the work place, as the source of domestic strife. Lerner's group hopes to provide a pro-family organization for liberals and progressives, the trade union movement, the liberal wing of the church, community service organizations, and minorities. The program centers around the connection of personal stress and the work world, while emphasizing justice, fairness, love, and mutual caring. The family has now come out of the liberal closet and is no longer just a public issue for conservatives.

Novak more conservatively praises the bourgeois or middle class family with its emphasis on the importance of private property, merit, child rearing, individuality, freedom from state control, and the belief that one's family position is not guaranteed by birth, but must be earned through effort and excellence:

> ...The Bourgeois family does make judgments. It does so not only in codes of ethical conduct and in schemes of self-improvement, but also in terms of practical achievement. The code of the bourgeois family is to measure - to measure in order to compete against oneself, to inspire self-improvement, to better oneself (1981:66-67).

The latest reports on the current state of our society and institutions indicate both a real caution and a new found sense of optimism that "new rules" are emerging regarding issues of the quality of our lives, in lieu of purely quantitative and materialistic concerns (Yankelovich, 1981). Many individuals appear to have come to some understanding of the psychic costs associated with useless competition and status striving, as well as the social costs of isolating their private lives from public involvements and support structures. The private search for self-fulfillment is eroding (Yankelovich, 1981).

This analysis highlights the importance of the relationship between our private and public morality and how marriage and family life mediates these two worlds. Even if we don't always live up to our intended standards and values in action, we must assume some responsiblity for our institutions. We often rationalize our actions or choose those values that fit our behavior without reflection. Muddled intentions and moral drift often result.

Excuses no longer work in a world of diminishing resources and complex interdependencies: although we may intend no harm by our individual actions, the consequences we build into public policies offer our children a concrete world they must cope with. Hiding behind bureaucratic rules or blaming the victim ideologies doesn't absolve each of us from the need for critical moral thinking about the kind of world we are creating. The link between our private and public worlds is more pertinent today than ever before (Berger, 1977). The forces tearing at the fabric of family life are public, social and structural and intimately affect the very grounding of our social future and commitment to a sane and better world (C. W. Mills, 1959).

B I B L I O G R A P H Y

Berger, Peter

1977   "Marriage and the Construction of Reality"
            in Facing Up to Modernity: Excursions
            in Society, Politics and Religion, New
            York: Basic Books.

Boss, Pauline G.

1980   "Normative Family Stress: Family Bound-
            ary Changes Across the Life-Span" in
            Family Stress: Coping and Adaptation.
            Hamilton I. McCubbin and Pauline G.
            Boss. National Council on Family Re-
            lations: Minneapolis, Minn. 17-22.

Bowman, Ted W.

1983   "Promoting Family Wellness: Implications
            and Issues" in David R. Mace (Ed.) Pre-
            vention in Family Services: Approaches
            to Family Wellness. Beverly Hills, CA.:
            Sage, 39-48.

Broderick, Carl F.,
Smith, James

1979   "The General Systems Approach to the
            Family" in Contemporary Theories About
            The Family: General Theories/Theoretical
            Orientations Vol. II Wesley R. Burr et al.
            (Eds.) New York: The Free Press, 112-129.

Buehler, Cheryl,
Hogan, M. Janice

1980   "Managerial Behavior and Stress in Fami-
            lies Headed by Divorced Women: A Pro-
            posed Framework" in Family Stress: Coping
            and Adaptation. (Eds.) Hamilton I. Mc-
            Cubbin and Pauline G. Boss. National
            Council on Family Relations: Minneapolis,
            Minn., 93-100.

23

Constantine, Larry,
Constantine, Joan

    1973   Group Marriage: A Study of Contemporary
                  Multilateral Marriages, New York: Mac-
                  millan.

Fishman, Barbara,
Fishman, Robert

    1983   "Enriched Marriage as a Reciprocally Re-
                  sonant Relationship" in David R. Mace
                  (Ed.) Prevention in Family Services:
                  Approaches to Family Wellness, Beverly
                  Hills, CA: Sage, 110-120.

Condon, Thomas

    1983   "Transforming Early Parenthood to Promote
                  Family Wellness" in David R. Mace (Ed.)
                  Prevention in Family Services: Approaches
                  to Family Wellness. Beverly Hills, CA:
                  Sage, 133-147.

Kantor, D.,
Lehr, W.

    1975   Inside the Family, San Francisco: Josey-
                  Bass.

Kenniston, Kenneth

    1977   All Our Children: The American Family
                  Under Pressure. New York: Harcour, Brace
                  Jovanovich.

L'Abate, Luciano

    1983   "Preventionas a Profession: Toward a New
                  Conceptual Frame of Reference" in David R.
                  Mace (Ed.) Prevention in Family Services:
                  Approaches to Family Wellness. Beverly
                  Hills, CA: Sage, 49-62.

Mace, David R.

    1983   "The Marriage Enrichment Movement" in
                  David R. Mace (Ed.) Prevention in Family
                  Services: Approaches to Family Wellness.
                  Beverly Hills, CA: Sage, 98-109.

24

Mace, David R.

1983   (Ed.) Prevention in Family Services:
          Approaches to Family Wellness. Beverly
          Hills, CA: Sage.

Martin, Shan

1983   Managing Without Managers: Alternative
          Work Arrangements in Public Organizations.
          Beverly Hills, CA: Sage.

McClain, Raymond,
Weigert, A.

1979   "Toward a Phenomenological Sociology of
          Family: A Programatic Essay" in Wesley
          R. Burr (et al.) (Eds.) Contemporary
          Theories About the Family: General
          Theories/Theoretical Orientations. Vol.
          II. New York: The Free Press. 160-205.

Mills, C. W.

1959   The Sociological Imagination, New York:
          Oxford University Press.

Mintzberg, H.

1983   The Nature of Managerial Work. New York:
          Harper and Row.

Minuchin, S.

1974   Families and Family Therapy. Cambridge,
          Mass.

Murdock, George P.

1949   Social Structure. New York: Macmillan.

Novak, Michael

1981   "The Bourgeois Family in Decline" Society,
          Vol. 18, No. 2, Jan., Feb.

Nye, F. Ivan,
Gecas, V.

1976   "The Role Concept: Review and Delineation.
        In F. Ivan Nye (Ed.), Role Structure and
        Analysis of the Family. Beverly Hills,
        CA: Sage.

Roberts, Marc

1982   Managing Conflict. San Diego, CA: Uni-
        versity Associates.

Selznick, D.

1957   Leadership in Administration. New York:
        Row, Pederson.

Skolnick, Arlene

1981   "The Family and Its Discontents" Society,
        Vol. 18, No. 2, Jan., Feb.

Sprey, Jetse

1979   "Conflict Theory and The Study of Marriage
        and Family" in Wesley R. Burr (et al.)
        (Eds.) Contemporary Theories About the
        Family: General Theories and Theoretical
        Orientations Vol. II. New York: The Free
        Press, 130-159.

Stephens, William N.

1963   The Family in Cross-Cultural Perspective,
        New York: Holt, Rinehart and Winston.

Stinnett, Nicholas

1983   "Strong Families: a Portrait" in David R.
        Mace (Ed.) Prevention in Family Services:
        Approaches to Family Wellness. Beverly
        Hills, CA: Sage, 27-38.

*Dr. Edgar W. Butler is Chair of the Sociology Depart-
ment, University of California, Riverside.

*Dr. Douglas B. Gutknecht is a member of the Sociology
Department and Coordinator of the M.S. Degree in
Human Resource Management and Development, Chapman
College, Orange, California.

CHAPTER 1

MARRIAGE: THE DREAM AND THE REALITY

Luciano L'Abate* and
Bess L. L'Abate*

The purpose of this paper is to review one of
the major areas of polarization in marriage that does
not seem to have received the attention it deserves.
This polarization, more often than not, takes place
along a continuum in which the husband pursues his
"Dream(s)"of success, i.e., money, achievement, power,
while the wife is left home to deal with the "Realities" of life, i.e., children, house, chores, etc.
The result of this polarization is an inability to
be or become intimate (L'Abate & L'Abate, 1979).
Trollope put it well a long time ago:

> A burden that will crush a single pair of shoul-
> ders will, when equally divided--when shared by
> two, each of whom is willing to take the heavier
> part--become light as a feather. Is not that
> sharing of the mind's burdens one of the chief
> purposes for which a man wants a wife? For there
> is no folly so great as keeping one's sorrow
> hidden.

Levinson, Darrow, Dean, Levinson, and McKee
(1978) have addressed themselves to the topic of the
function of "The Dream" in the formative development
of man's evolution in personality. Originally this
Dream has a "vague sense of self-adult-world...At the
start it is poorly articulated and only tenuously
connected to reality" (p. 35). Eventually, this
Dream becomes articulated within the channel of maxi-
mal exposure taken by the man, i.e., his occupational
choice. He dreams of winning the Nobel prize if he
is a physicist or biologist, becoming a renowned
writer, winning the Pulitzer prize, becoming a great
athlete, artist, businessman, etc. Levinson et al.
poignantly described the functions of "The Dream" in
the lives of the forty men they studied.

Part of the marital contract for such men, explicit or implicit, is that the wife will help the husband achieve his Dream, whatever it may be. Thus, in
this arrangement the marital relationship is initially
one-sided. The agreement is for the wife to "help"

the husband, as in the cases of nurse-doctor marriages, but there is no clear or explicit agreement that there will be reciprocity in this relationship. The woman initially may agree to help in exchange for material goods or vicarious rewards that may derive from the husband's success. But Levinson et al. (1978, p. 109) note:

> If in supporting his dream she loses her own, then her development will suffer and both will later pay the price. Dynamics of this kind often surface in transitional periods such as the Age Thirty Transition or the Mid-life Transition.

The foregoing quote speaks to the very point of this chapter. There are many marriages of hard-driving competitive, and ambitious executives, managers, achievement and success-oriented professionals who, through their workaholic investment in their jobs, hope, attempt, want, and oftentimes succeed in fulfilling their Dream. But, this fulfillment may be achieved at a great cost and sacrifice to the marriage and to the family. Failure to actualize the Dream may lead to feelings of inadequacy and failure that may be externalized in the marriage in the form of affairs, blaming wife for lack of support, among others.

Components of this Dream are enacted by the decision that to achieve this goal he will need courage, strength, and determination, as shown through the following characteristics: (a) reason and logic as the means through which the Dream is achieved; (b) strength, courage, determination are demonstrated by keeping his feelings to himself, and repressing, denying, and avoiding any expression of feelings that may possibly suggest vulnerability, weakness, or even worse, inadequacy!

A previous paper (L'Abate, 1975) explained part of family dysfunctionality in terms of the man's rigid inability to switch from a managerial role at work to a nurturant role at home. Further elaboration is needed about the roles of both men and women in coming to grips with issues of intimacy in marriage (L'Abate & L'Abate, 1979). The major dysfunction-producing aspects of this Dream seem to be: (a) drive and intensity of purpose, as shown by excessive and exclusive absorption in the occupational role; (b) inability to shift, differentiate, and integrate demands from work and from home; and (c) inability to experience feelings, to improve dialogue, and achieve intimacy in marriage.

I. THE POLARITIES OF MARRIAGE

Considerable effort is made by the husband to promote proper appearances. A good first impression is sought through clothing, car, and house. Thus, a great deal of his functioning is directed at presenting the self in as good a light as possible. The wife, on the other hand, is involved with more practical issues; those issues that exist below, or underneath, the flow of self-presentation and go beyond the first blush facade of appearance (L'Abate, 1976). The husband either neglects chores and responsibilities, or is apparently unaware of the trivia that occupy his wife's attention. The more she brings these "Realities" to his attention, the more he resists dealing with them.

One way wives demonstrate their initial involvement and collusion with The Dream is that most of them have no careers of their own. All of their selves have been given to the pursuit and sharing of The Dream without demands of reciprocity. Eventually, when the futility or irrelevance of the collusion hits them, the emotional toll and cost that this Dream has extracted from them usually provokes a depression. If the wives are not depressed at the beginning of therapy, usually they are still angry and frustrated. Eventually they will be able to become depressed, a sign that therapy is working. The husbands, of course, find it much more difficult to get in touch with their underlying feelings of depression. But if therapy is effective, they may be able to get in touch with the emptiness that determined part of the pursuit in the first place. The husbands' selves were given up for professional roles or titles to the extent that little self remains. In fact, many of these men and some of their wives have a hard time understanding the concepts of being, which will be discussed later on in this paper. Some of these existential issues have been considered by Crosby (1976).

Further polarities of the "Dream" role are a nice-nasty quality that covers the man's attempt to achieve success on the outside by being a "nice guy," and putting forth a self-presentational facade (L'Abate, 1976) of a "hail-fellow-well-met" glad-hander, with

29

all of the qualities that accompany such a role. This
stance, of course, polarizes the wife toward the
opposite extreme of nastiness. Her increasing frustration and loneliness are expressed in "bitchy,"
angry outbursts and blaming statements that are surprising and incomprehensible to the husband. How
could a "nice guy" like him be considered such a
lowdown creature? Why does she continue bugging him
about small, irrelevant details like plumbing, yard-
work, and the infinite little occurrences that take
place in the household every day? Why should he be
concerned with diapers and diaper rash? He is in
pursuit of the far greater Dream that cannot in any
way be detoured, sidestepped, or interfered with by
such petty irrelevancies. One husband, a worldwide
traveler tycoon, became enraged when his wife asked
him to deal with the gardening contractor, who for
$350.00 a month was not getting the job done. Imagine
him having to bother with such trifles! He was
involved in multimillion dollar projects all over the
USA and in foreign countries! How could she dare
bother him with a chore which clearly belonged with
the realm of her responsibilities and not his?

The wife's reactions oftentimes are so alien to
the picture that the man has of himself and of his
role that the discrepancy between the Dream picture
and the Reality presented by the wife becomes unac-
ceptable. He becomes unwilling to come to terms with
it and begins acting out by becoming even more im-
mersed in his job, picking up a mistress on the side,
drinking more, etc. If and when the wife is successful in bringing him into the therapy office, he feels
ganged up on by the therapist, if the therapist in
any way, subtle or otherwise, sides with the wife's
Reality.

These couples may display other polarities:

1. Intimacy and isolation - it is clear that
   many of these couples never dealt in their
   marriages with the issues of intimacy. Consequently, they are destined to be isolated
   from each other in what could seem an "arrangement" rather than a marriage.

2. Enmeshment with families of origin - many of
   these couples, even after more than ten years
   of marriage and thousands of miles from their
   families of origin, remain enmeshed to the

point of still spending vacation time with them and fighting with each other over them.

3. Delegation from parents and loyalty binding - Very often these couples present some of the aspects of delegation discussed by Stierlin (1974), to the point that their success is bound to the "failures" of their parents. Their parents' failures (either economic or interpersonal or both) need to be remedied by them.

4. Anniversary reaction or separation phase often-times the major precipitating reason for therapy is ostensibly fear of loss (i.e., finding husband has had an affair) or the children's reaching grade school age and leaving the wife.

5. Another dimension of the dream-reality continuum is the expressive-inexpressive (rational-irrational) distinction (L'Abate, 1980) emphasized for many years by Balswick (1980).

The wife's increasing worry about realistic details of everyday, routine household life (chores) points to another polarization between mates, i.e., pessimism-optimism whereby the wife begins to look at the dark side of family happenings, including the behavior of the identified patient (IP), usually one of their children, while the husband is bound to deny it, by belittling its severity or seriousness, thereby delaying, until the breaking point, any possible intervention (L'Abate, 1975). The IP, whether the wife or child, will need to escalate to the maximum level of noise (attempted suicide, being kicked out of school, flunking, etc.) to obtain the husband's attention and acknowledgement that something may need to be done. At this point professional help may be sought.

II. DISCUSSION

Some of these conclusions about the woman's role in a "workaholic" husband's life are supported by the research of Macke, Bohrnstedt and Bernstein (1979), who examined the cornerstone of traditional views of marriage that housewives experience their husbands' successes viccariously. Macke et al. maintained that the specific role requirements of traditional marriage may reduce a woman's self-esteem and render her more vulnerable to stress. To obtain more verification of

31

this hypothesis, Macke et al. obtained relevant information from 121 mostly upper middle class women, who are roughly similar to the couples we see in our clinical practice. They found that a husband's success affects a housewife's self-esteem positively, but only indirectly, through its effect on perceived marital success. Only the husband's income by itself had a positive effect on self-esteem. Apparently a housewife, according to Macke et al., can translate money into consumer products or other material means of increasing her status among peers, and thus indirectly her self-esteem. Macke et al. also found that other successes of the husband seem to work against the self-esteem of those wives who were not working. This finding, which parallels our findings with clinical couples, is enhanced by the finding that none of the above outcomes were present in working wives.

Boss, McCubbin, and Lester (1979) reviewed how the wives of corporate executives cope with their husbands' frequent absences and long work hours. Their major coping strategies, which we find absent in the wives we have observed in our clinical practice and on which we base our generalizations are: (a) fitting into the corporate life style (frequent entertaining and social group activities; (b) developing self (as independent from the husband); and (c) establishing independence (emotionally as well as socially).

III. DIAGNOSTIC IMPLICATIONS

Diagnostically, one important way of checking on the couple's overinvolvement with work, for the husband, or with children, for the wife (L'Abate, 1975), is to ask them about their priorities. What is more important to each of them in order of preference? Most men will reply: "My family and my work." Most women will say: "My husband and my children." Neither one of them usually mentions the self as an important aspect of priorities (L'Abate, 1976). If and when the concept of self is mentioned, the notion seems to be strange and questionable. However, when the problem is rephrased: "How can a bridge stand on weak pillars?", the point is driven home that the establishment of a functional self is just as important for the marriage as any other priority. When the question is raised: "How can parenthood be achieved without a partnership?", or "How can a partnership be achieved without personhood?", it becomes even clearer that

32

all of these issues have not been considered by the couple. In both mates the self is ill-defined, unclear, and essentially weak.

The woman may show signs of inadequacy, if not hatred, whereas the husband attempts to hold on to the occupational self to achieve a certain degree of selfhood. When the woman who defined herself as "housewife" is asked to find any definition of self that precedes "housewife," developmentally and in importance, she may have a great deal of trouble in coming up with a definition of self that includes concepts of womanhood, personhood, or individuality. The weaker she is in individuation, the more she relies on her husband and her children to define herself. Her selfconcept is essentially reactive and external to both sources of satisfaction. The husband will show just as much trouble in understanding the concept of manhood separate from occupational, marital, or tertiarily, familial functions (manager, lawyer, husband, father). It is crucial at this point to assert the importance of a self-concept on which to base the marriage (Crosby, 1976). This assertion is sometimes met by questioning glances. Oftentimes, it is then best to congratulate the couple for losing their selves for the love of the other: "You must have had a self if you lost it!"

The best empirical framework within which some of the above conclusions can be evaluated, and eventually tested, is that of Foá and Foá (1974). They not only have developed an exchange theory that can encompass some of the above, but have also developed tools to assess it. Briefly, this theory assumes six classes of resources: Love, Status, Money, Goods, Services, and Information. A revision of this theory (L'Abate, Sloan, Wagner, & Malone, in press) groups Love and Status as components of being, Information and Services as components of doing, and Money and Goods as components of having. Within this framework we can see that many of these couples function very effectively in the doing and having areas, but are quite defective or ineffective in the being area. They do not know how to be, as experienced by: (a) expression of deep or soft feelings, (b) relaxation and letting go in leisure time, whereas for them business and pleasure many times are mixed, (c) inadequate definition of self as separate from an occupational (manager, lawyer, etc., rather than "woman" or "person"). As noted previously (L'Abate, 1976), these priorities in resource exchange are mixed up, dif-

33

fused, fused, or confused. Their whole orientation
to doing and having is so uncritically ingrained that
understanding the implications of a being orientation
is as difficult as experiencing feelings or assuming
an "I" position.

IV. THERAPEUTIC IMPLICATIONS

What is the goal of therapy under these conditions? Obviously one goal is for the couple to learn
to negotiate realistic and functional objectives for
themselves, and for the husband to learn to give reciprocally while the wife learns to expect, request,
and demand this reciprocity from her husband. Ultimately, the goal will be for them to learn to share
their pain and depression. Previously the marriage
has been on a reactive see-saw or rollercoaster. When
one partner is up, the other is down. Eventually, in
the course of therapeutic intervention, the couple is
able to avoid such examples of affective polarization
and learn to share more emphatically their hurts and
pains (L'Abate, 1977; Frey, Holloy, & L'Abate, 1979).
At this point, the marriage may become a real marriage
and not an arrangement. To reach this point usually
both partners have to learn to negotiate important
issues without incongruent affect or avoidance of the
issues involved. Berkowitz (1977) has essentially
developed a position that is very similar to the present one. He stated that:

> A central developmental task of the family is
> to help its members develop the capacity to
> cope with the grief attendant on separation and
> loss...to work through such feelings, each mem-
> ber must be able to acknowledge the affect as
> present, internal, and belonging to the self...
> family members may avoid awareness of such
> feelings within themselves. The disclaimed
> emotions remain powerful unconscious motivators
> of behavior exerting their influence despite
> their denial.

The wife in many ways, at least in the beginning
of married life, has colluded with the husband by
agreeing with him that, explicitly or implicitly, she
would share "The Dream" with him and do whatever
would be necessary to help achieve it. How could she
now betray him? The sheer force of the Reality brought
about by household and childrearing responsibility
that can only increase with married life eventually
forces the wife to take a second look at herself and

the nature of the marriage. If she does not become aware of her collusion, she does become aware of her giving up of her own self to allow the husband's self to prevail unilaterally. Depression, and all of its concomitants (feelings of low self-worth, rejection, fear of abandonment, etc.) come to the forefront, forcing the husband to become involved whether he likes it or not.

Oftentimes, the wife will see individual therapists who unwittingly would enter into a collusion with the husband by accepting the wife as a "sick," dependent woman, the IP (L'Abate, Weeks, & Weeks, 1979). Under these conditions, the husband is now free, and treatment becomes a long-drawn affair between the woman and her therapist, where eventually she may get over her depression, but may be unwilling to accept her husband as he is and as he has remained, since no intervention has taken place to change his involvement and love affair with The Dream!

The hard-driving, success-pursuing, reasonable and logic-oriented husband is not only preoccupied by his Dream at the expense of performing his husbandly and fatherly chores, but he also cannot speak about it even though, as therapy unfolds, he comes to realize that his Dream serves to cover up a great deal of hurt and emptiness.

In treatment, the foregoing patterns persist and become, in fact, highlighted. The husband typically smiles a great deal and presents most of the aspects mentioned above. When the wife cries, he becomes embarrassed and either takes it as a personal affront or becomes angry, or avoids dealing with it, because he is unable to emphasize with her tears. He sees the wife's increased dependency and helplessness as a yoke around his neck that is slowing down the process of attainment of his Dream and interferes with his work and his ever-present job commitments. Some of these men (Supermen) are so convinced of their inherent power and attributes that it may take very extreme behavior on the IP's part to convince the husband to join and share the realities of everyday life.

The most difficult part in therapy of these couples is not to side with the wife, but to see her behavior as equally contributing to the overall trouble as the husband's. She needs to be supported without injury to the husband's feelings of inadequacy, or he may feel that both therapist and wife had colluded and "ganged up" on him.

V. CONCLUSION

We have presented a major polarization of marriage that allows us to put together into one conceptual framework diverse strands of clinical experience and empirical evidence about marriage, its successes and its failures.

B I B L I O G R A P H Y

Balswick, J.

 1980 "Explaining Inexpressive Males: A Reply
      to L'Abate." Family Relations, 29,
      233-234.

Berkowitz, D.A.

 1977 "On the Reclaiming of Denied Affects in
      Family Therapy." Family Process, 16,
      495-502.

Boss, P.G., McCubbin, H.I. &
Lester, G.

 1979 "The Corporate Executive's Wife's Coping
      Patterns in Response to Routine Hus-
      band-Father Absence." Family Process,
      18, 79-86.

Crosby, J.E.

 1976 Illusion and Disillusion: The Self in
      Love and Marriage. Belmont, CA:
      Wadsworth.

Foá, V., &
Foá, E.

 1974 Societal Structures of the Mind.
      Springfield, IL: C.C. Thomas.

Frey, J., Holley, J. &
L'Abate, L.

 1979 "Intimacy is Sharing Hurt: A Comparison
      of Three Conflict Resolution Methods."
      Journal of Marriage and Family Therapy,
      5, 35-41.

L'Abate, L.

 1980 "Inexpressive Males or Overexpressive
      Females? A Reply to Balswick." Family
      Relations, 29, 231-232.

L'Abate, L.

    1977   "Intimacy is Sharing Hurt Feelings: A
                 Reply to David Mace." Journal of
                 Marriage and Family Counseling, 3,
                 13-16.

    1976   Understanding and Helping the Indivi-
                 dual in the Family. New York: Grune
                 & Stratton.

    1975   "Pathogenic Role Rigidity in Fathers:
                 Some Observations." Journal of Marriage
                 and Family Counseling, 1, 69-79.

L'Abate, L., &
L'Abate, B.L.

    1979   "The Paradoxes of Intimacy." Family
                 Therapy, 6, 175-184.

L'Abate, L., Sloan, S.Z.,
Wagner, V., & Malone, K.

    In   "The Differentiation of Resources."
    Press   Family Therapy.

L'Abate, L., Weeks, G., & Weeks, K.

    1979   "Of Scapegoats, Strawmen, and Scare-
                 crows." International Journal of
                 Family Therapy, 1, 86-96.

Levinson, D.J., Darrow, C.N.,
Dean, E.B., Levinson, M.H.,
& McKee, B.

    1978   The Seasons of a Man's Life. New York:
                 Alfred Knopt.

Macke, A.S., Bohrnstedt, G.W.,
& Bernstein, I.N.

    1979   "Housewive's Self-esteem and Their Hus-
                 bands' Success: The Myth of Vicarious
                 Involvement." Journal of Marriage and
                 the Family, 41, 51-57.

Stierlin, H.

1974   Separating Parents and Adolescents: A
                Perspective on Running Away, Schizo-
                phrenia, and Waywardness.   New York:
                Quadrangle/The New York Times Book Co.

A P P E N D I X
Instructions for Workshop Format

In conjunction with this paper, which in various formats has been given to a variety of organizations, we have found it useful to translate the above abstractions into a direct workshop format. Here are the instructions used with couples (real or simulated). We hope they will help any reader who may want to apply them in a workshop or enrichment format.

How many are here with their spouses?

Those who are not will have to role play with one another.

Now I (We) hope everyone is more or less partnered.

1. For the next 5-10 minutes we want each couple
   to talk to each other about your dreams or
   life goals. This should be your personal,
   individual dreams--not goals as a couple.
   Possible and impossible.

2. Now talk about where you want to be 5 years
   from now, 10 years, 20 years. (5-10 minutes)

3. Now talk about the similarities or discrepancies of your dreams. (5-10 minutes)

4. Now discuss the realities that are interfering
   with your dreams. (5-10 minutes)

5. How much of your past or present life are you
   giving up or sacrificing for dreams to be realized in the future? Has your marriage paid
   a price for the dream? Have your children?
   Discuss whether it is or has been worth it.
   (5-10 minutes)

6. Discuss ways you can integrate your dreams
   and realities so that you both win in the
   present and the future. How many of you will
   continue these dreams at home?

7. Now it is feedback time. Would any one couple
   like to share with us anything they have
   learned about themselves or their marriage in
   these discussions? (Take as much time as it
   seems feasible.)

*Luciano L'Abate is Professor of Psychology and Direc-
tor, Family Study Center, Georgia State University,
University Plaza, Atlanta, Georgia 30303. Bess L.
L'Abate is in part-time private practice.

Reprinted from Family Relations, Vol. 30 (January,
1981: 131-136). Copyrighted 1981 by the National
Council on Family Relations. Reprinted by permission.

CHAPTER 2

THE GROWTH PERSPECTIVE OF INTERPERSONAL RELATIONSHIPS: A NEW VISTA

Herbert A. Otto*

The Growth Perspective on Relationships is an emergent concept. It is a revolutionary concept and it provides a new perspective. The growth perspective of human relationships rests squarely on the human potentiality's hypothesis. This hypothesis is very briefly that the average, well-functioning human being is functioning at from four to ten percent of capacity. William James, the well-known American psychologist, as the turn of the century made the statement that he believed we were functioning at ten percent. Margaret Mead, in an article she contributed to my book, Explorations in Human Potentialities in 1966 made the statement that she believed we were functioning at six percent of capacity. Since that time, we have had so many discoveries about the human potential, including those relating to biofeedback that now the current estimate is that we are functioning at four percent of capacity. This human potentiality's hypothesis is internationally accepted.

Among the people who suscribe to this hypothesis, and some of the names may be familiar, are the following: There is the father of the human potential movement, Gardner Murphy, the famous psychologist Gordon Alport, Margaret Mead, Abraham Maslow, and others. The human potentiality's hypothesis is by no means restricted to the U.S. This hypothesis is generally accepted and one of the countries that has done a great deal of research in this area is the USSR. This is a hypothesis of hope and, unfortunately, this hypothesis of the human potential is restricted to the educated segment of our population. It is opposed by the ruling classes and it is opposed by people who are of an elitest orientation. On the other hand, the human potentiality hypothesis forms the very basis for human evolution. Why this is, I develop below.

Each person has tremendous potential and I hope, in some ways, to be able to "turn you on" to what this may mean to you. So we will start out briefly

41

to get an idea what we mean by "the human potential."
What are some of the indicators of the human potential? Do you remember when you were a child and your
parents stepped into the room? Sometimes you knew
what they were going to say. More often you knew
exactly how they felt. Remember how good things
smelled; how your vision was different? We are continually taking in sensory cues on a subliminal level,
on a level of which we are not conscious. Our sensory apparatus is very highly sensitive, and as
children we were perhaps more sensitive than we are
today. Today, as part of the human potential movement, we have training in sensory awareness that can
re-awaken these sensory capacities.

Another indicator--there are Indian tribes that
are able to smell almost with the acuity of a hunting
dog. We all have a tremendously developed sense of
smell which, of course, we stifle due to the polluted
environment. All of us have tremendous reserves of
strength. There are cases on record of people listing
cars under emergency conditions that have weighed
thousands of pounds. There are neurological indicators that everything that has ever happened to us is
stored in the human personality in some way that is
not as yet fully understood. Six years ago we believed the storage area was the brain. Today we know
that there is also such a thing as muscular memory.
This has vast implications for psychotherapy. What I
am saying is that we have stored a tremendous mass of
data and, to use a computer analogy, we have not yet
learned how to program ourselves to use this tremendous storage of data for problem-solving purposes.

Psychosomatic research and psychosomatic concepts are a clear indicator of human potential. Most
doctors who are sophisticated and trained within the
last 15 to 20 years are aware that anywhere from 70
to 80 percent of the people who walk into a general
practitioner's office are suffering from functional
illness. This means they have a symptomology for
which no physical but an emotional basis can be found.
Psychosomatic concepts are of tremendous importance
because they indicate that it is not the bacteria,
not the germ, not the virus that is causing the illness. It is our total outlook about ourselves, and
the well known American psychiatrist Szaz, who is
currently a gadfly on the tail-end of the AMA and the
establishment, makes the flat statement that illness

is a symbolic way of asking for help. It is a symbolic way of saying, "I can no longer cope. I need love and caring." Of course, we all hate to disabuse ourselves of the myth and notion that germs, viruses, and bacteria cause our illnesses. Yet, we know that most of us have had tuberculosis but very few have utilized that disease in order to say "I need caring" to the world and perhaps to get it from the world.

Another indicator of the human potential is the whole area of extrasensory perception, parapsychology, psychokinesis, clairvoyance. This whole, vast area has received a great deal of attention in the USSR. In this country, we are still trying to prove that the so-called "psychic phenomena" exist. In the USSR, they no longer need the proof. They accept E.S.P. They call mental telepathy 'radio brainwave communication.' They are trying to help people to tap into these powers and to help the man on the street to utilize it--a totally new approach to the subject. We all know today that most children have extrasensory capacities and that these capacities are trained out of them fairly early in childhood. I want to open this up for your consideration because many of you here have these capacities.

We are using only a small fraction of our sexual potential and I think we all need to know this. If we accept that we are using a small fraction of our total potential, then, of course, this also has something to do with the whole area of sexual experiencing. My research has shown conclusively that if people begin to work in this area they can have huge increments of sexual pleasure; that the quality of their sexual experiencing can be raised considerably, even compounded. All this depends, of course, on the individual's self-investment in this process. Every person has tremendous creative capacities and powers which lie untapped and latent.

There is a great deal of solid core research showing that people can experience a creativity workshop (or a course) and come up with capacities that they didn't even know or suspect they had. There is also what I call a "Grandma Moses phenomena." The famous primitive painter Grandma Moses discovered that she had talents when she was in her sixties and seventies. Most of us have talents which we will take to our graves with us because we will never develop them.

43

What I also am saying then is that every person
is the artist of his or her own creation. You are
the artist of your own creation. We determine our
own life and death--and that is hard to take, but
that is where the responsibility is. It lies totally
within each one of us.

In the light of this recognition then, I hope
that the development of your personal potential will
be a lifelong adventure for you. Why is this so
important? Because now we come to something that we
call the short-circuit theory. It goes something
like this: the unused human potential may go into
organismic, self-destructive paths. Athletes know if
you don't use it, you lose it. That applies to all
of us!

The human being needs to be continually pointed
in the direction of actualizing potential. We need
to be continually engaged in this process--in this
search. The actualization of human potential is the
path of human evolution. This is the road of life
affirmation. This actualization of our possibilities,
of our latent powers is life supportive and life pro-
longing. It adds quality to life; it adds vitality
to us and it gives us joie de vivre. In other words,
it gives us the tremendous sense of WOW! It's won-
derful to be alive and living!

The emphasis needs to be on the process and not
on the outcome. We must not be outcome-centered but
process-centered in this adventure of actualizing our
possibilities. The very core of the human potentiality's concept has tremendous relevance to human relationships because the interpersonal relationship
matrix is the prime matrix for actualizing human potential. We actualize our possibilities through relationships with people. We grew into what we are
through relations with people and we grow into what
we can be through relations with people. If you think
about that, you will recognize that this is where the
truth lies. Ask yourself this question: What is the
purpose of human relationships? Here are some of the
answers that you will give: Companionship is the
purpose of human relationships. Human relationships
help me to define myself. They give me a self-defini-
tion. Human relationships are for pleasure, sexual
and otherwise. Human relationships are for survival.
They are a necessity. We can't do without them.
Yet, all of us know about the empty and shallow nature

44

of most patterns of human relatedness. The game-playing; the artificiality that is all around us in contemporary society.

Looking at this desert of stereotypes of human-relatedness, we again ask: What is the purpose of human relationships? And one basic answer emerges: The actualizing of human potential is the prime reason for the human relationships that we have. In other words, we relate to people in order to foster our and their personal growth; our and their personal unfoldment; our and their personal evolution. This process needs to form the basis of our relatedness. If you believe this, you need to undertake a fundamental reassessment of the quality, trust, and the nature of the human relationships in which you are engaged, because there are such things as toxic individuals who bring out disturbance and who create pathogenic processes in us. We need to be aware that there are such things as psychic vampires, people who do, indeed, suck our energies and take, and take from us and give nothing, or very little in return. They never change, and never grow. Conversely, we need to recognize that there are people who stimulate us, who enhance our growth, who challenge us, and who make us feel more creative, more alive. We need to seek out those people. We need to be with them. We need, in turn, to give to them as they give to us.

Recognition of the fundamental principle that direction determines outcome, is of the very essence of what we call the growth concept of human relationships. The fundamental principle is, that if we believe in this, then this indeed will be the outcome. Namely, "my relationships exist for my and the other person's growth. I bend my efforts in this direction." If we believe this, then the outcome is more likely to be that.

The growth perspective of human relations operates within the framework of a number of concepts: (1) open communication; (2) honesty (no games between people); (3) furnishing growth opportunities and experiences for each other. That means conscious thought and effort expended on the question, "How am I going to help that person to grow and how can that person help me grow as a person and unfold my possibilities?" Risk-taking is of the very essence of this type of growth. Openness to feelings is also. The next principle involves recognition that human beings are a mystery. You are a vast mystery. The exploration of this mystery is a tremendous adventure and the exploration the mystery of the person with whom you co-exist and who is your companion, that is, in part, where the excitement of life lies. We need to recognize that human relationships are an interplay of energy forms and that we give and receive energy. We need to recognize that there are masculine and feminine components in each one of us and we need to be sensitive and open to these components of ourselves. We need to unfold them, to celebrate and welcome them because they represent precious assets and precious possibilities. We need to use our intuitive capacities, our hunches, to the very hilt when we engage in human relationships and we need to use them, particularly, with strangers because our growth always takes place in the context of strangers who become intimates. There, again, lies the adventure and the challenge for each one of us. The fear of the stranger is the greatest taboo of the bankrupt and sterile society that it is used by such a bankrupt and sterile society to sustain "anomie," the greatest cancer of this culture.

What are some of the social implications of the growth perspective of human relationships? First of all, I think we are all aware that men and women's roles are changing. We need to be very much aware that contemporary research has proven conclusively that the woman is the stronger of the species by all criteria that have been and can be established. Mortality, morbidity, survival rate, number of pleasure centers, however you look at it, you find the man is the more fragile organism of the two. This also means that a reversal of the roles in the sense of "interpersonal outreach" has to take place. The responsibility for outreach to the opposite sex has, up to now, largely been the males. This has to be reversed.

Another social implication of the growth perspective of human relationships is the importance of short term, quality relationships. That is extremely important. We need to get away from the concept of exclusively long term relationships. We need to recognize that in terms of personal growth, in terms of intimacy, in terms of openness, in terms of actualizing human possibilities, a great deal can exist between two people and can unfold in a relatively short period of time. A period of time

46

characterizes real openness, real communication. We also need to recognize that long term relationships can turn into a matrix inimical to human growth. In other words, many long term relationships become dead and sterile. This can be reversed in some instances, but for the most part, I have a feeling it is irreversible.

We need to develop frameworks so that people can meet each other. I think Bob Rimmer's brilliant suggestions along those lines: social clubs in motels, human potential centers, this type of thing, this is where we need to move (see Chapter 19,23). We also need to move into an area that I call structured interpersonal experiences as a means of personal growth. For example, we could have such an experience by sitting down with a person with whom we want to be intimate, using our intuitive faculties and communicating to that person what we perceive as his or her strengths.

In our culture, the emphasis is always on what is "wrong" with us. How about on what is "right" with us? How about more emphasis on our strengths, our resources--they are indeed present! We need to confront each other in terms of our strengths and potentials. The other side, what's "wrong" with, our "weaknesses" and so on, we get that type of communication all the time. We need to share such experiences with each other as the most loving moment in our lives. That's very important. We need to share with each other the happiest sexual experience we've ever had because that may give us some indication where we may want to go. We need to share with each other what our sexual fantasies are because it also is a form of communication. We need to recognize that at the very core of the sexual experience lies an energy and affective exchange and that a lot more than we know about is taking place between two people. We need to be very aware and very much focused on the need and the importance of nourishing love and caring for each other. Love and caring for each other and for ourselves. How much love and caring do we give to ourselves? That is where growth often really starts.

I want to say then, in closing, you are faced with a tremendous challenge and that challenge is, can you make your human relations, growth experiences, a framework of growth, a framework of mutual growth, of growth for you, a means of growth for the person with

whom you are intimate? That, I think, is the greatest
challenge that is facing all of us.

*Dr. Herbert A. Otto, The National Center for the
Exploration of Human Potential, La Jolla, CA.   Reprinted from The Other Americans, 1978 by permission.

CHAPTER 3

INDIVIDUAL AND FAMILY WELL-BEING OVER THE LIFE COURSE:
PRIVATE AND PUBLIC DIMENSIONS

Douglas B. Gutknecht*

I. INTRODUCTION

Studying the individual within numerous life
paths and stages, including marital, familial, work,
and leisure is becoming a topic of interdisciplinary
interest in the social and human sciences (Brim and
Baltes, 1980; Kenniston, 1977). Sociologists, psychologists, health scientists, anthropologists, his-
torians, educational and policy researchers, each
reveal partial snapshots of a holistic picture, the
implications of which will promote a better understanding of the life-long process of optimum development and well-being, both personal and familial.
This chapter draws inspiration from the work of numerous pioneers in the field of life course research,
family studies, socialization, and developmental
psychology (Brofenbrenner, 1970, 1979; Elder, 1974;
Riley, et al., 1972; Clausen, 1972; Brim, 1966;
Riegal, 1975; Neugarten, 1969). The life course is
defined as including numerous paths and dimensions
including family, career, educational, leisure, public service, which provides opportunities, influences,
and obstacles in the unending search for personal
development and humanistic social change. The family
provides one of the major life paths and contexts for
personal development, as well as a challenge for humanistic affirmation of a viable future for unborn
generations to come. Numerous issues and problems of
life long development find expression at those points
in a life course where one begins to seriously consider living together permanently, taking a partner
in marriage, deciding to have children, matching
family and career paths, divorcing, starting second
families, or watching grown children leave the nest.

After briefly defining the concept of well-being
in part two, a discussion of the underlying assumptions of this analysis follows in part three. Then
part four introduces the relationship of generational
cohorts, economic and family life course well-being.
Part five probes the dimensions of self and well-
being; while part six discusses the importance of

49

social support systems for general life course well-being, obviously impacting the family.

II. WELL-BEING DEFINED

Well-being is defined as the opportunity to maximize one's potential and enlarge one's possibilities for meaningful transactions with self, family, and society. It requires self-knowledge, including the desire and opportunity for life long learning and meaningful involvement in personal goals, family life, meaningful work, and public activities. Well-being is rooted in a basic biological level of fitness, not just absence of disease. Well-being is based upon a flexible attitude when faced with ambiguous situations and stressful daily encounters. Individuals derive it from actively defining, interpreting, and constructing meaningful bridges to other humans beings through social involvement, whether in family, work, or community. Well-being is more than coping, although this is one tool or skill essential over the long haul; it includes involvement in active and challenging activities. Well-being is rooted in the awareness that aging by itself does not produce inevitable decline of one's human potential for active involvement and meaning. Role obligations at different stages of life provide both opportunity and obstacles for a life that is well, optimal, actualized, world affirming. This holistic definition is offered only as a starting point for your reflection and expansion.

III. ASSUMPTIONS REGARDING WELL-BEING OVER THE LIFE COURSE

This analysis builds upon fundamental assumptions regarding the humanistic pursuit of well-being over the life course. First, individual change, growth, and development is much more than chronological aging (growing old). The inevitability of change requires a look at self development in an experimental manner, rejecting a rigid view of externally imposed stages and an imposed set of stereotyped expectations.

Second, structured social processes, transitions, and patterns, and structures systematically influence and set the stage for personal development and well-being over the life course. Intrinsic dimensions of life course transitions include the timing, continuity, extent, and number of role relationships at different stages of life (Foner and Kertzer 1978). For

50

example, a movement from the role of single to married may create demands, expectations, and disruptions for individuals trying to adapt to other life changes, like school or employment. Recognition of such possible discontinuities permits a more flexible attitude towards family role experimentation, via dating or living together, in order to prepare oneself for new responsibilities of living in an intimate setting with another human being. Flexible practices that allow individuals to learn about future role obligations help individuals better adapt to changing social demands, and ultimately reduce possibilities of excessive role strain and stress. Adolescents and young adults need more flexibility and support from society in order to reduce the strains of role transitions and possible discontinuities. Learning how to anticipate and deal with role conflicts and strain is essential for individuals desiring to maximize their human potential. For example, divorce rates are highest for 15-19 year olds, who often lack both material resources and role skills needed to handle life's inevitable conflicts and stresses.

IV. DEMOGRAPHY, ECONOMICS, FAMILY, AND LIFE COURSE
    WELL-BEING

The idea of generation or cohort is heretaken as a starting point and for comparisons. Social and demographic studies of generational cohorts provide one perspective of how well-being is impeded or sustained over the life course. Picture society as a large python that swallows a huge pig (i.e., cohort) that moves the entire length of its body as a big bulge. This baby boom bulge is now moving through our American society python creating many consequences because of its large size. Likewise the well-being of individuals in this large post-war baby boom generation is affected by the numerous social and historical events existing at the time of entry and movement.

For example, those born between 1946-1964, called the post-war baby boom generation, experienced an element of communality, as a result of entering society during a time of economic growth, suburbanization, increasing use of automobiles and T.V., and expansion of public education. World War II led to a reduction and delay in childbirth which then spurred a post-war baby boom. Large numbers of baby boom children are

51

now moving through occupational and family roles;
this situation has created many opportunities and
obstacles.

Today many post World War II baby boomers occupy
social roles like college student for longer periods
of time because we have stretched the transition period of college as a result of graduate and professional training. Longer periods of schooling provides an
escape valve for society because the occupational
world can't absorb such large numbers of potential
workers. In addition, training requirements of a
highly technological society are greater. The consequences for individuals ready to experiment with adult
roles, love, sex, marriage, or living together is often negative. The inability to enter work and assume
adult occupational responsibilities creates transitional problems for those desiring to marry and begin
a family after graduation. More graduate school marriages, with excessive strains, leads to high divorce
rates among this cohort. Those who do enter the work
world experience increasing competition for promotions.

Our society must better educate and prepare
young adults for the responsibilities of being workers, lovers, friends, helpers, communicators, and
stress reducers at earlier ages. This task involves
teaching about the developmental tasks of fully functioning human beings before major problems arise.
Younger adults need to be challenged and given meaningful responsibilities for their own futures, including work, love, and society. Young adults themselves need to recognize that autonomy and informed
choice involves responsibility for the rights of
others. We must ask how prepared we are to assume
the responsibility for guiding the growth of others
and sharing intimacy.

This generation has fostered new arrangements
between family and work paths. Traditionally women's
lives revolved around the family, although the pattern
began to change after World War II. First older married women in their 40's and 50's began to enter the
labor force as they completed their childbirth responsibilities at earlier ages and had more years to
live after their children's departure. Later in the
1960's increases in consumer expectations, along with
post Vietnam War stagflation, contributed to the
additional increases in the number of women working.

The economy itself began to depend on women working, particularly in the service sector. Dual-career families began to plan family and work paths together in order to insure the quality of life, consumption and future options that middle class families came to expect as the Post World War II American dream. More women began to work while raising young children and the percentage of married working women exceeded 50% in 1984, up from 30% in 1960.

The changing nature of economic realities created altered patterns of life paths for both men and women, but particularly for women. Women began to enter the labor force in the 1960's, particularly in the service sector, supported by a growing welfare state mentality. During the late 19th and early 20th century women until the childbirth cycle began. World Wars I and II provided the emergence of development paths where women started work, stopped to have families, and started work again in later life, after children left the nest. The newly emerging pattern of planning career or work cycles in conjunction with family responsibilities began after World War II, but developed most rapidly in the 1960's. Traditionally men plan their involvement in family and career as simultaneous developments, because women assumed the primary responsibility for child rearing. Traditionally men's careers have always taken precedence over family life.

Today the need for women to contribute to the economic well-being of the family has created potential conflicts over how to integrate career and family responsibilities for both spouses. Likewise, the very fact that a woman contributes to family resources in the era of excessive inflation enlarges her power and decision making authority in the family unit. Women, because they now more often possess independent access to wages, can leave an undesirable marriage because they no longer fear starvation.

The changing patterns of career and family life paths creates potential for the exploitation of women because so many married women entered the labor force in jobs that might be characterized as low paid, low level, and dead-end. Many of these jobs are as clerks, receptionists, and secretaries in service industries such as health care, education, insurance, banking, sales, etc. Many of these low-level, white and pink collar jobs were temporary, part time, with

few fringes, and no future. However, because families often need a working wife to combat the ravages
of inflation, the old escape valve of leaving the
labor force to have children used by previous generations of women no longer proves available. Women
are now asked to accommodate their schedules to both
families and employers. Unlike men whose life patterns are altered little upon the decision to marry
or have children, women often must sychronize their
family and career paths, with possible conflicts and
role overload the result.

Role overload results in fatigue and other symptoms of stress which both spouses need to recognize.
Fatigue is the physical wear and tear on our bodies.
In addition, time pressure occurs because many individuals don't know how to organize their workloads.
Such overload resulting in competing loyalties to
home and career, and intensifies emotional conflict.
The solution requires spouses to clearly communicate
and negotiate the changing financial, social, and
emotional reasons for working or not working, which
might reduce guilt and allow the positive aspects of
the situation to stand out. Higher educated women
appear more likely to force changes in both public
and private worlds, because working provides both
financial and social - psychological gratifications.

Short-term discontinuities may create needed
changes in the long-run as women demand changes in
career and family life and men must renegotiate old
sex role, decision making, and authority patterns.
The implications of the increased work force participation, income, and ultimate power in family decision making may upset functional thinking that suggests the necessity in marriage and family life of
rigid and distinct spheres of activity or division of
labor between husband and wife. The husband can no
longer be seen as the sole link to the world of work
(i.e., the instrumental role), and the wife the
emotional helpmate (i.e., the expressive role), or
nurturer. Well-being may require both spouses to
utilize their undeveloped skills and attributes in
order to resolve the many conflicts that lie ahead.
The idea that every marriage is really two, his and
hers, or includes many marriages at different stages
(i.e., childless, childfilled, empty nest) in the
marital cycle, may finally gain acceptance.

Such conflicts may increase the divorce rate and create marital strains, in the short-run, particularly for working couples wedded in traditional sex roles. However, in the long-run all society will benefit by this change in the devalued roles associated with the private aspects of domestic life. Such is best accomplished not by rhetoric but by changes in both public and private dimensions of sexual inequality, in domestic role responsibilities, wages, career opportunities, public support systems for child care, and flexible work hours, etc.

The public realm must be utilized to lighten the burden of private troubles for families, particularly for wives and children. This occurs because a class based society pushes those at the bottom of the economic ladder, particularly single parent families headed by females, to work in order to survive. Yet the ideology of democratic equality assumes that somehow all families are equal and can prepare their children to compete for a better future. However, without public support, any private energy or initiative families may muster will soon be drained away and the rhetoric of a private sanctuary will become instead a living nightmare.

In this view both the private and public external realms need to become integrated. Personal and public change must both occur; the reordering of relationships between family and work provides one example of how these two dimensions can become integrated without relying upon super-mom, super-career-women. At this point let's examine the relationship of private and public well-being using a slightly different focus.

V. SELF, FAMILY, AND THE LIFE COURSE: INTRINSIC SOURCES OF WELL-BEING

Well-being over a lifetime is closely related to how we sustain our growing, active sense of self. Internal dimensions of well-being include a sense of meaningfulness, authentic feelings and emotions, caring attitudes, a high level of cognitive functioning and education, multiple role involvements, biological health, and high level of energy and vigor.

A sober yet hopeful assessment of our situation in the modern world suggests that:

Increasingly today, the members of our society know that we are not set, certain, irrevocable substantial selves. They increasingly recognize that who we are, what we are, is continually in the process of becoming through our continual struggles, are notable to dictate the outcomes of this flux . . . the flux is crucial in our everyday lives (Douglas and Johnson, 1977:66).

Framing this discussion within existential and clinical sociology, our intellectual focus must be toward the importance of direct, personal experience, the passion for living, making sense of the world, and responsibly accepting the consequences of our attitudes, values, social decisions, and actions. We construct ourselves as feeling beings in a social world. A belief in indestructability of our deepest being and the importance of our feelings and emotions (i.e., situated being or self), allows us to emerge as selves in process. This view of self rejects rigid reductionism and the belief that people can be reduced to labels. Such labels channel our attention away from our humanistic possibilities for growth and well-being. The possibility and purpose of life is intimately tied to the concepts of consciousness and meaning.

The consequence of blocking our sense of purpose, our vital system, results in the loss of public morality, responsibility, and meaning. By blocking larger purposes and meanings we elevate our own petty problems to unreal and fantastic proportions and become neurotic, anxious, and self preoccupied (Wilson, 1972:225).

We lose well-being as we lose consciousness of our social and human connections. Losing meaning often results in turning inward; we experience guilt, inactivity, and passivity. For example, those who begin to experience family problems often seem destructively prone to turn their gaze on themselves, to project their hostilities on other family members who function as merely mirror images of their own weaknesses. In this view consciousness loses its power to focus, to engage, to take the role of the other, to connect, to analyze with compassion, to join forces. In fact, "we let our robot take over," we become passive, bored, frustrated, spiteful, amplifying the bad messages and ignoring the good:

56

Man is a many-layered creature, whose highly complex structure is largely 'robitic.' The unconscious mind is an enormous computer, its circuits need to be 'triggered' by certain definite signals. The vital reserves . . . the mind, the whole needs to be exercised. The mentally healthy individual habitually calls upon fairly deep levels of vital reserves. An individual whose mind is allowed to become dormant - so that only the surface is disturbed begins to suffer from circulation problems (Wilson, 1972: 222).

The mind needs to amplify, to contact deep levels of vital reserves and energy - otherwise, the trivial, the daily hassles, raise their heads and lead to fragmentation, passivity, breakdown in dialog and communication, stress, and burnout. A meaningful future, provides a vision for caring about others and not giving up after things don't work out. Affirmation of possibilities, goals and visions of the future provides a link from our consciousness to the public social world.

Our attitudes toward energy, time, and commitment highlight the possibility of meaning, purpose, and well-being (Marks, 1977:921-926). Discounting the scarcity approach to these concepts, Marx develops an expansionary view of self and consciousness which argues that we expand energy and time by increasing our commitments and social involvements. The key is priority time--time we choose to share with significant others, and pursue meaningful careers can actually increase our energy, both physical and psychological. The scarcity view of time assumes that energy is severely limited. Again the adage in personal and family life becomes the quality of time spent with others, not just quantity. In this view activity traps become a boring routine that tires us, not something that rejuvenates us. Such rejuvenation can hardly appear, however, if individuals feel that activities are dumped on them. In contrast, fulfilling activity can actually produce energy because it is rooted in our cells and is triggered by adenosine triphosphate (ATP):

The body stimulates the production of A.T.P. from glucose only through the consumption of A.T.P. in activity; hence the process of production of human energy is inseparably a part of

57

the consumption of energy. Activity is thus
necessary to stabilize the production of human
energy. And even while we are spending it we
are also converting more of it for later use
(Marks, 1977:925-926).

Although healthy and nourishing foods and exercise are
obviously an important component of this holistic view
of mind-body integration, one can see that meaningful
projects, goals, values, attitudes, also call forth
vital energy reserves, and expand the vigor for life:

> Abundant energy is 'found' for anything to which
> we are highly committed, and we often feel more
> energetic after having chosen it; also, we tend
> to 'find' little energy for anything to which
> we are uncommitted, and choosing these things
> leaves us feeling spent, drained and exhausted
> (Marks, 1977:927).

Time itself is not scarce but varies with meaningful commitments, valued activities, attitudes towards tasks, cultural scripts and institutionalized
roles:

> Like energy it is flexible, waxing, abundant,
> or scarce, slow or fast, expanded or contracted,
> depending upon very particular sociocultural and
> personal circumstances (Marks, 1977:929).

Such a view is not entirely incompatible with notions
of time as a scarce commodity. We do often feel
stressed and overloaded. Thinking about the quality
and priority of time requires us to plan flexible life
patterns. We must think about ways to bargain with
ourselves, our families, employers, and government to
support trade-offs between clock measured, quantified,
obligated work time, leading to extrinsic rewards and
quality leisure time--that time we truly cherish,
which leads to intrinsic rewards, values, and enjoy-
ments.

Commitment is not a scarce commodity but requires some thought regarding its priorities. The
principal point here is the need to reconceptualize
the drain - scarcity metaphor, applied to energy,
time, commitment, and consciousness. Energy is expanded by meaningful life events, social connections,
family, love, friendship, and challenging relationships, which somehow work to fill us with enthusiasm

and motivation. Thus, well-being over the life course increases, as we risk moments for intimacy, love, friendship, public, social, and community involvements. The key is that we reflect upon and prioritize those meaningful commitments which will make a difference in our lives.

Human energy is neither infinite nor biologically constant, but instead circumscribed by sociocultural variables:

> The findings reported here lead empirical support to the proposition the involvement in multiple roles does not necessarily result in role strain . . . additionally, the flow of commitment across roles will shift depending on the stages of the life cycle. These and other factors tend to diffuse the flow of commitments across several activity clusters. While individuals may find general well-being in whatever roles they enact, the findings reported here lend oblique empirical support for Siber's (1974) role accumulation theory in the sense of predicting incremental benefits as a function of multiple roles (Spretzer, et al., 1979:147).

VI. WELL-BEING AND SUPPORT SYSTEMS: EDUCATION, WORK AND FAMILY LIFE

Well-being, both personal and familial, involves innumerable transitions and decisions, regarding co-mingling paths and time tables for education, family, career, leisure, consumption, and life style. Often transitions, involving new intensive obligations and enlarged tasks, create personal stress and reduce the quality of family life. Some individuals may break out of their rigid patterns by pointing the way to alternative tasks, time tables, transitions, and life paths. Such ground-breaking responses sometimes require larger social and structural changes in order to institutionalize support systems. Today we must recognize that family and personal well-being are intimately tied to the available structural and social support systems which either limit or enhance options and potentials.

It is important to have flexible life scheduling in order to break down the arbitrary patterns, time tables, and normative expectations associated with the "education-work retirement lockstep" (Best, 1980:

3-11). This lockstep is made up of old predetermined, institutionalized patterns, that once served a purpose, and are now difficult to change because traditions die slowly, long after their original reasons for existing disappear. The lockstep is a sequence of age and time graded activities - youth for education, adulthood for work, and older age for retirement. This stereotyped sequence is built upon a one-dimensional life plan (e.g., linear life plan), that wastes precious human resources, squanders human energy, and reduces flexible life options. The lockstep is built upon the metaphors of energy scarcity and drain. The option and joy of planning alternate life paths, time tables, and careers over the life course is ignored. Flexible life scheduling remains an undernourished alternative.

There are creative ways to reconceptualize the choices between education and work, work and retirement, education and retirement, which impact individual and family well-being. For example, computers, technology, and rapidly changing, increasingly sophisticated work environments, require new thinking about how education prepares one for work over a lifetime. Meaningful work, one of the most important components of individual well-being, can be promoted by such techniques as lifelong study, retraining, sabbaticals, better career planning, educational credits for work experience, and work credit for time spent in school, pursuing the enrichment of adult learning.

In addition, the idea of cramming all education into narrow arbitrary stages, like youth or early adulthood, prolongs boredom, irrelevance, inactivity, poverty, and practical knowledge of the world. Such lockstep beliefs about education requires a reevaluation of our beliefs that we are through learning once we complete college. Well-being is actually promoted by allowing students to work while in school, join cooperative education programs, and alternate periods of work and education throughout their lives.

Flexible life scheduling should be joined with public recognition of how social support systems encourage or discourage individual, family, and social well-being. We must learn to diversify our options by promoting assessment of individual and family needs, goals, and plans by experimental social and policy support programs:

60

Learning how to cope with stress, strain, and burnout also indicates the importance of providing support systems to assist families and workers on the job (Warr and Wall, 1975; Cobb, 1976; Seyle and Brecht, 1980; Payne and Cooper, 1980; Girdano and Everly, 1980; Chernis, 1980). Although scarcity metaphors and theories may not govern the use of human energy, the facts of work stress, overload, and role strain remain. Excessive amounts of alienating and meaningless work distract from a human feeling of competence and mastery, which decreases a sense of quality involvement with personal goals, family, friends, and community activities (French, Rosenthal, and Cobb, 1974). Options open to the individual as part of flexible life scheduling allow a better fit between changing needs, family, work responsibilities and social supports, particularly when the fit creates stress and strain. Let's explore the relationship between family and work.

One emerging emphasis in the organization literature is the importance of human resources and the mutual interaction of family life and work environments (Mouton and Blake, 1981). The family needs to be supported, not only because it promotes productivity and economic growth, but because workers with good family lives are often more motivated and involved workers. What is invested in families dramatically affects how individuals perform on the job. Likewise, what happens at work certainly impacts how individuals respond to each other at home, which in turn carries over into the next work day. Difficulties, conflicts, lack of assistance or resources, stress and strain, in either family or work life, creates an increasing deteriorating situation in both spheres. Our sense of satisfaction and the health of our society is intimately linked to the productive use of our societal and human resources. Our private and public lives do intertwine even if we act as though they are worlds apart (see also Introduction to Section III).

There are three links which respond to internal family and external work demands. The wife's work link, the husband's work link, and the family link:

Work links include stamina, one's orientation to the content of what one is doing, one's reaction to the organization where one is employed, and one's relations with the people with whom one

61

works: peers, supervisors, subordinates. The
family link, similarly, encompasses many different relations, including those with one's spouse,
one's children, and parents, and with the community . . . (Bailyn, 1978:121).

The traditional pattern has until recently emphasized
the accommodation of family links to work links. Frequency of residential movement, type and number of
schools attended, child care options, even family
life styles are often influenced by work related pressures and standards. However, the era of the organizational man and the homogeneous suburban family, with
one spouse commuting to work and one spouse remaining
home, appears over. The forces of inflation and high
economic expectations, along with the demands of dual
career families, and the resurgence of interest in
leisure life and personal enjoyment, have caused a
reevaluation of the value of career advancement, and
the need for geographic mobility.

New standards regarding work and family links
are supporting changes in couples' values and life
goals. For example, two wage earners in a family can
be more picky about trade-offs between more money
versus less family life. Women now spend more years
in the labor force, which has increased their sophistication in bargaining for equal pay for equal work,
and lessens the demand for the male to make bread
winner sacrifices for just "any old job." Issues of
housing costs, area living standards and potential
sources of support by the corporation or community,
now become real issues for dual career families.
When faced with the decision of moving or being fired
or denied a promotion, families are now choosing to
stay put.

The growing involvement of women in the world of
banking, insurance, and other service and white or
pink collar sectors of our post-industrial service
society, places enlarged demands on both private and
public organizations. Increasing numbers of women,
now over 50%, work in order to achieve economic and
social goals promised by our leaders throughout the
post World War II decades. Support systems are
emerging more frequently in the corporate world--
corporate day care; job sharing (Arkin and Dobrofsky,
1978:122-137); employee assistance, like financial,
legal, health, family, and drug counseling; flexible
"cafeteria" type benefit packages that allow trade-

offs between benefits such as child care versus pensions; relocation job opportunities for one's spouse; moving assistance expenses and cost of living bonus and adjustments.

Personal and social well-being over the life course is best facilitated by such progress which allows more meaningful involvement in personal work, community, and family life. The key is participation and learning to forge new relationships, open avenues of growth, and challenging institutions, like the work place, to offer needed supports. We must understand the forces that narrow our lives and place us in rigid work, family, and community roles and timetables. We can break out of the lockstep mentality. Stereotype and lockstep-thinking, about education, careers, health, family, retirement, and institutional change limit our ability to learn and change. Developing skills, resources, and support systems requires a lifelong commitment to personally meaningful change projects. Increasing rapid social changes, a fact of life in America for several decades, also requires the individual to assume more responsibility for personal and familial well-being. We must become more involved with those decisions that impact our personal, family and community life. This task calls for numerous assessment, decision making, organizational, and political skills. The problem of supporting family life in its various dimensions is essentially one of promoting development of our human potential.

BIBLIOGRAPHY

Arkin, W. and Lynne Dobrofsky

1978   "Job Sharing" in Robert and Rhona
            Rapoport (eds), Working Couples.   New
            York: Harper & Row.

Bailyn, Lotte

1978   "Accommodation of Work to Family" in
            Robert and Rhona Rapoport (eds),
            Working Couples. New York: Harper &
            Row.

Best, Fred

1980   Flexible Life Scheduling: Breaking the
            Education - Work - Retirement Lockstep.
            New York: Praeger.

Brim, O.

1966   "Socialization Through the Life Cycle"
            in Orville Brim and Stanton Wheeler,
            Socialization After Childhood: Two
            Essays. New York: Wiley.

Brim, O.G. and
D.B. Baltes (eds.)

1980   Life-span Development and Behavior
            (vol. 3), New York: Academic Press.

Bronfenbrenner, V.

1979   The Ecology of Human Development, Ex-
            periments by Nature and Design.   Cam-
            bridge, Mass.: Harvard University
            Press.

1970   Two Worlds of Childhood.   New York:
            Russel Sage.

Chernis, Albert

1980   Burnout in Human Service Organizations.
            New York: Praeger.

Clausen, J.

1972   "The Life Course of Individuals" in
            M. Ruby, M. Johnson, and A. Foner,
            Aging and Society III: A Sociology of
            Age Stratification. New York: Russel
            Sage.

Cobb, S.

1976   "Social Support as a Moderator of Life
            Stress." Psychosomatic Medicine, vol.
            3, no. 5:300-304.

Douglas, T. and
J. Johnson (eds.)

1977   Existential Sociology. New York:
            Oxford.

Elder, Glen

1974   Children of the Great Depression.
            Chicago: University of Chicago Press.

Foner, A. and
D. Kertzer

1978   "Transitions Over the Life Course:
            Lessons from Age Set Societies."
            American Journal of Sociology, vol. 83,
            March: 1031-1104.

French, J.R.P.,
W.L. Rosenthal,
and S. Cobb

1974   "Adjustment as Person--Environment
            Fit." In G. Coello and D. Hamburg and
            J. Adams (eds.), Coping and Adaptation.
            New York: Wiley.

Girdano, D. and
G. Everly

1980   Controlling Stress and Tension. New
            York: Prentice Hall.

Glick, Paul

1979 "Future American Families" The Wash-
     ington COFO Memo. 2 (3):2-5.

Highet, Gilbert

1976 The Immortal Profession. New York:
     Weybright and Talley.

Kenniston, K.

1977 All Our Children: The American Family
     Under Pressure. New York: Harcourt
     Brace Jovanovich.

Klapp, O.

1979 Opening and Closing: Strategies of
     Information Adaptation in Society.
     New York: Cambridge University Press.

Marks, S.

1977 "Multiple Roles and Role Strain: Some
     Notes on Human Energy, Time, and Com-
     mitment." In American Sociological
     Review, vol. 42 (Dec.): 921-936.

Mouton, J.S.
and R.R. Blake

1981 Productivty: The Human Side. New
     York: A.M.A.C.O.M.

Neugarten, B.L.

1969 "Continuities and Discontinuities of
     Psychological Issues Into Adult Life,"
     Human Development, 12:121-130.

Payne, R. and C.L. Cooper

1980 Stress at Work. New York: John
     Wiley & Sons.

Pearing, A.

1982   "New Claremont College MBA/Ph.D., Pro-
            gram Mixes Business and The Humanities
            to Produce Well-Rounded Leaders." The
            Executive, February, p. 100-102.

Reigel, K.F.

1975   "Toward a Dialectical Theory of Devel-
            opment," Human Development, 18:50-64.

Riley, Matilda White
M. Johnson and A. Foner

1972   Aging and Society III: A Sociology of
            Age Stratification. New York: Russel
            Sage.

Seyle, H., and R.A. Brecht

1980   Stress and the Manager: Making it Work
            For You. New York: Spectrum Books.

Spretzer, E., E. Snyder
and D. Larson

1979   "Multiple Roles and Psychological Well-
            Being" Sociological Focus, Vol. 12,
            No. 2.

Warr, D. and T. Wall

1975   Work and Well-Being. Baltimore: Pen-
            guin Books.

Wilson, C.

1972   New Pathways in Psychology, Maslow and
            the Post Freudian Revolution. New
            York: Taplinger Publishing Co.

*Department of Sociology, Chapman College, Orange,
California.

CHAPTER 4

EDUCATION FOR CHOICE: IMPLICATIONS OF ALTERNATIVES IN LIFESTYLES FOR FAMILY LIFE EDUCATION

Eleanor D. Macklin*

Given the increasing range of lifestyle alternatives available in contemporary society, it is important that family life educators prepare individuals to make wise lifestyle choices. The article reviews the contemporary alternatives to the traditional family, notes some of the skills and knowledge required by these alternatives, and suggests a format for preparing students to make appropriate lifestyle choices. The following lifestyle options and their implications for family life education are reviewed: to marry or not to marry, to parent or not to parent, to co-parent or single-parent, to make a lifelong or openended commitment, degree of androgyny, to be sexually exclusive or nonexclusive, gender of partner, and to live alone or with others. An educational approach is proposed, based on a humanistic perspective and designed to foster knowledge about available alternatives, increased awareness of individual values, and the development of decision-making and conflict-negotiation skills.

One of the major trends in recent years has been the growing range of available lifestyle options from which to choose and the increasing freedom with which to make that choice (Macklin, 1980). This has important implications for the youth in our society and for those seeking to prepare them to deal realistically with their futures.

Traditionally, our dominant culture has assumed that its adult members would select a mate of the opposite sex, marry, have children, be sexually exclusive, live together till death did them part, and acknowledge the male as primary provider and ultimate authority. Although it is clear that many did not, in fact, live this way, the majority did so and little support was given to those who did not. Given such a world, it was appropriate that family life education would focus primarily on such topics as mate selec-

69

tion, parenting, home management skills, and the developmental phases of the nuclear family.

But the above is no longer the case, for increasingly the traditional pattern is neither the reality nor the ideal for many. In 1978, fewer than one-third of the U.S. households consisted of a married couple with children under 18 (compared to 40% in 1970), and in over half of these the mother was in the labor force (U.S. Bureau of the Census, 1979a, Table A; U.S. Department of Labor, 1979). Almost one-quarter of the households consisted of persons living alone, and increasing numbers were living as single parents or as partners of persons to whom they were not married. By 1990, close to one-third of all children will experience the divorce of their parents (Glick, 1979a), and large numbers of these will, in turn, become members of stepfamilies.

The field is alive with new terminology as researchers seek to identify the seemingly endless variations currently evolving. Dual-career families, commuter marriage, the binuclear family, blended families, group marriage, sexually-open marriage, gay fathers, lesbian mothers, the open family, and the urban commune are only a few of the many present forms. Preparing persons to deal constructively with the complexity of the new pluralism and to make informed choices for themselves with regard to lifestyle is the challenge of family life education in the '80s. The question becomes how best to meet the challenge. This article will review the available lifestyle options, suggest some of the skills and understandings required to deal with them effectively, and propose a format for introducing students to these.

Contemporary Lifestyle Options

What are the lifestyle choices which persons must be prepared to make today? It is not easy to organize the multitude of alternatives into some logical and meaningful series of options. A helpful approach is to view the alternatives as variations on the traditional nuclear family. One is then led to the following list (see Table 1):

70

Table 1
Contemporary Lifestyle Options

The "Nontraditional" Alternative	The "Traditional" Alternative	The Choice Which Students Must Be Prepared to Make
Never-married singlehood; non-marital cohabitation	Legally married	To marry or not to marry
Voluntary childlessness	With children	To parent or not to parent
Single-parent (never-married once-married); joint custody and the binuclear family; the stepfamily	Two-parent	To co-parent or single-parent
Renewable contract; divorce and remarriage	Permanent	To make life-long or open-ended commitment; to stay married or to divorce; to remain single or to remarry
Androgynous marriage (e.g., O'Neill's "open marriage," dual-career marriage, commuter marriage	Male as primary provider and ultimate authority	Degree of androgyny
Extramarital relationships sexually open marriage, swinging, Ramey's "intimate friendship"	Sexually exclusive	To be sexually exclusive or non-exclusive

Table 1
Contemporary Lifestyle Options (continued)

The "Nontraditional" Alternative	The "Traditional" Alternative	The Choice Which Students Must Be Prepared to Make
Same-sex intimate relation-ships	Heterosexual	Gender of partner
Multi-adult households (e.g., multilateral marriage, communal living, affiliated families)	Two-adult household	To live alone or with others, and with how many others

To Marry or Not to Marry

Although once viewed as a sign of abnormality in men and undesirability in women, singlehood is increasingly seen as an acceptable option today (Libby, 1977; Stein, 1978). The average age at marriage is gradually advancing (of women aged 20-24, 29% were still single in 1960, 36% in 1970, and 49% in 1979-- U.S. Bureau of the Census, 1980: Tables A and B). Thus, people are single longer, and although the vast majority will still choose to eventually marry, it is predicted that 8 to 9% of those presently in their twenties will experience a lifetime of singlehood (Glick, 1979b). In addition, large numbers of adults experience being single as a result of divorce or widowhood (e.g., in 1976, 30% of the adult males and 37% of the adult females were either never-married, divorced, or widowed--U.S. Bureau of the Census, 1977).

There are also increasing numbers who choose to live with a partner without being married (Macklin, 1978; Yllo, 1978; Jacques & Chason, 1979; Newcomb, 1979). The great majority of these persons will eventually marry, although not necessarily each other, but some will choose for a variety of reasons to cohabit as a permanent alternative to marriage, particularly those who have experienced a previous marriage and divorce. It is estimated that at the present time, unmarried-cohabiting couples represent only about 3% of all "couple households" in the U.S. (U.S. Bureau of the Census, 1980, p. 3-5), but almost 50% of a recent sample of marriage license applicants in Los Angeles had lived for some time with their current partner before marriage (Newcomb & Bentler, 1980).

The above realities have a number of obvious implications. For instance, students need guidelines for assessing their own readiness for marriage and the extent to which a committed partnership with another is currently or potentially an appropriate life choice for them. If the decision to cohabit and/or to marry is to be a thoughtful one, individuals must have a realistic understanding of the relative costs and benefits, both socio-emotional and legal/financial, of these lifestyles. In addition, both males and females must plan their lives with the anticipation that at some point in their adult years they may be voluntarily or involuntarily single, and

73

be encouraged to develop the skills and resources
needed for a successful independent life.

To Parent or Not to Parent

Although it was traditionally assumed that marriage would inevitably lead to parenthood, and couples
who were without children were either to be pitied
or criticized, voluntary childlessness is becoming
a more common phenomenon, at least among urban educated
professionals (Veevers, 1979). The '70s witnessed a
definite trend toward postponement of childbearing
(among ever-married women aged 25-29, the percentage
remaining childless increased from 16% in 1970 to 25%
in 1978--U.S. Bureau of the Census, 1979b: Table 7).
It is currently estimated that about 10% of all
couples will remain voluntarily childless (Veevers,
1979). However, because of the strong pronatalist
orientation of our society (Calhoun & Selby, 1980),
research uniformly reports that voluntary childless
complex experience some degree of disapproval from
others (e.g., Ory, 1978). If one accepts that parenthood is not equally appropriate for all, education
must foster an atmosphere which supports childlessness
as an acceptable option, and so do what it can to
help individuals determine whether parenthood is, in
fact, the best option for them.

To Co-parent or Single-Parent

There has been a dramatic increase in the number
and proportion of single-parent families during the
past decade, due to an increase in separation and
divorce and in the number of families headed by
never-married mothers. In 1979, 19% of all households with children under 18 were maintained by
single parents (17% by mothers, 2% by fathers), and
it is predicted that 45% of all children born in 1977
will spend some time as a member of a single-parent
family (Glick, 1979a). The most pressing problems
experienced by such families are economic, coupled
with the struggle of fulfilling parental roles while
living in a society which still maintains negative
attitudes toward single parents and their children
(Parks, Note 1). Students need to be prepared for
the increasing prevalence of this family form, understand its commonly experienced problems, realize that
it can be a viable lifestyle for both fathers and
mothers, and be aware of sources of community support
for such families.

74

It should be noted that many so-called single-parents are, in fact, functioning as co-parents, although the other parent is not an official member of the household. An example would be those divorced couples who elect joint custody (where the court assigns divorcing parents equal rights to, and responsibility for, the minor child--Milne, 1979) and who are living as a "binuclear family" (where the child is part of a family system composed of two nuclear households with varying degrees of cooperation between and time spent in each--Ahrons, 1979). Students should be challenged to think creatively about ways of maintaining family when the spousal unit dissolves, realize that co-parenting is an option in the event of divorce, and recognize the factors which predict the success of such an option.

In this context it should be noted that stepfamilies (where one or both of the married adults have children from a previous union with primary residence in the household) now comprise about 10 to 15% of all households in the U.S. (Glick, 1979a), and this number increases greatly when one includes all remarriages in which one of the two adults was a parent in a previous marriage. Clinical experience suggests that the stepfamily is structurally and psychologically different from the traditional nuclear family and that an understanding of its special complexities is necessary for its success (Visher & Visher, 1979), yet few persons are prepared for this reality. With so many presently involved in stepfamilies, it is crucial that persons be helped to understand the special characteristics of this unit, that teachers be aware that many members of their classes may be actively involved in such households, and that persons be prepared to cope effectively with the stresses predictable for that unit.

To Make Lifelong or Open-ended Commitment

The idea of renewable couple-written contracts is not new (e.g., Weitzman, 1974), but is not yet fully recognized within our legal system. The State still holds that when persons marry, it is for life (unless the State decrees otherwise) and with certain universally designated obligations to one another. However, increasingly, couples are being encouraged informally to develop for themselves clearly specified contracts, spelling out their expectations and promises to one another, in a wide range of areas such as economic, task-sharing, child-rearing, social life, and career development, including specified periods for renegotiation and evaluation and techniques for dealing with any conflicts which may arise (Whitehurst, Note 2).

Classroom exercises which give the student the experience of thrashing out such a contract serve to alert the individual to the range of potential problem areas, give practice in negotiation, and elicit discussion about the possible criteria for termination of a relationship. Since unexpressed and often unconscious expectations brought into a relationship are a common source of problems in relationships (Sager, 1976), it is crucial that students be taught the importance of being in touch with their own needs and expectations, learn to verbalize these, and be open to hearing the needs and expectations of the other. One might also argue that given the short-lived nature of many relationships in present society, and the prevalence of divorce, time should be spent exploring the concept of commitment and the dynamics of termination.

Degree of Androgyny

Our society has made significant strides toward removing sex-role stereotyping and achieving more sharing of child-rearing and household responsibilities, although there has been more change in attitude than in practice (Scanzone & Fox, 1980). In 1979, nearly half of all wives 16 years old and over (with and without children) were working or looking for work, and slightly over half of all children under 18 living in two-parent families (60% in one-parent families) had mothers who were in the labor force (U.S. Department of Labor, 1979). As women come to espouse the same career goals as men, and as parental and professional roles are seen as equally appropriate for both sexes, increasing numbers of families will be confronted by the conflicting priorities of home vs. work, and of wife's career development vs. husband's (Gross, 1980; Skinner, 1980).

Akin to the concept of the androgynous, or non-gender-roled, relationship is the widely discussed "open marriage," a relationship characterized by functioning in the "here and now" with realistic expectations, respect for personal privacy, role flexibility, open and honest communication, open companionship, pursuit of identity, mutual trust, and equality of power and responsibility (O'Neill & O'Neill, 1972). It is interesting to find that, although the past decade has witnessed much support for many of the values inherent in open marriage, research suggests that few college-educated couples actually evidence these characteristics (Wachowiak & Bragg, 1980).

Similar to open marriage is the concept of "open family," with its emphasis on flexible role prescriptions across both age and gender, clear communication with extensive negotiation and decision by consensus, open expression of emotion, and mutual respect (McGinnis & Flannegan, 1976; Constantine, 1977). But, once again, in spite of increasing lip service given to these values, there is little evidence that American families reflect them in actual practice.

It seems clear that education must continue to sensitize students to the issues of gender equality and prepare them to deal realistically with the conflicts they are likely to experience if they seek to live more androgynous lives. It also seems clear that if more egalitarian relationships are to be a reality of our society, there must be a more conscious fostering of this ideal and training for such relationships.

Whether to be Sexually Exclusive

Among the well-documented realities of modern life are the increases in reported sexual interaction with someone other than one's spouse or primary partner (particularly for women), the fact that the first incident is occurring at a younger age, and the finding that rates for women are becoming similar to those for men (Athanasiou, Shaver, & Tavris, 1970; Hunt, 1974; Bell, Turner, & Rosen, 1975; Levin, 1975; Maykovich, 1976). Moreover, research has made it clear that extramarital sex is not necessarily indicative of or contributive to a poor primary or marital relationship (Johnson, 1970; Hunt, 1974; Bell et al., 1975; Levin, 1975; Glass & Wright, 1977; Atwater, 1979). There are, in fact, couples who have made a mutual decision to allow one or both to have openly acknowledged non-competing sexual relationships with satellite partners (Ramey, 1976), believing that such a relationship maximizes the opportunity for both personal growth and emotional security. It is also clear that for many persons such a lifestyle is not functional. The viability of non-exclusivity as a lifestyle appears to depend on such variables as the quality of the primary relationship, the demands of the outside relationship, and the personalities of the individuals involved (Knapp & Whitehurst, 1977).

Given the above, it follows that persons need to be prepared for the reality that, at some point in their lives, they or their loved ones may violate the traditional norms of sexual exclusivity, and to be given the skills and perspective necessary to deal constructively with such an eventuality. Students need to be taught that there are, in fact, viable alternatives to traditional exclusivity, but that these do not work well for many. In order that they can better determine whether a nonexclusive lifestyle is likely to be appropriate for them and/or their partner, they must gain a knowledge of the kinds of problems which can be anticipated, an understanding of the personal characteristics associated with success, and a realistic appraisal of their own needs and limits.

Bernard (1977) has suggested that since in today's society it is difficult to achieve both sexual exclusivity and permanence, and since to insist on sexual exclusivity seems to lead to a pattern of serial monogamy, we would be wise to redefine marital fidelity to mean "living up to one's vows." If one were to follow this suggestion, it appears that one function of family life education is to help students think clearly about what promises they can realistically make to their partners. It is possible, for instance, that instead of promising a lifetime of exclusivity, a couple might agree to the process by which they will deal with any desires for extramarital intimacy. Thus, it becomes necessary for the curriculum to include the teaching of communication and conflict-negotiation skills (e.g., Gordon, 1970; Guerney, 1977; Mace & Mace, 1977; Miler, Nunnally, & Wackman, 1979) and that some consideration be given to constructive approaches to the problems of jealousy and possessiveness (Mazur, 1977).

Gender of Partner

Until recently, gender of partner would not have been considered a choice which persons voluntarily

78

made, nor would the selection of a same-sex partner have been viewed as an acceptable alternative. But the '70s ushered in important changes with regard to the viability of gay relationships and the social acceptability of homosexuality as a personal life-style (Bell & Weinberg, 1978; Harry & Lovely, 1979; Masters & Johnson, 1979). It is anticipated that there will be an increasing number of individuals who experience intimate relationships with persons of the same sex at some point in their lives, who choose to live as acknowledged homosexuals, and who challenge the laws which discriminate against them. Family life education can do much to increase society's understanding of such persons and help to eliminate the myths and prejudices surrounding this lifestyle.

Given the above goal, it follows that family life curricula should ideally include activities geared to help young persons understand those who differ in choice of sexual partner, appreciate the similarities between homosexual and heterosexual relationships, and accept themselves should their choice be atypical. Students need to realize that there are many, often as yet poorly understood, reasons for sexual preference, and that sexual preference is not necessarily consistent throughout a lifetime. They need to make the necessary distinctions between gender identity, sex-role identity, and gender of preferred sexual partner, and to recognize that one's sexual preference is distinct from one's degree of masculinity or femininity. And, so that they may participate as informed citizens, they need to understand the issues related to the legal rights of gay persons, particularly those concerning marriage and parenthood.

To Live Alone or With Others

The relative strength of one's needs for emotional closeness and for personal space is basic to the decision of whether to live alone or with others, and, if with others, with how much obligation to the others. Multiadult households, such as communes and multilateral marriage, are instances of living patterns based on an expectation of high degrees of sharing and togetherness. For many, the communes associated with the late '60s and early '70s resulted from a desire for community, and those few which survived usually evidenced a high degree of social organization and subordination of the individual to the group (Kanter, 1972, 1973; Mowery, 1978; Ruth, 1978). Multilateral or group marriage (Constantine & Constantine, 1973; Constantine, 1978), a lifestyle characterized by three or more partners each of whom considers him or herself personally committed to more than one of the other partners, necessitates a high energy investment in consensual decision-making.

It is important to note that most of these more complex living ventures have not continued for long. While much of their demise can be traced to poor organizational and interpersonal skills, even more basic may be the fact that persons came into them with little awareness of the demands of these living arrangements and with high hopes for a sense of togetherness coupled with a firm personal commitment to individual freedom--mutually exclusive needs which will inevitably clash if not consciously reconciled. Helping persons recognize the importance of assessing their own needs and limits, in particular their relative needs for intimacy and autonomy, as they make a choice of living pattern, can be an important function of family life education.

A Suggested Approach

The challenge of preparing persons to deal constructively with contemporary alternative lifestyles is a difficult one. The issues are controversial, the requisite skills and understandings are many, and resources are limited. There are many who will argue that even to acknowledge the existence of alternatives is to legitimize them, and that such legitimation works only to further erode the stability of an already over-stressed society. They suggest that to present the student with a smorgasbord of choice will serve merely to further confuse and to foster a climate of normlessness and anomie. There are others who will say that the purpose of education is to inform, and that to deny students an opportunity to explore and discuss the realities of contemporary society is to ill-prepare them to move intelligently within that society. The question is: How can we help students examine the available alternatives in a way which will simultaneously enhance both their awareness and understanding and their sense of personal competence and direction?

The approach to be presented here is based on a humanistic perspective operating within a Kohlberg framework (see Englund, 1980). Thus, the intention is to maximize the opportunity for personal growth and individual choice while pressing for an awareness of the values underlying one's choices and the effect of these choices on the larger social system. The proposed format seeks to stimulate both cognitive and affective learning (Olson & Moss, 1980), and equal emphasis is devoted to the development of values, skills, and knowledge. The goal is for students to become sufficiently aware of their own values, of the decision-making process, and of the available alternatives that they can make mature, informed, functional lifestyle choices for themselves and understand those who make choices different from their own.

The proposal is envisioned as a first course in family life education, thereby laying a foundation for later courses which would focus in more depth on such topics as parent education and couple relationships. Having developed in their first course an appreciation for the wide range of current family forms, students in the advanced courses would be less likely to fall into the present trap of discussing parenting only within the traditional nuclear family, or viewing couple relationships as only premarital or first-marriage.

Establishing a Supportive Environment

In order that students may grow in self-awareness and experience an unbiassed exposure to the various options, staff must create a classroom atmosphere of mutual acceptance, conducive to self-disclosure and mutual sharing. It must be clearly understood that no one lifestyle is necessarily correct for all and that each lifestyle has its own particular set of costs and benefits, both for the individuals involved and for society. It is often helpful to begin such a course with a discussion of the guidelines to be followed during the course, and to have these posted in a conspicuous spot. The list should be generated with the students and include those procedures which they think are necessary if they are to feel safe sharing their ideas and experience with one another. Students should be encouraged to speak for themselves rather than for others (e.g., "It is difficult for me to imagine myself ever feeling comfortable living with a guy if I wasn't married to him" rather than "I can't

81

imagine anyone ever feeling comfortable..."), and judgmental comments should focus on process rather than content (e.g., "You have not told us why you would prefer to have a wife who didn't work" rather than "You are really old-fashioned if you don't want your wife to work"). It is important that the teacher model the agreed-upon principles and help students to act upon them.

Getting in Touch with Values

Just as the instructor makes decisions regarding classroom procedures based on his/her value system, so students must come to realize that they will make their lifestyle choices based upon a particular system of values. For them to make conscious and consistent choices, it will be necessary that they have some conception of the value system from which they are operating.

Because so much of an individual's value system and role expectations are influenced by the family in which s/he grew up, it seems reasonable to begin such a course with an analysis of one's family of origin. Assignments can include such activities as: construction of a family genogram, depicting the members of the family and their structural relationship to one another; observation of one's family in interaction, with particular attention to communication patterns, roles, power, rules, cohesion, and how family members deal with conflict (Carnes, 1981); interviews of significant family members regarding importance attached to marriage and family and their views of the family's roles, rules, and traditions.

As students share the structure and roles within their family system, the wide variation in family patterns in modern society should become vividly obvious. The teacher can take the opportunity to diagram in detail some of the described patterns, noting, for instance, the complexities of the stepfamily with its frequent role ambiguities and loyalty conflicts. Students can learn the basic concepts used to analyze family functioning and those components of healthy family process which appear to operate irrespective of family structure (e.g., Lewis, Beavers, Gussett, & Philips; 1976; Olson, Sprenkle, & Russell, 1979). Most importantly, they can begin to articulate the value patterns which have been modeled by their family and which are likely to play a significant role in their own life choices. Values clarification and moral development will be fostered throughout the course as the teacher seeks to elicit a diversity of opinion, explores a variety of lifestyles, and raises questions designed to encourage students to consider the possible reasons for, and personal and societal consequences of, the various lifestyle options.

Decision-Making and Conflict-Negotiation Skills

The ability to make decisions, both for one's self and with others, is a crucial skill in a society which espouses freedom of choice and respect for the needs of others. It is, therefore, necessary that students learn the basic skills associated with decision-making and conflict-negotiation: the ability to send complete, congruent "I" messages, the ability to listen to a message and to confirm that it has been received accurately, and the ability to identify and evaluate alternatives (Miller et al., 1979). Taught relatively early in the term, these skills can be practiced in the course of later class discussion. Journals in which students keep a record and analysis of their own communications with significant others, and of their observations of the communications of others, will serve to keep these skills in focus and allow an opportunity to monitor student progress.

Knowledge of Alternative Family Forms

If students are to make informed decisions for themselves, they must have knowledge of the various options open to them. It is suggested that class time be given to consideration of each of the eight life-style choices listed in Table 1. Discussion should seek to place each lifestyle option in historical perspective, noting the societal and psychosocial factors that led to the development of the tradition-al way and its alternatives, identify the personal and social costs and benefits typically associated with each, and review the available research. The extent of such coverage will vary with the nature of the student body.

It is important during the above discussion to note that the various options are not theoretically mutually exclusive. Thus, it would be possible to "mix and match" the alternatives in any number of different combinations. One can, for instance, choose to stay single, have children, co-parent, make a permanent commitment, be sexually non-exclusive, have a same-sex partner, and live communally. It is possible, therefore, given the increased acceptance of pluralism in modern society and a careful choice of associates, to write one's lifestyle script in any of a number of ways. One must also realize that the particular life-style one ends up living is not always a matter of choice, and may be thrust upon one by circumstances or the wishes of others--some lifestyles results from ideology and personal choice, while some are borne of necessity. Students should also understand that life-style choices are not necessarily made "once and for all." Given the rapid social change and inevitable personal developmental changes, choices made at one point in life may not be the choice and/or the reality at another point in life.

In addition to the above cognitive focus, it is suggested that students be provided some first-hand experience with persons living these various alterna-tives. This can be provided in several ways: persons living a given lifestyle can be asked to come to class to share with the students their own particular exper-ience, or students can interview persons living in various lifestyles and then share their observations with the class. One class period might include, for instance, reports from students who have interviewed single-parent fathers, in which they describe the nature of the living arrangement, the history of that arrangement, and the problems and satisfactions ex-perienced. Given such information, the class could speculate about the viability and the prevalence of the particular lifestyle in the future.

There are numerous assignments which could be given near the end of the course to help students articulate and summarize what they had learned about their own lifestyle preferences. A role play in which they are asked to develop a premarital or precohabita-tion contract with another class member would encour-age them to review those lifestyle issues which cou-ples should discuss and negotiate prior to a long-term commitment. This would require that each individual take a position on such questions as whether and when to have children, child care and house maintenance roles, use of leisure time, and the nature of accept-able outside relationships, thus establishing their current view on these matters. The act of negotiating with their "partner" would also provide a good indicator of their current skill at constructive communication. In addition, students might be asked to write a summary paper, indicating their anticipated choice for each of the lifestyles options, with reasons for that choice.

Conclusions

Although the dominant family pattern in our society continues to appear very traditional (with the majority choosing to marry, remain married, have children, live in single-family households, and be sexually exclusive and heterosexual), there have been significant changes which must be reflected in education for contemporary family life. First, there have been dramatic increases in the proportion of working wives, single-person households, divorce and remarriage rates, stepfamilies and binuclear families, and persons living together unmarried, each with its own set of complexities and personal and social implications. Second, there has been an increased emphasis on quality of interpersonal relationships within marriage and the family, with little preparation in how to achieve this. Third, and most important, there has been a continued evolutionary movement toward individual freedom of choice, with a growing awareness of lifestyle options and acknowledgement that lifestyle choices made at one point in life may not be appropriate at another point. This means that, irrespective of one's preferred lifestyle, individuals today are faced with greater expectations of family life but little knowledge of how to meet these, the stress of continual decision-making and negotiation, the uncertainty that comes from having few available role models for many of the newer lifestyles, and the insecurity that comes from venturing in new directions with little societal support.

If we are to equip students to deal effectively with these realities, it is important that family life educators:

1. foster an awareness of the range of family living patterns within our society and of the personal and societal implications of this growing pluralism;

2. provide as much information as possible about the available alternatives, so that students can make informed decisions for themselves

85

and react intelligently and supportively to the lifestyle decisions of others;

3. help students become aware of the values, needs, and expectations which grow out of their own socialization, and understand the impact which these will have on their own choice of lifestyle and family pattern;

4. focus on building those basic decision-making and communication skills needed to constructively negotiate familial conflict and generate creative lifestyle solutions; and

5. provide some understanding of the basic components of healthy family functioning which appear to operate irrespective of lifestyle and family form.

It will not be easy for educators to do the kind of educating which has been indicated, and much of it cannot be accomplished solely within the secondary or college curriculum. Many of the lifestyle issues which confront persons today do not become a reality until adulthood, and although it is important that they be introduced earlier, instruction will be most relevant when the individual is actively involved in decision-making. Many constituencies will be uncomfortable with the open approach which is espoused here, and hence, modifications will frequently be necessary. What is suggested is an ideal based on the assumption that individuals have a right to make decisions about how they will live, that it is only through personal and societal exploration of new ways that necessary adaptation and evolution occurs, and that given sufficient factual information, opportunity for experience, and skills with which to process that experience, persons will, in general, make wise, functional lifestyle choices. It is hoped that family life educators can gradually move to implement this ideal.

REFERENCE NOTES

1. Parks, A. Single parent families: Meeting the challenge of the 1980's. Unpublished paper presented at The Groves Conference on Marriage and the Family, 1981. (Available from the author, Parents Without Partners, 7910 Woodmont Ave., Bethesda, MD).

2. Whitehurst, R. N. Relationship contracts: Making, keeping, and breaking them. Unpublished paper presented at The Groves Conference on Marriage and the Family, 1981. (Available from the author, Dept. of Sociology, University of Windsor, Windsor, Ontario, Canada N98 3P4).

B I B L I O G R A P H Y

Ahrons, C. R.

1979   "The binuclear family: Two households, one family." Alternative Lifestyles, 2, 499-515.

Athanasiou, R., Shaver, P., & Tavris, C.

1970   "Sex." Psychology Today, 4, 39-52.

Atwater, L.

1979   "Getting involved: Women's transition to first extramarital sex." Alternative Lifestyles, 2, 38-68.

Bell, A. P., & Weinberg, M. S.

1978   Homosexualities: A study of diversity among men and women. New York: Simon & Schuster.

Bell, R. R., Turner, S., & Rosen, L.

1975   "A multi-variate analysis of female extramarital coitus." Journal of Marriage and the Family, 37, 375-384.

Bernard, J.

1977   "Some moral and social issues." In R.
      W. Libby and R. N. Whitehurst (Eds.),
      Marriage and alternatives: Exploring
      intimate relationships. Glenview, IL:
      Scott, Foresman.

Calhoun, L. G. &
Selby, J. W.

1980   "Voluntary childlessness, involuntary
      childlessness, and having children: A
      study of social perceptions." Family
      Relations, 29, 181-183.

Carnes, P. J.

1981   Family development I: Understanding
      us. Interpersonal Communication Pro-
      grams.

Constantine, L. L.

1977   "Open family: A lifestyle for kids and
      other people." The Family Coordinator,
      26, 113-121.

Constantine, L. L.

1978   "Multilateral relations revisited: Group
      marriage in extended perspective." In
      B. I. Murstein (Ed.), Exploring intimate
      life styles. New York: Springer.

Constantine, L. L., &
Constantine, J. M.

1973   Group marriage: A study of contemporary
      multilateral marriage. New York:
      Macmillan.

Englund, C. L.

1980   "Using Kohlberg's moral developmental
      framework in family life education."
      Family Relations, 23, 7-13.

Glass, S. P., &
Wright, T. L.

1977   "The relationship of extramarital sex,
        length of marriage, and sex differences
        on marital satisfaction and romanticism:
        Athanasiou's data reanalyzed." Journal
        of Marriage and the Family, 39, 691-703.

Glick, P. G.

1979   "Children of divorced parents in demo-
        graphic perspective." Journal of Social
        Issues, 35, 170-182.

Glick, P. C.

1979   "Future American families." The Washing-
        ton COFO Memo, 2, 2-5. (b)

Gordon, T.

1970   Parent effectiveness training: The
        "no-lose" program for raising respon-
        sible children. New York: Peter H.
        Wyden.

Gross, H. E.

1980   "Dual-career couples who live apart:
        Two types." Journal of Marriage and
        the Family, 42, 567-576.

Guerney, B. G., Jr.

1977   Relationship enhancement; Skilling
        training programs for therapy, problem
        prevention, and enrichment. San
        Francisco: Jossey-Bass.

Harry, J., &
Lovely, R.

1979   "Gay marriages and communities of sexual
        orientation." Alternative Lifestyles,
        2, 177-200.

Hunt, M.

1974   "Sexual behavior in the 1970's."
        Chicago: Playboy.

Jacques, J. M., &
Chason, K. J.

1979   "Cohabitation: Its impact on marital
        success." The Family Coordinator, 28,
        35-39.

Johnson, R. E.

1970   "Some correlates of extramarital
        coitus." Journal of Marriage and the
        Family, 32, 449-456.

Kanter, R. M.

1972   Commitment and community: Communes and
        utopias in sociological perspective.
        Cambridge, MA: Harvard University Press.

Kanter, R. M. (Ed.)

1973   Creating and managing the collective
        life style. New York: Harper & Row.

Knapp, J. J., &
Whitehurst (Eds.)

1977   "Sexually open marriage and relation-
        ships: Issues and prospects." In R. W.
        Libby and R. N. Whitehurst (Eds.),
        Marriage and alternatives: Exploring
        intimate relationships. Glenview, IL:
        Scott, Foresman.

Levin, R. J.

1975   "The Redbook report on premarital and
        extramarital sex: The end of the double
        standard?" Redbook, October, 38-44,
        190-192.

Lewis, J., Beavers, W. R.,
Gussett, J. T., & Philips, V. A.

1976   No single thread: Psychological health
            in family systems. New York: Brunner/
            Mazel.

Libby, R. W.

1977   "Creative singlehood as a sexual life-
            style: Beyond marriage as a rite of
            passage." In R. W. Libby and R. N.
            Whitehurst (Eds.), Marriage and alter-
            natives: Exploring intimate relation-
            ships. Glenview, IL: Scott, Foresman.

Mace, D., &
Mace, V.

1977   How to have a happy marriage: A step by
            step guide to enriched relationships.
            Nashville: Abington.

Macklin, E.D.

1978   "Non-marital heterosexual cohabitation:
            A review of research." Marriage and
            Family Review, 1, March/April, 1-12.

Macklin, E. D.

1980   "Nontraditional family forms: A decade
            of research." Journal of Marriage and
            the Family, 42, 905-922.

Masters, W. H., &
Johnson, V E.

1979   Homosexuality in perspective. Boston:
            Little, Brown.

Maykovich, M. K.

1976   "Attitudes vs. behavior in extramarital
            sexual relations." Journal of Marriage
            and the Family, 38, 693-699.

Mazur, R.

1977   "Beyond jealousy and possessiveness."
In R. W. Libby and R. N. Whitehurst
(Eds.), Marriage and alternatives:
Exploring intimate relationships.
Glenview, IL: Scott, Foresman.

McGinnis, T. C., &
Finnegan, D. G.

1976   Open family and marriage: A guide to
personal growth. St. Louis: C. V.
Mosby.

Miller, S., Nunnally, E. W., &
Wackman, D. B.

1979   Couple communication I: Talking together.
Interpersonal communication Programs.

Milne, A. L. (Ed.)

1979   Joint custody: A handbook for judges,
lawyers, and counselors. Portland:
Association of Family Reconciliation
Courts.

Mowery, J.

1978   "Systemic requisits of communal groups."
Alternative Lifestyles, 1, 235-261.

Newcomb, M.D., &
Bentler, P.M.

1980   "Cohabitation before marriage: A comparison of married couples who did
and did not cohabit." Alternative
Lifestyles, 3, 65-85.

Newcomb, P. R.

1979   "Cohabitation in America: An assessment
of consequences." Journal of Marriage
and the Family, 41, 597-603.

Olson, D. H., Sprenkle, D.H., &
Russell, C. S.

1979   "Circumplex model of marital and family
systems I: Cohesion and adaptability
dimensions, family types, and clinical
applications." Family Process, 18, 3-28.

Olson, T. D., &
Moss, J.J.

1980   "Creating supportive atmospheres in
family life education." Family Relations, 29, 391-395.

O'Neill, N., & O'Neill, G.

1972   Open marriage: A new life style for
couples. New York: M. Evans.

Ory, M. G.

1978   "The decision to parent or not:
Normative and structural components."
Journal of Marriage and the Family,
40, 531-539.

Ramey, J. W.

1976   Intimate friendships. Englewood Cliffs,
NJ: Prentice Hall.

Ruth, D. J.

1978   "The commune movement in the middle
1970s." In B. I. Murstein (Ed.),
Exploring intimate life styles. New
York: Springer.

Sager, C. J.

1976   Marriage contracts and couple therapy.
New York: Brunner/Mazel.

Scanzoni, J., &
Fox, G. L.

1980   "Sex roles, family and society: The
seventies and beyond." Journal of
Marriage and the Family, 42, 743-756.

Skinner, D. A.

1980   "Dual-career family stress and coping:
            A literature review." Family Relations,
            29, 473-481.

Stein, P. J.

1978   "The lifestyles and life chances of the
            never-married." Marriage and Family
            Review, 1, July/August, 1-11.

U.S. Bureau of the Census

1977   "Marital status and living arrangements:
            March 1976." Current Population Reports,
            Series P-20, No. 306. Washington, D.C.:
            U.S. Government Printing Office.

U.S. Bureau of the Census

1979(a)   "Household and family characteristics:
            March 1978." Current Population Reports,
            Series P-20, No. 340. Washington, D.C.:
            U.S. Government Printing Office. (a)

U.S. Bureau of the Census

1979(b)   "Fertility of American women: June 1978."
            Current Population Reports, Series P-20,
            No. 341. Washington, D.C.: U.S.
            Government Printing Office.

U.S. Bureau of the Census

1980   "Marital status and living arrangements:
            March, 1979." Current Population Re-
            ports, Series P-20, No. 349. Washing-
            ton, D.C.: U.S. Government Printing
            Office.

U.S. Department of Labor

1979   "Multi-earner families increase." News,
            October 31. Washington, D.C.: Office
            of Information.

Veevers, J.E.

1979   "Voluntary childlessness: A review of
            issues and evidence." Marriage and
            Family Review, 2, Summer 1-26.

Visher, E. B., &
Visher, J. S.

1979   Stepfamilies: A guide to working with
            stepparents and stepchildren. New
            York: Brunner/Mazel.

Wachowiak, D., &
Bragg, H.

1980   "Open marriage and marital adjustment."
            Journal of Marriage and the Family,
            42, 57-82.

Weitzman, L. J.

1974   "Legal regulation of marriage: Tradi-
            tion and change." California Law Re-
            view, 62, 1169-1288.

Yllo, K. A.

1978   "Non-marital cohabitation: Beyond the
            college campus." Alternative Life-
            styles, 1, 37-54.

*Eleanor D. Macklin is an Assistant Professor, Depart-
ment of Family and Community Development, University
of Maryland, College Park, MD 20742.

Reprinted from Family Relations, Vol. 30 (October,
1981):567-577. Copyrighted 1981 by the National
Council on Family Relations. Reprinted by permission.

SECTION II

PROBLEMS AND ISSUES FACING INDIVIDUALS AND FAMILIES

Douglas B. Gutknecht* and
Edgar W. Butler*

I. INTRODUCTION

The chapters in this section are concerned with framing some of the fundamental challenges facing both individuals and the family in mid 1980's and beyond. The modern age of enlightened relationships and progressive freedoms has also spawned its own discontents, failures, exploitation and alienation. These discontents have led many to search for simple solutions. These solutions, when severed from the context of modern social and economic relations, doom modern family members to opt for a far too narrow view of personal transformation on the one hand, or on the other hand calling for an end to the family because it oppresses everyone. The issues of concern to us in this section revolve around love, sexual relations, sex roles and stereotyping, the decision to remain voluntarily childless, one-child families, divorce, remarriage, child custody, and alcoholism.

Chapters five and six cover topics generally grouped together -- sexuality, love and sex roles. Chapter five expresses the topic of sexuality by focusing upon 1) forms of sexual expression, including masturbation, nocturnal orgasm, petting, sexual relations; 2) the relationship of love to sex; 3) sexual myths related to topics such as sexual stimulation, orgasm, age discrepancies in male and female sexual patterns; 4) sexual dysfunctions, including impotence, premature ejaculation, orgasmic dysfunction, birth control; 5) contraceptive devices and techniques, including diaphragm, pill, IUD, condoms, etc; 6) abortion; 7) birth control and sterilization; 8) and sex education. Chapter 6 discusses the topics of sex and gender roles by focusing upon models of sex role development, sex role stereotypes and the possibility of overcoming these narrow, straight-jacket stereotypes through androgyny and male consciousness raising.

Chapters seven and eight also cover similar issues regarding how family and society impact personal

97

lifestyle choices--whether to have a family or not, and, of course, how many children are desirable if the former choice is affirmative.

In Chapter seven the first difficult relationship is expressed--should we voluntarily remain childless? A small sample of eleven in-depth interviews provides the reader insight into the important relationship issues that often come prior to the final decision to remain childless--images of motherhood, attitudes toward children, role models for childlessness, unconscious assumptions about conventional marriage, postponements of children, precipitating events and the search for justification and understanding. Chapter eight explores the issue of another lifestyle choice that contradicts traditional ideals of family size and explores the advantages and disadvantages of the one-child family.

Chapters nine and ten can also be grouped together because they focus on current family problems. Chapter nine discusses several issues pertaining to the divorce process--trends in interpreting divorce statistics, divorce and the law, effects of divorce on children, factors contributing to divorce, custody issues, biological childsnatching, and remarriage. Chapter ten probes the important topic of alcohol abuse and family structural adjustments, including children's roles, significant others' roles, and treatment implications.

II. CONTEMPORARY MARRIAGE THEMES AND THE FUTURE

A number of changes have occurred in U.S. families over the past three generations. First, there has been an emerging emphasis on developmental ideology with respect to childhood. Second, there has been an increasing stress on sharing household tasks and a concomitant decrease in specialization of husband-wife roles. Third, there appears to be more risk-taking by families. Fourth, there is more planning taking place now than previously in economic matters, family planning, and so on. Fifth, there is more open communication taking place, although it is accompanied by greater conflict. In an evaluation of these changes, Hill and his associates (1970) explicitly reject the notion that the family is disintegrating or becoming functionless.

Accompanying societal trends are a reduction in birth rate, morbidity, and mortality, and structural changes as follows:

1. More women are working for pay resulting in a loss or reduction of male power and dominance in the family.

2. Not only are more women working outside of the home, more of them are working in supervisory and higher level jobs.

3. More women are working at jobs not for survival but because they want to work outside of the home; there has been a decline in the economic dependence of women.

4. The government is increasingly providing services formerly provided by the family male.

5. There has been a steady increase in leisure time.

6. There is an increasing dispersion of leisure and social activities outside the family unit.

Structural changes have been accompanied by an increasing emphasis on human rights and individualism. Legal blocks to equality by race, sex, and age are being removed. Overall there has been a movement toward equalitarianism within society and in the family. As associated initial result has been the increasing number of marital separations, divorces, family violence, alcoholism, serial marriages, and alternative life styles. Child care increasingly takes place outside of the home unit, and children are having more early childhood experiences outside of the home, resulting in a broader world view. Marriage has been taking place at older ages than previously. One thus finds both positives and negatives resulting from such structural changes in family life.

Within the family, equalitarianism is growing, with more power accruing to females, and sexual standards are becoming more nearly equal for men and women.

There is increasingly less supervision of children by adults, especially regarding sexual activities. Fertility control, both by adults and younger people is becoming standard, and family planning of both the timing and number of children is the norm. Generally, even with all these trends it appears that the traditional nuclear family is here to stay, albeit with modified values, behaviors, and attitudes. The main reasons are that it is necessary for socialization, emotional security, and affectional needs. Other forms will emerge but probably with a minority of persons involved. There are several other main themes or threads that can be distinguished in contemporary marriage that need to be considered in discussing the future family. These themes are as follows:

1. With very few exceptions divorce is a painful and confusing experience; this is also true for professionals in the field.

2. There is universal dissatisfaction with the divorce process and its legal complications and procedures, which need simplification.

3. The choice of mate is often made when an individual does not have maturity and reason to make a good choice.

4. Current socialization practices in our society lead to expectations of marriage that are unrealistic. Partners expect too much of each other and are disappointed because their needs cannot be met through marriage.

5. Notwithstanding the increases in the divorce rate, the dissatisfaction of marriage, and the belief that it is a wretched institution, four out of five persons who get a divorce expect to remarry "within a reasonable time" (Otto, 1970:1-3)

Tyler (1975) suggests a simple plan that he believes would save marriage. Whether he is serious or not, his plan has merit since it would bring together people who are presumably sexually compatible. "At about 20-25 years of age, a man would contract his first marriage to a woman of 40-45 who is leaving her first marriage. A woman of 20-25 years of age would contract her first marriage to a man of 40-45 who is leaving his first marriage. Presto! Revolving mates. At 60-65 years of age, both men and women would leave the system to marry each other in third marriages, if they wish, or to enjoy retirement and well-earned

100

single bliss." There are substantial advantages to this plan. First, it faces squarely sexual realities as we now know them. That is, men appear to attain their greatest sexual vigor at about the age of 20, while women reach a sexual peak in their 40's. This plan would match men and women at their sexual peaks.

Another possibility is companionate marriage (Mead, 1966), which is based on earlier notions of trial marriage (Lindsey and Evans, 1927; Russell, 1929). There would be two steps: (1) A simple ceremony would be followed by a trial marriage in which members would have limited economic responsibilities, easy access to divorce, and no children. (2) Couples who were ready for the lifetime obligations of parenthood and economic interrelationships would enter a parental marriage, which would be difficult to break off and would entail continued responsibility for children. A third step might be a legitimized cohabitation consisting of a short-term contractual arrangement which would precede the other two steps. This trial relationship might be required for a year. Such apprentice periods have been proposed so that partners can explore each other before an actual marriage takes place. Perhaps one of the most famous trial marriage experiments was the fictional one proposed in the novel The Harrad Experiment; college students lived with computer-selected roommates of the opposite sex on a trial basis (Rimmer, 1966).

Progressive or serial monogamy may already be substantially under way (Alpenfels, 1970). People marrying, divorcing, and remarrying is a popular pattern. While people may become unhappy with a particular marriage, to be married is still a goal that dominates the life of most men and women. The basic structure and interaction networks in our society are for couples, and people need a "steady" that they go to functions with. These primary reasons for progressive monogamy suggest that it will be a viable future pattern.

In view of conflicting predictions, the safest and most accurate assumption is that there will be pluralistic models of the family in the future (Morgan, 1975:229ff). There will be a variety of nuclear family forms, modified extended families, dual career families, open families, and loose or tight networks of families. In addition, communal experiments will continue to develop, ranging from completely economic

101

self-sufficient communes with complex marriage and love relationships to looser and more temporary arrangements. In the immediate term such changes may suggest the family is failing but the situation is certainly more complex than simply relying on the obvious indicators of family disruption and disorganization like statistics on divorce, alcoholism, and violence.

III. CONCLUSION

We expect that the dominant family form in the future will continue to be the nuclear form as it now exists - a husband and wife and child or children. However, changes in society will alter many of the basic values, expectations, attitudes, and behaviors within these nuclear family units (Lasswell and Lobsenz, 1976). Similarly, many, if not most, of those who enter nuclear families probably will enter the nuclear family with a clearer notion of its advantages, disadvantages, and limitations.

The decline in family sex role differentiation will continue unabated, and while the basic tasks that need to be accomplished in the family unit will remain, who does each task will become less of a sex-linked characteristic and more of a personal preference by marital partners. The trend toward equalitarian families with shared powers and decision making is expected to grow as "personal growth" becomes a dominant value in our society. Associated with more democratic families will be more females working outside of the home. By virtue of this work, the female will accrue more power within the family unit and this will enhance the equalitarian marriage.

The growth of equality in sexual relations, both within and outside of the marriage, will profoundly affect the family of the future as well as all other human relations (Clavan, 1972). As equalitarianism becomes the mode and as power in the family becomes more equally distributed, the "open communication," so much revered by therapists and others, will become more of a reality, and it will strengthen rather than weaken the marital bond. As this open communication becomes more extensively practiced, males will find themselves, of necessity, agreeing that their spouses should have the same freedoms that they do.

The future family is one that is evolutionary and still assumes that the nuclear family is the most effective unit for residential living, consumption, and social functions, as well as for raising children. It is a family that is not a radical departure from current forms and thus allows maintenance of the family unit for raising children, intimate relations, security, friendship, companionship, and sexual access (Constantine and Constantine, 1973:231).

In summary, the "reports of the death of marriage are, to paraphrase Mark Twain, greatly exaggerated" (Hunt, 1971). The evidence is overwhelming that old-fashioned marriage is not dying but that there is a continuing evolution and a rebellion against certain aspects of it (Toffler, 1970). The evolutionary aspects may be considered as patchwork modifications enabling marriage to serve the needs of contemporary people without being unduly costly or painful. In spite of the current divorce rates and the many problems involved with contemporary family, the future family may be as follows:

> The marriage of the future will be a hetero-sexual friendship, a free and unconstrained union of a man and a woman or companions, partners, comrades, and sexual lovers. There will still be a certain degree of specialization within marriage, but by and large the daily business of living together--the talk, the meals, the going out to work and coming home again, spending their money, the love-making, the caring for children, even the indulgence or non-indulgence in outside affairs--will be governed by this fundamental relationship rather than by the lord-and-servant relationship of a patriarchal marriage. Like all friendships, it will exist only as long as it is valid: it will rarely last a lifetime, yet each marriage, while it does last, will meet the needs of the men and women of the future as the earlier form of marriage could have. Yet, we who know the marriage today will find it relatively unfamiliar, comprehensible - and very much alike (Hunt, 1971).

Changes taking place in marriage forms do not reflect immediate impulses on the part of married people but, instead, reflect genuine needs for growth and change in the family. There are basic needs that hu-

103

man beings have and these needs apparently are being expressed. The need for love, affection, recognition, respect, sexual satisfaction, and security remain vitally important for people in most marital relationships. This section will explore some of the problems, changes and projections regarding the future of the family in American society. Along the way we also hope to examine some policy issues that impact the health of the family and its ability to meet the stresses, strains, and challenges of the 1980's.

BIBLIOGRAPHY

Alpenfels, Ethel J.

1970   "Progressive Monogamy: An Alternate
            Pattern?" In Herbert A. Otto (Ed.),
            The Family in Search of a Future.
            Englewood Cliffs, N.J.: Prentice-Hall
            (Appleton), pp. 67-73.

Bosserman, Phillip

1977   "Changing Core Values in American So-
            ciety: 1876-1976," unpublished paper.
            Salisbury State College, Salisbury, MD.

Clavan, Sylvia

1972   "Changing Female Sexual Behavior and
            Future Family Structure." Pacific So-
            ciological Review, 15 (July): 295-308.

Constantine, Larry L., &
Constantine, Joan M.

1973   Group Marriage. New York: Macmillan.

Edwards, John N.

1967   "The Future of the Family Revisited."
            Journal of Marriage and the Family,
            29 (August): 506-511.

Hill, Reuben and
collaborators

1970   Family Development in Three Genera-
            tions. Cambridge, Mass.: Schenkman
            Publishing.

Hobart, Charles W.

1963   "Commitment, Value Conflict, and the
            Future of the American Family."
            Marriage and Family Living, 25
            (November): 405-412.

Hunt, Morton

1971   "The Future of Marriage." Playboy,
            18 (August).
                        105

Lasswell, Marcia, &
Norman M. Lobsenz

1976   No-Fault Marriage. Garden City,
              New York: Doubleday.

Lindsey, Ben B., &
Wainright Evans

1927   The Companionate Marriage. New York:
              Liveright.

Mead, Margaret

1966   "Marriage in Two Steps." Redbook,
              July.

Morgan, J.H.J.

1975   Social Theory and the Family. London:
              Routledge & Kegan, Paul.

Otto, Herbert A.

1970   "Introduction." In Herbert A. Otto
              (Ed.), The Family in Search of a
              Future. Englewood Cliffs, N.J.:
              Prentice-Hall (Appleton), pp. 1-9.

Rimmer, Robert H.

1966   The Harrad Experiment. Los Angeles:
              Sherbourne Press.

Russell, Bertrand
1929   Marriage and Morals. New York:
              Liveright.

Toffler, Alvin

1970   Future Shock. New York: Random House.

Tyler, Robert L.

1975   "The Two-Marriage Revolving-Mate
              Generation-Bringing Plan to Save
              Marriage." In Jack R. De Lora and
              Joann De Lora (Eds.), Intimate Life
              Styles (2nd ed.), Pacific Palisades,
              Calif.: Goodyear, pp. 406-410.

*Doug Gutknecht, Department of Sociology, Chapman College, Orange, California; Edgar W. Butler, Department of Sociology, University of California, Riverside, California.

CHAPTER 5

VIEWING LOVE AND SEXUALITY TODAY AND TOMORROW

Douglas B. Gutknecht* and
Edgar W. Butler*

I. INTRODUCTION: SEXUALITY

The social science perspective on sexuality up until very recently followed the popular model. From this perspective, sexuality supposedly represents the instinctive or animal side of human nature, which is in contrast to higher forms of learned and cultural behavior. Generally, even social scientists have subscribed to the point of view that sex is a powerful, natural drive, perhaps necessary for reproduction, but that it must be socially controlled (Skolnick, 1973:154). According to this view, the socialization process, or learning of culture, is a mechanism to control this instinct and not an influene on sexuality. The theory of sexual behavior as instinctive assumes that such behavior is biologically determined. It is, of course, a fact that hormones do help shape the bodies of men and women and are associated with secondary sex characteristics of body and facial hair, voice depth, and so on. However, it is not necessary to make a leap in inference and state that sexual desires and choice of sex partners are biologically or hormonally determined.

The current trend among social scientists is to move away from the view of hormonal control over sexual behavior and more toward the belief that higher centers of the brain control sexual behavior by learning and symbolic processes (Gecas and Libby, 1976). That is, sexual behavior is related primarily to how people interpret and construct the social context in which they exist. Thus, there is a current emphasis on social and psychological factors in erotic arousal, the importance of imagination and what turns people on, and a deemphasis of biological differences (for a review that stresses biological impacts, see Shuttleworth, 1959).

Substantial differences exist in what cultures expect and prohibit in the way of sexual behavior. In some societies, for example, children are encouraged to masturbate and play at having intercourse so that they will be ready for the real behavior when they reach sexual maturity (Ford and Beach, 1951:153-166). Obviously, such practices are not in keeping with current socialization patterns in the United States, where most parents attempt to discourage masturbation and to keep children from observing sexual behavior and from other forms of sexual behavior that involve other children. Societal prohibitions discourage children from having sexual interests or knowing about sex until the teen years. This only forces sex underground.

II. FORMS OF SEXUAL EXPRESSION

Masturbation

Men and women generally discover masturbation at an early age and usually enjoy it in spite of the prohibitions against it. In the past it was believed that masturbation caused people to get acne, lose their hair, go crazy, and even end up in an insane asylum. Undoubtedly, many young people who believed this continued to masturbate anyway. While there is still a general prohibition and a feeling in our society that one should not masturbate, other societies encourage children in self-stimulation to orgasm (Ford and Beach, 1951). Masturbation is a substitute for sexual intercourse, and for younger people it may be their only sexual outlet. Currently, most sexual authorities believe that masturbation is not harmful and that for both males and females it may be beneficial, pleasurable, and a useful way to learn about one's own sexuality. Many men and women masturbate even though they have a sexual partner.

Men tend to masturbate less frequently as they grow older, while women tend to masturbate more frequently up to middle age, after which the frequency remains relatively constant. Kinsey et al. (1953) found a great variety in masturbatory participation by females; some masturbate only once or twice in their lifetime while others have multiple orgasms in a single masturbatory session. The average is about every two to four weeks regardless of age or marital status. More recent research evidence than the Kinsey studies suggests that there has been an increase in the frequency of masturbation among single women and

110

men in the age range mid-20 to mid-30 (Hunt, 1973). Some people believe that masturbatory activity will cause people to be unresponsive to actual sexual intercourse. Generally, experience has proven this not to be true. In particular, women who have experienced masturbation or orgasm before marriage are more likely to reach orgasm through sexual intercourse during the early years of marriage.

Nocturnal Orgasm

Nocturnal orgasm takes different forms depending on one's gender. Men have direct evidence of their "wet dreams" in the form of ejaculation; women may not even have a memory of it. A person who masturbates is not likely to have nocturnal orgasms. Especially in men, pressure builds up if sexual release has not been obtained in some other way. In the Kinsey study, about 55 percent of the women had experienced dreams ending in orgasm, and about 70 percent reported having had sexually related dreams. Virtually all men at some time or another have had nocturnal orgasm.

Heterosexual Petting

Sexual contact between a man and a woman not culminating in intercourse, or petting, is a form of sexual activity that almost all people in our society have experienced. The Kinsey studies showed that well over half of the men and almost 90 percent of the college-educated men had experienced what they called deep kissing and that virtually all the men had felt a woman's breasts. There was more variation regarding mouth-breast contact and manipulation of a woman's genitals. If one compares the Kinsey research with more recent work, there has been a significant increase in the number of people engaging in oral-genital petting. In general, college-educated men and women are more likely to have experienced heavy petting and a variety of sexual experiences than less educated people. Various research results suggest that men usually have more petting partners throughout their life than women do. (Who are the women with whom they pet?)

111

Premarital Heterosexual Relations

There are conflicting values and attitudes in our society regarding premarital sexual intercourse(Reiss, 1967, 19:200). Some, still subscribing to abstinence, believe it is wrong for both males and females. Some adhering to the double standard, believe it is acceptable for men but not women. Others believe that premarital sexual behavior is permissible when there is love or strong affection or when couples are engaged. Finally, there are those who believe in permissiveness and that, affection aside, physical attraction alone justifies premarital intercourse for both men and women.

A range of attitudes and values exist for both physical and emotional intimacy. Peoples' attitudes toward premarital sexual intimacy are thus related to their standards and attitudes about appropriate physical and affectional limits. However, sexual values and attitudes don't always guide our sexual behavior. Just as we find a wide variety of physical and emotional sexual standards, one finds a wide variety of premarital sexual behavior.

Udry (1966) asks the interesting question of whether premarital sexual experiences makes any difference in subsequent marital satisfaction; but the information is inconclusive in that the data do not consistently show that premarital experience increases or decreases subsequent marital satisfaction. The most obvious consequence of premarital intercourse is pregnancy. In approximately one out of every four marriages that occur in this country, the woman is pregnant; for younger persons who are still in high school when they get married the number is as high as four out of five. Of course, there are many additional births with couples who do not get married. The influence of premarital pregnancy upon subsequent "adjustment" in marriage is also inconclusive; some report that it may result in better sex when married and better overall adjustment. One question is whether subsequent marital satisfaction is affected by the premarital sexual relationship between spouses or by sex with other partners in addition to the subsequent spouse. Generally, people with similar sexual needs have a more satisfactory marital adjustment if their spouses also have intense sexual needs. Similarly, a

112

person with fewer sexual needs must have a mate whose needs are also compatible.

It appears that the number of young people of both sexes engaging in sexual relationships prior to marriage is increasing, although the increase appears greater among women than men (Zelnick and Kanter, 1980). However, Clatworthy (1983) surveying college students and the percentage of females engaging in premarital sex fluctuate from 20% in 1965 to a high of 80% in 1975 and again drops to 50% in 1980-81. It is doubtful that young individuals today are any more promiscuous than in the past. The normal number of sexual partners is not increasing drastically and the belief that affection and commitment should occur with sexual relations appears strong. However, the definition of affection is more varied with today's young person--formal engagement is no longer the sole criterion of affection. Let's briefly explore the nature of love and its relationship to affection and building health sexual relationships. We must remember, however, that love and sex are not the same thing.

III. CONTEMPORARY DEFINITIONS OF LOVE

The word love comes from the Sanskrit world Lubhyat, which means desire. But love means many things to many people: a strong commitment; a strong emotional attachment; a positive emotional experience by several people in an interpersonal relationship. One quite comprehensive definition of love was suggested by Meerlo (1952:83):

> I love you. Sometimes it means: I desire you or I want you sexually. It may mean: I hope you love me or I hope that I will be able to love you. Often it means: It may be that a love relationship can develop between us, or even, I hate you. Often it is a wish for an emotional exchange: I want your admiration in exchange for mine, or I give my love in exchange for some passion, or I want to feel cozy and at home with you, or I admire some of your qualities. A declaration of love is merely a request: I desire you, or I want you to gratify me, or I want your protection, or I want to be intimate with you, or I want to exploit your loveliness. Sometimes it is the need for security and tenderness or

113

parental treatment. It may mean: My self-love goes out to you. But it may also express submissiveness. Please take me as I am, or I feel guilty about you, or I want through you to correct the mistakes I have made in human relationships. It may be self-sacrifice and a masochistic wish for dependency. However, it may also be full affirmation of the other, taking the responsibilities for mutual exchange of feeling. It may be a weak form of friendliness, it may be the scarcely even whispered expression of ectasy. "I love you," wish, desire, submission, conquest, it is never the word itself that tells all the meaning.

Love may mean the proclamation of ownership of the other person--you are to do my bidding from now on. In our society, where there is always an emphasis on the sexual aspects of any relationship, some believe that sex apart from love cannot exist. Sexual attraction, certainly a part of love between a man and a woman, is often mistaken for love. Some argue that those who claim to have fallen in love at first sight actually were only sexually attracted. Love may grow from such an attraction, but it certainly is not the first emotion felt, in spite of the fact that many people seem to believe in the concept of love at first sight.

One interesting test of interpersonal interaction is how much time the couple spends gazing into each other's eyes. Similarly, it is suggested that any strong emotional state, anger, fear, bliss, jealousy, or whatever, can produce feelings of what some would call passionate love. Yet de Rougemont (1949) called romantic love one of the most pathological experiments that a civilized society has ever imagined, especially in regard to basing marriage upon such passing fancy. He argued that people in this country are seduced by the romantic ideal into ignoring the practical considerations that in the past helped to insure successful marriages.

McCary (1975) argues that there are three types of love: infatuation, romantic love, and mature love. Infatuation is generally one person's unrealistic idealization of another without any real interaction necessarily occurring between them. According to McCary, everyone has experienced infatuation in life and can recognize it, especially in hindsight. Infatuation operates on the belief that love is totally unknowable; that is, it cannot be fathomed what creates the love. Some call infatuation the roller coaster of love because there is the exhilarating thrill of the ride and the abrupt jolt when the ride stops.

Romantic love, in contrast to infatuation, operates on the assumption that love is mysterious and elusive. As McCary points out, romantic love has several distinguishing characteristics. First, the belief that in all the world, only one "soul mate" was predestined for the other person. This leads to a belief in love at first sight, since when one first meets this soul mate, one immediately knows him or her. If the relationship becomes intense and marriage occurs, and it turns out to be unhappy, one logical explanation is that this partner was not the soul mate at all but an imposter, and divorce is the only solution.

As with infatuation, romantic love tends to lead toward an idealization of the loved one rather than viewing that person in realistic terms. Generally, women tend to be more idealistic than men about the person they love, although men apparently become attracted quicker. Romantic love, which leads to the notion that "love is blind," may also lead to problems when the daily routines and ordinary tasks and activities of marriage enter the picture. As time passes, a couple finds that their love diminishes as reality settles in. Yet most people in this country still believe that romantic love is necessary for a successful man-woman relationship.

Many marriages, even in contemporary America, are not based solely on romantic love. In falling in love, women seem to be more selective than men; and this leads to a reversal of the traditional American stereotypes about males and females and romantic love (Rubin, 1973:204). Generally, women make more stringent demands on what they want in a mate and a romance. Women appear to be more concerned about getting a date who is intelligent, has high status, is a good dancer, and dresses well. Generally, males are concerned primarily about physical attractiveness. Substantial research evidence shows that men typically fall in love quicker than women. Rubin has pointed out that this may be because when a man marries, he chooses a companion, perhaps someone to help him throughout his life, but a women is choosing not only a companion but a standard of living. Perhaps it is important or even necessary for a woman to be mercenary in the mate-selection process. Generally, males are more romantically inclined than women are in our society (Hobart, 1958; Kephart, 1967).

Beigel (1951) argues that much in the negative point of view of romantic love is not necessary. First, courtly love and romantic love (not identical with puppy love) are expressions of sociopsychological processes aimed at the reconciliation of basic human needs with frustrating social conditions. Secondly, he argues, the romantic function of love has not harmed the relationship of the sexes; rather, it has enhanced the status of women and softened the impact on the marital union of factors that endanger the ideological basis of marriage and related institutions but do not provide substitute values. Thus, Beigel believes that romantic love is actually very functional in contemporary marriages.

Currently, many authorities and authors believe that romantic love and conjugal (mature) love are logically separate, with the former being folly and fraud and the later sanity and truth (Hunt, 1962:94). Yet, there are some grounds for doubting the sense of this argument. Those who do family counseling report that an extremely common complaint concerns the way in which tenderness, expressiveness, and intensity in a marriage gives way to boredom and dullness. Most typically it is the wife who complains of this; husbands also have been known to complain, but less frequently because they have outside substitute satisfactions. Many women typically say "he's a good enough husband and father" and than ramble on about a hundred things all of which imply he isn't the kind of lover that he used to be. Many people who have been married for some time report that they miss the element of romantic love in their marriage.

Hunt feels that romantic love may have more to it than has been noted by its critics. First, romantic love accepted women as human beings of value rather than merely as sexual objects; it stressed the concept that lovers should serve and please each other rather than seek to conquer each other. While this made sex more difficult, it also allied concepts of loyalty

116

and friendship and made love a source of reassurance and genuine affection especially in a marriage. The more notions about romantic love that were absorbed within marriage, the more it came to seem an ideal state and the primary source of individual happiness. Hunt is not necessarily arguing against mature, or conjugal, love and its notions of adjustment, task specialization, and accommodation; rather he believes that these things by themselves constitute a grossly insufficient portrait of what most people in our society want and need from marriage.

While marriage probably cannot continuously partake of romantic love, it certainly makes people strive for and maintain romantic elements. Some married couples, even after 20 or more years, still have affection and romantic feeling for each other, which they act out in a multitude of ways; not necessarily by clinging and caressing in public, but by subtle friendliness, proudness, and admiration for the other person.

Mature love, the third type of love McCary describes, is the interaction between two emotionally mature individuals whose relationship is based upon creativity, mutual esteem, and erotic fulfillment (see also O'Neill and O'Neill, 1972). Mature love requires that there be free and honest communication with a minimum of restrictions or inhibitions affecting the relationship or individuals. While romantic love involves falling in love, mature love is an "ever-constant process of personal growth and awareness of the other's feelings and needs" (McCary, 1975:136). Obviously, mature love can only be experienced by mature people; it involves self-worth, self-love, and self-respect. Many have pointed out that love for others is possible only when one feels love for self. Mature love does not necessarily view sex and love as the same; however, there is no guilt over sexuality or sexual relations, and sex is viewed neither as perversion nor rebellion. In contrast with romantic love, which is an undulating series of highs and lows, mature love consists of moderation and is evenly balanced and tempered. "Where romantic love is hot, mature love is warm; mature love is not an extreme, but a way of life" (McCary, 1975:137).

When people are asked what they believe love is, ignoring what poets, philosophers, psychologists, or

117

sociologists are telling us, 40 percent report a
strong feeling or an attraction; 20 percent stress
companionship and compatibility, 20 percent suggest
that love is giving to each other; 17 percent say
that love equals security; and 3 percent say love
means a realistic or practical relationship with each
other (Udry, 1966:177).

Some Questions About Love

A variety of questions that have been asked about
love have not yet satisfactorily been answered--even
though love plays such a prominent part in most of
our lives. Among these unanswered questions that we
might reflect upon and try to answer are:

1. Is falling in love an interpersonal process?
   and how does one attribute to another the
   characteristics that that person does not
   have?

2. Are there sex differences in falling in love?

3. How does love enter into mate selection?

4. What are some of the functional aspects of
   love in relationship to marriage, and similarly, are there any dysfunctions of love,
   especially in marriage?

5. Can a marriage exist without love?

6. Is it possible for a person to have multiple
   lovers? of the opposite sex? of the same sex?

7. Can love be measured and compared by degrees?
   (McCrary, 1975:123)

8. If you can love more than one person, does
   that mean you can love one more and the
   other less? (Rubin, 1973)

9. Or does it mean that your commitment to one
   person is different from your commitment to
   another? (Rubin, 1970)

A number of these unanswered questions have led
to myths about love and sex (Safilios-Rothschild,
1977). Let's return to our topic on sexuality.

118

IV. SEXUAL MYTHS

There is substantial ignorance in the United States, among both younger people and adults, about sexual activities and sexuality. Several myths surround sexual stimulation, orgasm, differences in male and female sexuality, birth control, and sexuality.

Sexual Stimulation

McCary (1975:211) points out that one of our most dangerous myths is that oral-genital contact is homosexual behavior. According to all studies from Kinsey forward, the people who participate extensively in oral-genital sexual behavior include homosexuals, bisexuals, and heterosexuals. In fact, there appears to be a consistent relationship between higher educational levels and the likelihood that a person will participate in oral sex. Generally, for people of both sexes, oral sex is almost as satisfactory as ordinary sexual intercourse. Many women who do not achieve orgasm during sexual intercourse may climax during oral-genital contact and find it intensively satisfying. Both _fellatio_ (orally stimulating a man's penis) and _cunnilingus_ (orally stimulating a woman's clitoris) are sexual behaviors that are participated in by extensive numbers of people. At times, oral-genital sex may be a substitute for sexual intercourse. For example, during the last few weeks of pregnancy, oral sex allows for sexual release both for husband and wife when actual sexual intercourse may be dangerous for the mother and child yet to be born.

Orgasm

Another myth that seems to be a perpetual one is that each time sexual relations occur it should end in orgasm for both partners. Many now believe that sexual activity can and should be engaged in for its own sake; that is, sexual activity provides pleasurable stimulation and does not necessarily always have to lead to an orgasm. For example, a person may enjoy manual stimulation, oral-genital sex, or even sexual intercourse without an orgasm and still find the experience pleasurable. A number of women are capable of orgasm while masturbating but not during intercourse. The obvious solution for them is to relieve their own sexual tension through orgasm either by

119

masturbating or by manual or oral stimulation by their
sexual partners.

Perhaps one of the most damaging myths about
orgasm is that the male and female should have or
reach a simultaneous orgasm. The actual truth is
that it is extremely difficult for partners to reach
simultaneous orgasm, and it does not necessarily provide the most emotional satisfaction. For most people
the attempt to reach a simultaneous orgasm is a lesson
in futility. Similarly, when a person reaches orgasm,
he or she is more concerned with his own physical
responses and not inclined to be concerned with the
partner's well-being. On the other hand, when one
climaxes at one time and the other climaxes at another
time, each person can experience the other person's
orgasm.

Orgasmic experience evidently varies from person
to person. Among women, the variations of orgasmic
response are great, with some women having extremely
intense orgasms while others are not quite sure whether or not they had an orgasm. In women who have multiple orgasms, subsequent orgasms generally are more
intense than the first one. Up until relatively
recently, it was believed that the vagina was the
leading erogenous zone of females and that in order
for the transition to womanhood to be successful, the
vagina had to supersede clitoris as the focus of sexuality. According to Freud and others, women who did
not go through this process were "psychosexually im-
mature." However, recent research by Masters and
Johnson (1966) shows that this is incorrect. They
studied 487 women and made the following generalizations about female orgasms:

1. The dichotomy of vaginal and clitoral orgasms
   is false since all orgasms anatomically are
   centered in the clitoris regardless of whether the pressure is direct or indirect and
   resulting from the thrusting of the penis
   during intercourse or from generalized sexual
   stimulation of other erogenous zones of the
   body such as the breasts.

2. Women are naturally multiorgasmic. That is,
   it is possible for many women to experience
   several orgasms in rapid succession, and this
   is not an exceptional occurrence but one

120

which most women are capable of, given the right conditions.

3. Women's orgasms do not vary in kind but vary in intensity. The most intense orgasms of most women are experienced by masturbatory manual stimulation, (secondary is) manual stimulation by the partner, with the least intense...being experienced during intercourse.

4. There is an infinite variety of female sexual response in regard to intensity and duration of orgasms.

The Masters and Johnson study destroyed several major myths about female orgasm. However, as Lydon (1974) pointed out, this knowledge has not necessarily been incorporated by most American males. (For a variety of sexual techniques and coital positions, see Comfort, 1972, and Comfort, 1974; for critiques of marriage manuals, see Brissett and Lewis, 1970, and Gordon and Shankweiler, 1971.)

Age Discrepancies in Male and Female Sexual Patterns

One misunderstood area in marital relationships in our society involves the differences in male and female sexual patterns. It appears that in general males are most likely to have their greatest sex drive in their teens while females peak in their late 30s and 40s. If actual sex behavior is used as a guide, the sex drive of males is gradually decreasing at about the same time that the sex drive of women is increasing. Once a woman reaches her peak of sexual interest and capacity, it continues into her later years, and physiologists report that a woman may have as many orgasms at age 80 as she does at age 20. Males also experience sexual desires well into their 80s. Generally, when women in their 40s and 50s have a decrease in sexual interest the cause is often a result of their partner's rather than their own loss of sexual interest. However, a good relationship should allow opportunities to maintain a vital and healthy sexual involvement.

Each couple should explore their own sexual needs, desires, and expectations before marriage. McCary (1975) points out that a young male may feel rejected
121

because his young bride is not ready for intercourse as frequently as he is; the bride, on the other hand, may feel that she married a sex maniac. Later on in life, however, the woman's sexual appetite may increase substantially while the man's decreases somewhat. At this point there may be a matching of sexual needs, after which the woman's may become greater as the male's is decreasing. Frustration, confusion, and other problems can occur through all years of the marriage as a result of such mismatching. However, the key element becomes one of interest, imagination, and good communication which allows for different patterns to be worked out. Both men and women can create meaningful sexual relationships based upon mutual goals throughout their adult years.

V. SEXUAL DYSFUNCTIONS

A variety of sexual dysfunctions can interfere with sexual satisfaction and performance either on an episodic or a chronic basis (Kaplan, 1974). Sexual dysfunctions can be physiological or the result of social factors. The major kinds are discussed below:

Sexual impotence is generally defined as the inability of a male to obtain or maintain an erection for sexual intercourse (Kaplan, 1974:255). Impotency has been found to have a variety of causes. The rarest kind of impotence is caused by anatomical defects in the reproductive or central nervous system of the male. Functional impotence may be due to a nervous disorder, deficient hormonal functioning, circulatory problems, physical exhaustion, or even by the excessive use of alcohol and other drugs. However, the most frequent causes of impotence are emotional inhibitions and psychological factors. A distinction has to be made between males who are impotent at certain episodes and those who have chronic impotency. Almost every male at some time or another is unable to attain or to continue an erection long enough to have sexual intercourse.

If a man begins to fear that he will not be able to get and continue an erection, he is moving into an emotional area that could lead to even greater impotency. Some men in the later years erroneously believe that they are too old to function sexually and actually become impotent because of their beliefs rather than because of any physiological or organic reason. The most frequently cited causes of impotency are anxiety and concern about sexual abilities rather than any organic physiological reason. Generally, impotency caused by social or psychological factors can be treated by trained therapists, and Masters and Johnson (1970) report a success rate of almost three out of every four instances.

Premature ejaculation is another form of sexual dysfunction reported quite frequently for males (Kaplan, 1974:289ff). This is a condition in which a man cannot delay ejaculation long enough after penetration to satisfy his partner (Masters and Johnson, 1970). This can cause anxiety and stress for many men and women. What is important to recognize however, is that what is premature is socially defined and varies from individual to individual. For many women, premature ejaculation is not a problem since they do not reach orgasm by sexual intercourse anyway and are more likely to do so through oral-genital or manual manipulation.

The Kinsey study (1948) reported that about 75 percent of all men ejaculate within 2 minutes after penetration into the vagina, while most women require almost 15 minutes of sexual intercourse to have an orgasm. As noted previously, as men get older they are able to maintain an erection for a longer period of time without ejaculation. Perhaps this is where the belief that older men make better lovers comes from. The causes of premature ejaculation are highly varied, but virtually none of them are organic; they are primarily social or psychological in nature. Control of premature ejaculation is more a matter of self-training and overcoming emotional fears. Masters and Johnson (1970) report that they had almost a 98 percent success rate in treatment for premature ejaculation.

Orgasmic dysfunction is a condition in which a woman fails to go beyond the plateau phase in sexual response and have an orgasm (Masters and Johnson, 1970; Kaplan, 1974:374ff). One has to be very careful in diagnosing orgasmic dysfunction; some husbands or male partners think that if a woman does not have an orgasm every time they have sexual intercourse, she has this condition. From a clinical point of view, orgasmic dysfunction is the diagnosis if a woman seldom or never is able to have an orgasm. Having an orgasm

123

only once or twice a week is not considered as an orgasmic dysfunction. As with most other sexual dysfunctions, the general consensus is that female orgasmic dysfunctions are psychological in nature rather than a result of organic problems, and that they substantially derive from the socialization process in which women from a very early age are taught to suppress sexual feelings and inhibit sexual desires. Even in later life, a woman may know intellectually that sex is good and that she likes it, but she still may be unable to respond orgasmically because of these earlier learned emotionally inhibiting factors. One mechanism in helping a woman overcome orgasmic dysfunction is to use stimulative methods such as oral-genital contact, mechanical vibrators, manual manipulation, sensate focus, and so on. If these home methods do not make a woman orgasmic, generally the advice is that professional sexual treatment should be obtained.

Other sexual dysfunctions are vaginismus, painful contractions of muscles in the vaginal tract, and dyspareunia, which can occur in men or women but is more common among women. Vaginismus is almost always due to emotional factors rather than any physiological or organic problem. Generally, successful treatment of vaginismus is near the 100 percent level, with the majority of women able to reach orgasm after treatment (Masters and Johnson, 1970). In dyspareunia there is severe pain during orgasm, usually related to anxiety, fear, and apprehension over sexual intercourse rather than any physiological causes. Painful coitus in a woman can also be a result of scar tissue or other problems in the vagina.

VI. BIRTH CONTROL

Richards and Willis (1983) cite many reasons why teenagers make excuses about the dangers of possible pregnancy:

. because it seems more romantic not to think about or plan birth control;

. because they feel uncomfortable talking to their sex partner about sex;

. because their partners don't want them to use anything;

124

- because they're embarrassed to go into a drug-store and ask for birth control products;

- because they don't know where to find a family planning clinic;

- because they are afraid their parents or friends will find out;

- because they think that workers in the clinic won't treat them well;

- because, whether they know it or not, they want the pregnancy to happen.

Birth control methods include contraceptive devices, sterilization, abortion, and abstinence. The last is obviously an extremely safe and foolproof form of birth control; for most people, however, it is the least popular.

Contraceptive Devices and Techniques

Contraceptive techniques and devices vary in their effectiveness. The diaphragm is a thin dome-shaped rubber cup designed to cover the mouth of the womb, or cervix. To be effective, it must be measured for fit and comfort. Generally, diaphragms do not interfere with the pleasure of intercourse for either partner. Some people use diaphragms with a contraceptive cream or jelly that seals off the cervix and prevents sperm from entering the womb; this is generally very successful. Using the diaphragm with contraceptive foam, which also improves its effectiveness, is an extremely safe birth control measure. It works effectively about 95 percent of the time and also protects against venereal disease. In addition, the side effects associated with the pill are avoided.

The pill, or oral contraceptive, mainly consists of synthetic progesterone and estrogen. These prevent ovulation by mimicking the hormonal state of the body during pregnancy; thus, no ovum is released and pregnancy cannot occur. Generally, the pill is the most popular contraceptive method (Hawkins, 1970); it is considered 100 percent effective, a success rate that no other birth control method can match.

Unfortunately, for some women there are side effects of nausea, headaches, and irregular bleeding. Another serious side effect is that estrogen in the pill may increase the coagulatory action of the blood, thus increasing the risk of blood clotting, particularly in the legs. Longterm side effects of the pill are unknown at this stage. Additional evidence indicates a slightly increased risk of high blood pressure, heart problems, or stroke. This is the reason that doctors should prescribe the pill based on a comprehensive exam and medical history.

IUDs (intrauterine devices) are small mechanical devices of various shapes and sizes that are designed to fit the womb. The IUD acts as an irritant to prevent the implantation of the fertilized ovum in the uterine wall. It is not as effective as the pill, but approaches 99 percent effectiveness. Its cost is minimal, and once implanted, its effectiveness continues. Some have been concerned with the fact that the IUD works on the principle of irritation, which is also the cause of certain kinds of cancer. IUDs must be fitted by a physician and replaced every one to three years. Some women's bodies reject the IUD and thus are less often recommended for women in their teens or those not yet experienced in childbirth.

Condoms are probably still the most popularly used contraceptive in this country. Used with foam it is 97 percent effective in preventing pregnancy. Even without foam it is 80 to 85 percent effective. A condom is made either of thin rubber or sheep's intestine; it measures about 7 1/2 inches and fits over the penis. Its effectiveness as a contraceptive is not as good as that of IUDs, pills, or diaphragms, but in addition to the birth control use, condoms are perhaps the best method of preventing the spread of venereal disease. Many people use coitus interruptus as a method of birth prevention; the male withdraws the penis from his partner's vagina just before ejaculating. The danger in this technique is that sperm may be ejaculated before the male is able to exercise any control. Withdrawal is thus not a very good method of birth control. Douching is also used by many as a contraceptive measure, but it is not very effective because sperm move too quickly for a douche.

Several religious groups advocate the "rhythm" method, which requires that a couple abstain from sexual intercourse during the time in a woman's menstrual cycle when she is capable of conception. The problem with this method is the difficulty of correctly evaluating the "safe" period to have sexual intercourse. In conjunction with the rhythm method, a woman's temperature may be taken to determine what point of the menstrual cycle she is in; but for many women this is not effective and does not work since their temperatures do not fluctuate that much. Having intercourse during the menstrual period is another risk technique for birth control because ovulation can occur toward the end of a long menstrual period.

Abortion

Abortion is generally defined as a spontaneous or induced explusion of an embryo or fetus from the uterus before it has developed sufficiently to survive (McCary, 1975:202). While some may disagree with the recent Supreme Court decision that eliminated state laws prohibiting induced abortion, perhaps one of the major benefits of it is that it has taken abortions out of illegal and often unsterile situations and allowed them to be performed in sterile conditions by trained medical personnel. Abortion under sanitary conditions poses less of a mortality hazard to a woman than childbirth.

Of course, this is a very important contemporary issue in the United States. The status of legalized abortion is very uncertain, and is likely to remain so for some years. The January 1973 decision by the Court prohibiting state governments from outlawing abortions no matter what the grounds is an example of recent trends toward increasingly liberalized attitudes, behavior, and laws. Over the past decade or so, many states have changed to more liberal laws that allow abortion on demand, and some states have thrown out all laws prohibiting abortion. While eliminating all previous laws prohibiting or regulating abortion and accelerating the trend toward liberalization, the 1973 decision did not solve all the issues involved in abortion, and it even raised some additional questions.

Abortion is a heated issue that involves several overlapping elements. It is obviously a legal ques-

127

tion, and many people consider it a moral and/or religious question. Insofar as legalities are concerned, the elements of privacy, civil liberties, and personal freedoms are the major issues. Insofar as moral and religious beliefs are concerned, a substantial part of the question is determining when life begins and what constitutes a human being. Relatively ignored is the medical view of when life actually begins. A related question is what the dangers of abortion are at different stages of pregnancy.

Generally, those in favor of liberalized abortions see primarily the legal issues-civil liberties, individual decision making, and the privacy of a patient's decision - and argue that whether or not a fetus is a human being and at what point it does become a human being are unanswerable questions and thus not relevant to the issue. They generally believe that such behavior is private and poses no threat to others and that laws attempting to regulate abortion are unenforceable and an attempt to legislate private morality.

From the antiabortion perspective, however, there is a total rejection of the civil liberties argument; abortion is equated with murder, and certainly there is no question about the illegality of murder. Generally, antiabortionists believe that at the moment of conception, a human being exists and should have equal status with all other humans. Some believe that the unborn child is a potential person and therefore has a right to life regardless of when it is conceptualized as a human being. Antiabortionists also reject the private morality argument; they believe that there are two people involved, the mother and the fetus. For some, there is an unspoken belief that pregnancy is a just punishment for illicit sexual behavior and that allowing easy abortion lets the "sinner" escape her deserved punishment (Wells, 1975:180). Unstated or unrecognized, however, is the fact that many if not most illegal abortions prior to the Supreme Court decision were sought by married middle-class women rather than single and/or poor women.

Wells (1975:180) points out that laws attempting to regulate or ban certain kinds of private moral behavior may do a great deal of harm to individuals and to society by driving the behavior in question underground and thus creating a black market. An offshoot of the black market in abortions was a high mortality rate since those who generally were carrying out abortions were amateur practitioners. One very obvious change that resulted from liberalized state abortion laws prior to the Supreme Court decision was a sharp decline in mortality related to abortion. Significant declines were also reported in the rates of illegitimacy, indicating that in addition to the married women who felt that their families were large enough already, many single women were also taking advantage of the new laws.

Birth Control and Sterilization

Sterilization as a birth control measure generally entails a surgical procedure to make an individual incapable of reproduction. For men, the most likely procedure is vasectomy, which involves cutting and tying the ends of small vas deferens tubes. Generally, this operation can be performed in a doctor's office. It results in some soreness in the scrotum for a few days, but after a few hours, does not usually interfere with a man's activities. Except in a psychological sense, a vasectomy does not affect a man's sexual functioning; his ejaculate, or production of sperm is unchanged. The surgical procedure in the vasectomy prevents the sperm from being transported to the ejaculatory ducts, and thus sperm are absorbed into the body and the male becomes sterile.

For women there are several surgical sterilization procedures. In a tubal ligation, the fallopian tubes are cut and tied. This requires hospitalization. Perhaps, a man's decision that the woman should have a tubal ligation rather than for him to have a vasectomy results from the double standard, which gives women the responsibility for contraception, birth, and child care. A more recent method of sterilization for women is laparascopy. In this procedure, incisions are made in the women's abdomen, and fallopian tubes are severed and cauterized by an electrical instrument. This is generally called a "bandaid operation," and the woman needs to be in the hospital only until she becomes fully awake from the anesthetic. There are other techniques, some of which are much more severe than those already indicated. Certain procedures that result in sterilization are primarily used to correct abnormalties, such as the surgical removal of the ovaries, uterus, or fallopian tubes.

Generally, all sterilization procedures are irreversible. There are reported cases in which vasectomy was not successful and was reversed, but in general, once sterilization takes place, it must be considered a lifetime measure. This is very diferrent from birth control pills and from an IUD, which can be removed if and when a person desires to have a child.

VII. SEX EDUCATION

Kirkendall (1984:26) suggests the following changes are needed in sex education programs:

1. Sex education must be defined more broadly and include much more than physiological information and orientation to procreation.

2. Communication about sexuality must take into account our growing control over the outcome of sex. A wider range of activities is now accepted, as many of the presumed 'dangerous consequences' diminish.

3. The moral climate must be reassessed. Any future sex education program needs to grapple with moral values and keep in mind its particular audience. Without a doubt, parental values should be taken into account.... Parents, for the most part, must be realistic about sexual expression - their own and that of their children. If sexuality is life enhancing for them, then they should be able to acknowledge that to their children. Furthermore, their children as sexual beings will experiment with their sexuality not simply because it is sex but because they need, enjoy and mature through engaging in touch and body closeness.... Will we try to deny these experiences, or will we accept them and educate our children to express their sexuality responsibly. It will be an important task of any program of sex education to spell out responsibility in contemporary terms.

Scales (1981:563) argues that the key issues in sex education in the 1980's must move beyond prevention of ill health like V.D. and pregnancy to a positive health promotion and wellness emphasis:

(a) Knowledge about sexuality is helpful, not harmful, and controversy is an integral part of dealing with difficult issues;

(b) Self-esteem is central to effective decision making (people who feel poorly about themselves more readily succumb to pressure;

(c) Sex is not the same as love (this confusion has rarely been addressed in contemporary sex education, with the result that many people engage in sexual experiences when they are more generally searching for simple belonging, caring, trust, and the sense that they can both give and receive these qualities;

(d) Children must learn how to make distinctions in the kinds of relationships they want with different people, including platonic relationships, sexual friendship and passionate love;

(e) Communication and assertiveness skills are essential in enacting decisions (a decision not to have a particular sexual experience, for example, is hardly effective if one can neither communicate this to his or her partner nor deal with the physical pressure to have unwanted sexual experience).

Rossman (1983) argues that new information technologies such as computers and video discs can help defuse the debate regarding sexual education. A computerized sex education course could supplement the traditional sources of information regarding sexuality such as personal experimentation, observing those older, film, television, popular books, magazines, and pornography. The programs could be custom designed to fit the developmental level of each learner and would include the following dimensions:

First, each pupil will have access to what Leonard calls 'a full bank of the basic, commonly agreed-upon cultural knowledge.' The content of

131

this easily accessible electronic 'textbook' on the 54,000 pages or frames of a video disc, much more sophisticated and comprehensive than present materials will include films, slides, graphics, and a complete encyclopedia of scientifically established facts related to sexuality.

Second, a specific learning program, tailored for the individual, would consist of a computer dialogue that not only poses specific questions but also provides learners with the opportunity to ask any question they wish....

Third, even though each particular pupil is working on a specially designed program at the computer terminal, the learning process is far from being solitary work. Learners still work as a group in classroom, but they can have privacy and solitude when needed.... Sex education, therefore, will take place in a mixed-media learning environment involving teacher, computer, counselor, videodisc, other members of the class, and books, too (Rossman, 1983:73)

VIII.   CONCLUSION:

Plummer (1975:56-57) offers the following conclusions about sexual behavior:

1. People are born with a varying biological capacity for sexual experience including the physiological capacity to respond to a variety of different stimuli.

2. People are born into what is called a historically created "objective reality" which contains socially constructed series of sexual meanings. These meanings may include contradictions and variations, although there are natural orders.

3. The process of becoming a sexual person is like all other human social activities - a learning process.

4. Sexual experiences are variously interpreted by different people, and thus, sexual meanings are built up in interaction with significant other individuals.

5. A stable sexuality pattern is possible because of the emergence of attachments, the development of sexual perspectives and commitments, and the formulation of a relatively dimly understood sexual world view.

Generally, sexuality and sexual relations are being redefined in our society. Sexual behavior in general is coming out of the closet and is now a topic of conversation at all levels in our society. One primary result is that there can be seen on the horizon a more realistic convergence between the ideal verbalized values and the actual behavior in our society. A more psychologically healthy population most probably will be the consequence of this convergence.

[1]Some of the material presented in this chapter is revised from Butler's book, Traditional Marriage and Emerging Alternatives.

133

BIBLIOGRAPHY

Beigel, Hugo G.

1951   "Romantic Love," American Sociological
            Review, 16, June:326-334.

Brisset, Dennis, and Lionel S. Lewis

1970   "Guidelines for Marital Sex: An Analysis
            of Fifteen Popular Marriage Manuals,"
            Family Coordinator, 19, January, 41-48.

Comfort, Alex

1974   More Joy. New York: Crown.

1972   The Joy of Sex, New York: Simon &
            Schuster.

De Rougement, Denis

1949   "The Crisis of the Modern Couple," in
            R. N. Ashen (ed.), The Family: Its
            Function and Destiny, New York: Harper
            & Row.

Ford, S. Clellan, and Frank A. Beach

1951   Patterns of Sexual Behavior, New York:
            Harper & Row.

Gecas, Viktor and Roger Libby

1976   "Sexual Behavior as Symbolic Interac-
            tion," The Journal of Sexual Research,
            Vol. 12, no. 1:33-49.

Gordon, Michael, and Penelope J. Shankweiler

1971   "Different Equals Less: Female Sexuality
            in Recent Marriage Manuals," Journal of
            Marriage and the Family, 33, August:459-
            466.

Hobart, Charles W.

1958   "The Incidence of Romanticism During
            Courtship," Social Forces, 36, May):
            362-367.

Hunt, Morton

    1962   Her Infinite Variety: The American Woman
                 as Lover, Mate and Rival, New York:
                 Harper & Row.

    1973   "Sexual Behavior in the 1970s, Part II:
                 Premarital Sex," Playboy, 20, November:
                 74-75.

Kaplan, Helen S.

    1974   The New Sex Therapy, New York: Brunner/
                 Mazel, Publishers.

Kephart, William M.

    1967   "Some Correlates of Romantic Love,"
                 Journal of Marriage and the Family, 29,
                 August:470-474.

Kinsey, Alfred C., W. B. Pomeroy, and C. E. Martin

    1948   Sexual Behavior in the Human Male,
                 Philadephia: Saunders.

Kinsey, Alfred C., and Paul H. Gebhard

    1965   Sexual Behavior in the Human Female,
                 Philadelphia: Saunders.

Kirkendall, Lester A.

    1984   "The Future of Sex Education: The Compu-
                 ter Can't Do It All" The Furist, Feb.

Lydon, Susan,

    1974   "Understanding Orgasm," in Arlene
                 Skolnick and Jerome H. Skolnick
                 (eds.), Intimacy, Family and Society,
                 Boston: Little, Brown:157-162.

Masters, H.W., and V. E. Johnson

    1970   Human Sexual Inadequcy, Boston: Little,
                 Brown.

    1966   Human Sexual Response, Boston: Little,
                 Brown.

McCary, James L.

1975   Freedom and Growth in Marriage, Santa
            Barbara, Calif.: Hamilton.

Meerlo, J. A. M.

1952   Conversation and Communication, New
            York: International University Press.

O'Neill, Nena, and George O'Neill

1972   Open Marriage, New York: Avon Books.

Plummer, Kenneth

1975   Sexual Stigma: An Interactionist Account,
            London: Routledge & Kegan Paul.

Reiss, Ira L.

1967   The Social Context of Premarital Per-
            missiveness, New York: Holt, Rinehart
            and Winston.

Richards, Arlene Kramer and Irene Willis

1983   Under 18 and Pregnant. New York: Lothrop,
            Lee & Shepard Books.

Rossman, Parker

1983   "The Future of Sex Education: Computer-
            izing the Facts of Life," The Futurist,
            Dec.:69-73.

Rubin, Zick

1973   Liking and Loving, New York: Holt,
            Rinehart and Winston.

1970   Measurement of Romantic Love," Journal
            of Personality and Social Psychology,
            16, no. 2:265-273.

Safilios-Rothschild, Constantina

1977   Love, Sex, and Sex Roles, Englewood
            Cliffs, N.J.: Prentice-Hall.

Shuttleworth, Frank K.

   1959   A Bisocial and Developmental Theory of
             Male and Female Sexuality." Marriage and
             Family Living, May:163-170.

Udry, J. Richard

   1971   The Social Context of Marriage, Philadel-
             phia: Lippincott.

Wells, J. Gipson

   1975   Current Issues in Marriage and the
             Family, New York: Macmillan.

*Douglas B. Gutknecht, Department of Sociology, Chapman
College, Orange, California; Edgar W. Butler,
Department of Sociology, University of California,
Riverside, California.

137

CHAPTER 6

SEX AND GENDER ROLES: TOWARD EQUALITY?

Edgar W. Butler*
and
Douglas B. Gutknecht*

A distinction must be made between gender and sex roles. Gender identity specifies whether a person is male or female. Most people's maleness or femaleness is obvious, and in the newborn, generally anyone can tell the difference by the genitalia. When one utilizes the term sex roles, however, there is a subtle shift from the idea of male and female gender identity to notions of masculine and feminine roles. It is assumed that gender characteristics are physiological and biological in nature; whereas masculinity and femininity are learned scripts which tell us what is expected of men and women in a given society. Gender identity characteristics are assumed to be unchangeable (except by an operation) whereas sex roles, being socially prescribed and individually learned scripts acquired through the socialization process, are changeable. Sex roles are not innate and not always related to gender (Chafetz, 1974:4).

With present evidence and data, one cannot usually draw a precise line between characteristics caused by gender and role. However, as Chafetz points out, proving the influence of gender is up to those who believe in innate behavioral, attitudinal, emotional, or intellectual traits, because these supposedly innate traits vary greatly among societies and cultures. For example, the variety of ways that human mothers treat children suggests that there is no such thing as maternal instinct. Similarly, results of cross-cultural research show no reason to believe that males are necessarily more innately aggressive than females or that females are biologically or physiologically more passive or maternal than males. While there is no question that females must bear children, there is no biological reason that females must do the mothering of children. Raising children is both a male and female task in many societies.

I. SEX ROLES: DEVELOPMENT AS DIFFERENCES

Sex roles are patterns of expected behavior that vary by gender. It appears that every society has sex-role differentiation. Biological differences in males and females obviously predispose them to behave in somewhat different ways. Nevertheless, most people learn sex roles in the family and in other small groups. Thus we learn early what is means to be masculine and feminine, to practice the learned scripts on expectations attached to our gender role.

Physical attributes generally desired by parents for males include tallness, muscular physiques, and facial and body hair. Females, in order to be feminine, must have an attractive face and body, be pretty and small, and have little extraneous facial or body hair. For males in our culture, money equals success: Gould asks "does it also equal masculinity?" (1976:113). His answer is yes, to the extent that men are measured by their money and what they are able to earn or command in the market place, rather than by their potential as human beings. His view is that both men and women would be better off if masculinity was associated with "a man's sensitivity and his emotional capacity to respond to others rather than with dominance, strength, or ability to provide material goods."

In our society, sex-role definitions begin at birth, if not before (Spezzano, 1981). Parents even before birth may begin picking out female and male names. Almost immediately after birth, socilization into male or female sex roles begins. For boys, the blanket is blue, for girls, pink (Grambs and Waetjen, 1975:1). Rarely does one find a pink blanket even on a one-day-old male child. As seemingly innocent as this may seem, it is only an indicator of the vast myriad of behavior patterns related to a person's gender identity. Parents and other people respond to the child in sex-role terms, allocating sex-stereo-typed toys and sex-appropriate clothes.

In addition to the colors the child is given for clothing, bedding, a room decor, and toys, sex roles also influences the speech patterns parents and other use in talking about and to the child. How much self-reliance, nurturance, and independence the child will be given depends on whether the child is a boy or girl. It does not take much imagination for each of

140

us to recall from our own experiences such pervasive cultural imperatives regarding sex roles.

In the organization of children's play activities, boys play outdoors far more than girls (Lever, 1976). Though boys and girls both spend about 20 percent of their time alone, when involved in social play, boys more often play in larger groups. Boy's play occurs in more diverse age groups, and younger males must learn how to interact with older boys and girls. Boys are more likely to plan competitive games, and, generally, boys' games last longer.

The leisure patterns of boys and girls lead to the development of particular adult social skills and capacities. Boys' games help prepare them for successful performance in a wide range of settings in modern society. Girls' games prepare them primarily for working in the home and their probable future roles as wives and mothers. Boys' games provide many practical work lessons. Girls' games provide a training ground for the development of socioemotional skills.

Boys learn what they must not be before they gain knowledge of what it is they are supposed to be (Hartley, 1976:235). Boys restrict their interests and activities to masculine roles, even in kindergarten, while girls only gradually learn feminine patterns, perhaps four or five years later. In other words, more stringent demands are made on boys than on girls insofar as sex roles are concerned. At these early ages, boys are not able to understand the reasons for or nature of such demands. Almost from the cradle, boys are not able to participate in feminine or womanly things. Few boys have an understanding of the complimentary relationship between male and female roles. By overemphasizing the differences between the sexes we ignore the similarities. Although sameness is not the issue, many interpret the attempt to eliminate sex role stereotypes as the attempt to make us all the same. Conflicting sex-role pressures and rigid socialization of male children can lead to marked interpersonal communication difficulties and hostility toward so-called feminine sex role traits and behavior. This becomes particularly evident in adolescence where a wide range of potential characteristics are down played in favor of narrower ranges of gender scripts and behavior. This uncertain situation increases the likeliness of conflict and disagreement between the sexes at a time when intimacy is being learned.

II. MODELS OF SEX ROLE DEVELOPMENT

Several different models and theories have been utilized by social scientists to account for culturally learned behavior and attitudes (Skolnick, 1983). According to the "social-learning" model, a child learns sex-role behavior the same way a person learns any other type of behavior--through a combination of reward, punishment, imitation, and observation of what other people are doing and saying. This approach involves modeling; behavior is based on what the person may see occurring within a household, peer group, and other primary-group relationships. This view is rather consistent with the view that masculinity and femininity are the result of socialization and cultural factors.

Another approach is the "cognitive-developmental" model, which has been summarized as follows (Kohlberg, 1966): (1) Gender identity as a boy or girl is the critical and basic organizer of sex-role attitudes. (2) Gender identity results from basic, early, and simple cognitive judgments that are relatively irreversible and that are maintained by reality judgments, regardless of social reinforcements and parent identifications. If it is assumed that gender self-categorization organizes sex-role attitudes, then it can also be assumed that basic gender self-categorization determines basic values. One children categorize themselves as male or female, they then give a positive value to objects and acts consistent with their gender identity. They behave with a tendency toward cognitive consistency.

This approach suggests that sex-role concepts develop from children's active structuring of their own experience. In this view, children organize their perceptions and categorize the rest of the world and their place in it. In structuring experience, a person may examine how other people behave and interpret it through what they have learned up to that point. Thus, some young children believe that one's sexual identity is something that can change, like one's age, over time. Learning to be male or female is a process of understanding and interpreting rules defining sex roles--explicit rules as well as those implicit in interaction between other people. While

emphasis is on a child structuring his or her experience, this view is not necessarily in conflict with
a socialization-process model. It is consistent with
the cultural variation that exists in sex-role differentiation.

These orientations are also consistent with research showing that children with the same physiological or anatomical structure can be assigned to
either sex. That is, a psychologically and physiologically abnormal member of one sex may grow up as a
member of the other sex, in spite of his or her anatomical structure. Money (1972) has gone so far as to
report that every child is "psychosexually neutral" at
birth. More recently, having modified this position
somewhat, he belives that masculinity and femininity
are neither naturally unfolding nor innately biological processes, but processes with a heavy social
component.

In American society it is considered feminine to
be artistic, emotional, and nurturant. In other cultures men, not women, are supposed to be emotional,
expressive, and artistic. A classic study of sex
roles in three cultures was carried out by Mead
(1935). In one New Guinea tribe, the Arapesh, both
men and women were cooperative, unaggressive, and
gentle. On the other hand, in the Mundugumor tribe
of New Guinea, both sexes were ruthless and aggressive
and treated each other severely. This tribe had
applied characteristics that we would describe as
masculine traits to both males and females. In the
New Guinea Tchambuli tribe, there were sex-role con-
trasts--but the reverse of those in our society. Women
were aggressive, domineering, and managed the household; men tended to be artistic, dependent, sensitive,
and nurturant. Thus, Mead's study illustrates that
even on one South Pacific island, a variety of sex-
role patterns exist. Obviously they are not attri-
butable to the biological differences among tribes
but to cultural differences.

Clearly, some sex characteristics are physiological and are biologically derived. It is obvious,
at least in our society, that such external characteristics give a person a basic sense of gender
identity. However, to what extend to these influence
subsequent values, attitudes, and behavior? Cultures
demonstrate a large range of variations. In our
society, where substantial variation in the masculin-

143

ity-feminity aspects of sex and sex roles exists, people conform to the standard sex roles expected of them in their interests, attitudes, and behavioral characteristics. Different characteristics are identified as masculine and feminine in different societies.

In summary, the view that sex role learning begins at birth, if not before, sees most infants behavvior as guided by parents who have a sex-role view of the world. Girls are more often protected more than boys. They are less likely to be encouraged to become independent, are counseled against being adventurous, and are inhibited in exploratory behavior. Males are encouraged to be interested in things, to have extensive childhood experiences, and to be achievement oriented. These are systematic differences influenced by cultural variation in socialization. Substantial evidence exists suggesting that some relatively universal sex differences are biological in origin. However, these are relatively few in number and primarily involve child-bearing and care of children. Subsequently, most sex role differences that exist in our society, and in other societies, appear to be culturally and societally determined by the value system of that society. Thus, most sex role differences can be considered as social in origin. In our society we can trace back to almost the very first day of birth the different socialization processes that males and females go through. These different socialization processes and values and behavior patterns result in the differing perspectives of males and females.

III. SEX ROLE STEREOTYPES

Chafetz (1974) carried out research examining the variety of steretyped sex role traits associated with masculinity and femininity in our society. She asked a number of small groups the following question: "What kinds of words and phrases do you think most Americans use to characterize males compared to females or "masculinity" versus "femininity?" The results of her analysis are shown in Figure 1. Certain attributes have more importance attached to them than others. For example, under physical characteristics, the predominant character traits given were being strong for masculine and being nonathletic and worrying about appearance and aging for feminine. The primary functional traits given were being a bread-winner for masculine and being domestic and involved with chil-

144

dren for feminine. Dominant sexual characteristics given were aggressive and experienced for masculine and virginal inexperienced, and accepting the double standard for women. Women were supposed to be emotional, sentimental, and romantic; men were supposed to be unemotional and stoical and not cry.

Intellectually, women were supposed to be idealistic and humanistic; men, logical, intellectual, rational, objective, and scientific. The dominant interpersonal feminine traits were to be pretty, flirty, coy, gossipy, catty, sneaky, fickle, dependent or protected, unresponsive, status conscious, uncompetitive, refined, and adept in the social graces; the dominant interpersonal masculine traits were to be a leader, dominating, independent, free, and individualistic. Other traits associated with being masculine were to be aggressive, success oriented, and ambitous; feminine traits were to be self-conscious, easily intimidated, modest, shy, sweet, patient, and vain.

If the Chafetz results can be generalized for our society, Chafetz argues that there are more "blatantly negative" connotative words used to describe femininity, and somewhat fewer positive terms. A general impression emerges that the masculine sex role stereotype is positive, whereas the feminine one is either negative or passive. A basic dualism in female sexuality exists since women are held to be sexually passive and uninterested while at the same time being seductive and flirtatious. This theme, of course, runs through the history of Western civilization and various stories concerning "good" and "bad" females do not have a parallel for males.

One place where the dominant sex role beliefs of our society can be ascertained is in the mass media (television, magazines, etc.). Popular rock music lyrics, rock video pictures, describe what younger people believe and react to in sex role stereotyping. The male is considered as primarily sexually aggressive and adventuresome with secondary characteristics of being nonconformist, rigid, and egotistical; he does not do domestic work. On the other hand, the females are often viewed as victim, vamp, or being dominated as a sex object. In popular songs women conform substantially to being passive and dependent with secondary characteristics of being domestic, flirtatious, insecure, and idealistic. In general, in our society, masculine and feminine traits, stereo-

145

FIGURE 1: Stereotyped Sex-Role Traits

Characteristics	Masculine Traits	Feminine Traits

I. Physical	Virile, athletic, strong*
	Sloppy, worry less about
	  appearance and aging
	Brave
		Weak, helpless dainty,
		  nonathletic*
		Worry about appearance
		  and aging*
		Sensual
		Graceful

II. Functional	Breadwinner, provider*	Domestic* Maternal, involved with children* Churchgoing

III. Sexual	Sexually aggressive,
	  experienced*
	Single status acceptable;
	  male "caught" by spouse
		Virginal, inexperienced,
		  double standard*
		Must be married, female
		  "catches" spouse
		Sexually passive, uninterested
		Responsible for birth control
		Seductive, flirtatious

IV. Emotional	Unemotional, stoic, don't
	  cry*
		Emotional, sentimental,
		  romantic*
		Can cry
		Expressive
		Compassionate
		Nervous, insecure, fearful

V. Intellectual	Logical, intellectual,
	  rational, objective,
	  scientific*
	Practical
	Mechanical
	Public awareness, activity,
	  contributor to society
	Dogmatic
		Scatterbrained, frivolous,
		  shallow, inconsistent,
		  intuitive*
		Impractical
		Perceptive, sensitive
		"Arty"
		Idealistic, humanistic*

VI. Interpersonal	Leader, dominating*
	Disciplinarian*
	Independent, free,
	  individualistic*
	Demanding
		Petty, flirty, coy, gossipy,
		  catty, sneaky, fickle*
		Dependent, overprotected,
		  responsive*
		Status conscious and competi-
		  tive, refined, adept in
		  social graces*
		Follower, subservient,
		  submissive

VII. Other Personal	Aggressive*
	Success oriented, ambitious*
	Proud, egotistical confident
	Moral, trustworthy
	Decisive
	Competitive
	Uninhibited, adventurous
		Self-conscious, easily intimi-
		  dated, modest, shy, sweet*
		Patient*
		Vain*
		Affectionate, gentle, tender,
		  soft
		Not aggressive, quiet, passive
		Tardy
		Innocent
		Noncompetitive

*Attribute listed by five or more of the groups.
Source: Janet S. Chafetz, Masculine/Feminine or Human? Itasca, IL: F.E. Peacock,
   1974, pp. 35-38.

typically delineated, are thought of as belonging almost exclusively to one or the other sex. In many respects, however, these traits are not distributed in a dichotomous way but are distributed continuously. Thus, stereotypes do not always fit current individuals.

Early socialization within most families stresses sex role stereotypes. Religion, science, and other major institutions in our society aid and abet sex stereotyping. While this might or might not be considered desirable, much sex stereotyping of females is negative. This negativism has led to economic inequality and job discrimination, even against women with equal education, skills, and abilities. Stereotyped sex roles for women are, in fact, devalued activities and traits; this devaluation appearently carries over into other spheres--inequality in income and job distribution; lack of females at top level positions, whether in underground newspapers, large corporations, or educational institutions; inequalities in the fields of law, the political arena, and in the other major societal institutions.

How can a long-term, loving relationship develop between a female and a male whose roles are based on sex stereotypes? For to survive in our society, and for a marriage to survive, partners have to overcome traditional sex role stereotypes and strike out in a direction that will allow both partners to explore their full human potential. The first step is to establish equality between marital partners. The woman must either work or establish self-fulfilling activities outside the home to achieve this equality. In order to fulfill her personal needs, she has to develop more self-confidence.

Stereotyped masculine and feminine traits also have an impact upon the relationship between parents and children. In most American families, the early socialization process is directly related to the stereotyped sex traits we have already discussed. The female child may begin learning almost immediately that motherhood is fulfillment by receiving her first doll. If jobs were discussed, they are along the lines of the helping professions and so forth. Similarly, the male child is almost immediately socialized into the stereotyped traits especially insisted upon by fathers in our society.

147

Socialization patterns based on sex role stereotypes have an impact on friendships between people of
the same sex. From very early childhood, males are
encouraged to form friendships in peer groups with
other males and to cooperate with them to achieve
desired goals, often in competition with other all-
male groups. They are also encouraged to shun the
companionship of females for ordinary friendship
purposes. However, certain sexual stereotypes seriously limit the scope, content, and intensity of male
relationships, which consist primarily of activities
done together with very little importance attached to
discussions, especially about feelings, but also a-
bout other serious issues (Booth, 1972:186).

When males are together, most of the time is
spent in activities that satisfy recreational and
other needs. Very little time is spent discussing
insecurities and emotional needs. Males are discouraged from showing emotions and expressing dependency. Sex stereotypes in our society discourage
males from having an intense intimate and personal
relationship with each other.

Females, it appears, face different problems in
friendships. Females do get to know other females
and do form close friendships. Chafetz (1974:185)
believes this is possible because the feminine sex
role stereotype encourages women to express emotions,
needs, and problems without necessarily feeling
threatened and worrying about competition. Thus, in
contrast to what one finds with males, females will
talk to each other about the males they love rather
than about those with whom they've had fleeting and
casual relations.

IV. ANDROGYNY AS A LIFESTYLE: OVERCOMING SEX ROLE
    STEREOTYPES

An androgynous society can be defined as one
with limited sex role differences and few stereotypes
between males and females that are based on gender
(Osofsky and Osofsky, 1972:411). If changes currently underway in sex roles continue, such an androgynous lifestyle may actually become a viable lifestyle
option. Changes in stereotyped patterns of female
and male behavior that are occurring are altering
definitions of sex role development and ultimately
may have an affect on the socialization process. Of

course, traditional sex role behavior continues in many areas of work and family life and continues to indicate the differences between the ideal and real world--we often verbalize our beliefs in equality of the sexes but act in ways that contradict our expressed beliefs.

However, we remain optimistic regarding changes occurring in societally accepted roles for men and women encourage their joint participation in work outside the home and more sharing of traditional household responsibilities within the home (Haas, 1980). All of this will certainly broaden the societal definitions of expected behavior for men and women. While they may create consternation for some parents and relatives, such an increase in opportunity may allow individuals to find new opportunities for lifelong well-being. Obviously, benefits of such lessened sex role differences will have great impact on all institutions.

The early socialization process will be the key point in breaking down sex role stereotypes of the past. Part will occur in the family and part will probably be taken up within the school system. Children are being exposed more and more to male and female teachers at all school levels. Similarly, textbooks show females and males participating in many different positions and work role situations in society, not only in traditional roles. Similarly, we see more nonsexual types of lifestyles, based primarily on abilities and interests. While counselors may have traditionally encouraged females not to take careers seriously and to pursue family lines, today more women are encouraged to utilize all their abilities by attending graduate and professional schools and joining professions once dominated primarily by males.

Our society and many individuals within it are changing quite rapidly. Yet, in the future, some people undoubtedly will continue to folow traditional sex stereotyped roles. On the other hand, many others will not and they will develop new patterns. Hopefully, the occurring changes in sex role behavior will further the development of individuals so that people in a variety of roles can contribute to a humanistic development of our greatest asset--people.

Part of the decreasing emphasis on rigid male

149

and female sex roles is due to the women's liberation movement, which may have two possible main effects on the role of the father: First, the traditional role of the patriarchal father might disappear. Second, men may assume, at least in part, an expressive, affect role and thus enrich the emotional development of their children. On the other hand, men might collapse into resentment and frustration, rejecting such roles and leaving their children without their emotional support. However, it appears that close to 1 million men are now accepting the total responsibility of raising their children as single parent fathers (Oakland, 1984).

Another recent change in sex roles has been the development of the male liberation movement. This movement calls for men to free themselves of the sex role stereotypes that limit their ability to be human (Sawyer, 1976:287). Men involved in this movement believe that all men need to overthrow the dominant view males are ideally called upon to learn through sex role stereotypes. They argue for an alternative system in which men share, among themselves and with women, instead of striving for domination. They believe that men must be able to freely cry, be gentle, and show weakness, not because they are effeminate or masculine but because they are human beings with all the strengths and weaknesses that each and every person has. They are arguing for a fuller concept of humanity, recognizing that all men and women are potentially both strong and weak, both active and passive, both dominant and passive, and that these human characteristics are not the province of either sex (see Goldberg, 1979).

The importance of understanding how sex roles influence family life is clear. In the future, if gender is no longer important to what people do within the family unit, whether it be nuclear or otherwise, tasks will have to be assigned or rotated without regard to gender, releasing everyone to function based upon their interests, motivations, skills, and competences. If sex role stereotypes disappear, children obviously will be raised to explore the full potential of their humanity. Differences will certainly exist between the sexes but sex itself will not determine one's potential to fully participate in life's adventure. Men and women can learn to relate to each other as individual human beings rather than using sex role stereotypes.

BIBLIOGRAPHY

Booth, Alan

1972   "Sex and Social Participation," _American
        Sociological Review_, 37, April:183-192.

Chafetz, Janet S.

1974   _Masculine/Feminine or Human?_ Itasca, IL:
        F. E. Peacock.

Goldberg, Herb

1979   _The New Male: From Macho to Sensitive but
        Still All Male_, New York: New American
        Library.

Gould, Robert

1976   "Measuring Masculinity by Size of a Pay-
        check," in Deborah S. David and Robert
        Brannon (eds.), _The Forty-Nine Percent
        Majority: The Male Sex Role_, Reading,
        MA: Addison-Wesley:113-118.

Grambs, Jean D., and Walter B. Waetjen

1975   _Sex: Does It Makes a Difference?_ North
        Scituate, MA: Duxbury Press.

Haas, Linda

1980   "Role-Sharing Couples: A Study of
        Egalitarian Marriages," _Family Rela-
        tions_, 29:289-294.

Hartley, Ruth E.

1976   "Sex Role Pressures and the Socializa-
        tion of the Male Child," in Deborah S.
        David and Robert Brannon (eds.), _The
        Forty-Nine Percent Majority: The Male
        Sex Role_, Reading, MA: Addison-Wesley:
        235-244.

Kohlberg, Lawrence

1966   "A Cognitive-Developmental Analysis of
            Children's Sex Role Concepts and Atti-
            tudes," in Eleanor E. Maccoby (ed.), The
            Development of Sex Differences, Stanford,
            CA: Stanford University Press:82-98.

Lever, Janet

1976   "Sex Differences in the Games Children
            Play," Social Problems, 23, April:478-487.

Mead, Margaret

1935   Sex and Temperament in Three Primitive
            Societies, New York: New American Library
            (Mentor Books).

Money, John,

1972   "The Determinants of Human Sexuality,"
            in C. J. Sager and H. S. Kaplan (eds.),
            Progress in Group and Family Therapy,
            New York: Brunner/Mazel.

Oakland, Thomas

1984   Divorced Fathers: Reconstructing a
            Quality Life. New York: Human Sciences
            Press.

Osofsky, Joy D., and Howard J. Osofsky
1972   "Androgyny as a Life Style," The Family
            Coordinator, 21, October:411-418.

Sawyer, Jack

1976   "On Male Liberation," in Deborah S. David
            and Robert Brannon (eds.), The Forty-Nine
            Percent Majority: The Male Sex Role,
            Reading, MA: Addison-Wesley:287-290.

Skolnick, Arlene

1983   The Intimate Environment, 3rd edition,
            Boston: Little, Brown,

Spezzano, I.

1981   "Prenatal Psychology: Pregnant with
            Questions," Psychology Today, May:
            49-57.

Wallace, Ruth A., and Lengerman, Patricia Madoo

1983   Gender in America: Social Control and
            Social Change. New York: Prentice
            Hall.

*Douglas B. Gutknecht, Department of Sociology, Chapman
College, Orange, California; Edgar W. Butler,
Department of Sociology, University of California,
Riverside, California.

CHAPTER 7

VOLUNTARY CHILDLESSNESS:
SOME NOTES ON THE DECISION MAKING PROCESS

Patricia Thomas Crane, Ph.D.*

I. INTRODUCTION

There has been a growing trend among married couples to postpone childbearing for an extended period of time (U.S. Bureau of the Census, 1981; Wilkie, 1981). Little is known of the process of fertility delay, except as it relates to a declining desire to have children (Freshnok and Cutright, 1978), and the decision to remain voluntarily childless (Veeres, 1973; Bram, 1974).

Even though childbearing plans tend to be formulated before marriage, they are not likely to be implemented until after marriage, at which time it is likely they will be revised to reflect one's current attitudes and the effect of intervening experiences. Apparently, the longer a woman waits to have her first child, the fewer children she will over time, prefer--regardless of her earlier family size goals. Poston (1976) and Hunt (1978) have found that for childless wives, the percentage expecting to remain childless permanently, dramatically increased with duration of marriage. An interesting theoretical question is then, what is it about the passage of time, within the context of a marital relationship, which makes voluntary childlessness become more likely the longer a couple is married? Cramer (1980) has charged that most fertility models have ignored the processes by which plans are formed, an issue of considerable importance when one considers that fertility plans are likely to be more dynamic than static, and when the trend toward postponed first births is increasing.

Until very recently, the phenomena of childlessness has been virtually ignored as a field of study. Research concerning childlessness is limited whereas historically, the literature on the family has been characteristically devoted to inquiry into other facets of parenthood. Thus, voluntary childlessness represents a structural variation of the traditional family form about which little is known specifically

155

with regard to the dynamics involved in the process
of making the contranormative decision.

II. THE ANALYTICAL FRAMEWORK - DECISION AS SOCIAL
PROCESS

The following analysis constitutes a partial look
at several of the contingencies involved in the process leading to a decision to remain childless. Such
a process is conceived to have began in childhood
(i.e., early socialization experiences) and continues
after one identifies oneself as voluntarily childless.
This paper, however, shall be confined to the process
leading to the decision.

A process perspective, then, will be utilized to
trace the development of the respondent's attitudes
toward motherhood and children, as well as the signi-
ficance of role models which may have contributed to
an awareness of such an alternative. Then, issues
relevant to this process during courtship and marriage
shall be examined.

III. SAMPLE

Because voluntarily childless couples constitute
only an estimated 5 percent of the population, and
because they possess deviant attitudes with regard to
parenthood--they are difficult to locate for research
purposes. Thus, because there is no defined population of childless wives, large, representative samples
are very difficult to obtain. Eleven in-depth interviews of voluntarily childless wives have been obtained and analyzed to date.

IV. PROCESS ISSUES TEMPORALLY PRIOR TO COURTSHIP AND
MARRIAGE

Initially I assumed that the forthcoming issues
discussed in this section were part of the process of
becoming deliberately childless, and had temporally
preceded the actual identification of ones' self as
deliberately childless. However, the questions in the
interview did not specifically ask for temporal place-
ment with regard to the development of one's image of
motherhood or attitudes toward children. Doubtless,
however, one's attitudes toward children and motherhood constantly undergo renegotiation over time--in
the true sense of a process--as opposed to their being
specifically temporally identifiable and then not
changing. 156

A. Images of Motherhood

The issue of what motherhood means to those who deliberately choose to remain childless is an important one. On the outset of conducting my research, I assumed that motherhood would not likely be described favorably by the wives because such a favorable attitude toward motherhood would be inconsistent with refusal to enact it as a role. Respondents were asked to discuss their conception of how "motherhood" was generally conceived. What I found impressive about their comments was a rather condescending recognition that "society" has a "vested interest" in presenting motherhood as appearing in a manner that conventional couples would be attracted to it. However, when queried about their own views of motherhood, it was apparent that they perceived the two views as being quite discrepant. What was particularly striking about the wives' characterization of motherhood was their implicit suggestion that they held a more "realistic" view of motherhood. Such negative characterizations may reflect a defense used to protect themselves against pro-natalist arguments (Veevers, 1975.)[1] At the very least, however, the data from my sample suggests that the voluntarily childless conceive of themselves as mavericks within their own culture.

B. Attitudes Toward Children

One's attitude toward children is certainly of relevance in trying to understand why women voluntarily forego motherhood. Initially I expected the deliberately childless to view children unfavorably. This general lack of appeal on the part of children, I assumed, led one to discover new priorities that would supplant the traditional career of motherhood for women. However, five of the eleven wives interviewed contend they either don't care for children or feel uncomfortable being around them, yet six respondents either expressed no opinion or noted that they liked children. Thus, on the basis of my sample, liking or disliking children does not seem to account for whether or not one will choose to remain childless. The simple explanation that a woman just doesn't like children and that is why she is not having them is not borne out by this data, which suggests that other considerations are taken into account when one makes a decision to remain childless.

157

C. Role Models for Childlessness

Sociologists often explain behavior that runs counter to the norms of the group in which they are socialized by taking into account the likelihood that the individual may have identified with and assumed the values of another group or reference individual. With regard to this issue, I speculated that childlessness, as an alternative family form, is partly a function of having early contact with others who for one reason or another never had children.

Eight of the eleven wives interviewed reported that they had known someone, or usually some couple (usually during childhood or adolescence) who, for some reason, never had children. I suggest that these people served as role models, or at least played some part in introducing the possibility of childlessness as an alternative to conventional marriage.

One striking characteristic of the wives' descriptions of the couples they had known who were childless was a description of the "glamourous" lifestyle that the wives were noticeably impressed with. Their glamourous lifestyle was commonly attributed to their not having children. Of relevance here is the concern among the wives of achieving for themselves a glamourous lifestyle as a result of foregoing procreation (Crane, 1978:23).

V. PROCESS ISSUES OCCURRING DURING COURTSHIP AND MARRIAGE

Not surprisingly, there was no single path to a decision to remain childless. Rather, there were multiple paths leading to a decision from which certain patterns could be delineated. The following represents aspects of this process.

A. Assuming They Would have a Conventional Marriage

Although the data suggests that the process leading to the decision to remain childless begins prior to courtship, it appears that most of the respondents I interviewed identified courtship as the first stage of the process (at least it was the first time the issue had relevance for them). Nine of the eleven wives interviewed reported they had assumed during courtship, and even several years following marriage that they would eventually have children.[2]

One interesting feature of the data was that more than just assuming they "would go the way of every other girl they had ever known" eight of the wives reported that they had never discussed the prospect of eventually having children with their husbands while they were dating or engaged. This important conversation never occurred between those eight wives and their fiancees. Thus, the dual aspects of assuming, on the one hand, that they would eventually procreate and then never discussing plans for parenthood prior to marriage with their fiancees was characteristic of the wives interviewed.

Most of the wives reported that there was no apparent point in time when a decision was actually made not to have children.[3] When the interview guide was constructed, I assumed (albeit naively) that respondents could tell me exactly when it was that they and their husbands sat down and decided not to have children. I also expected many wives to relate tales of how difficult it was to find a potential spouse that would be willing to go along with such an unusual decision.[4] Rather, what I did discover was that when asked "when did you decide to remain childless?" six wives were unable to pinpoint an exact time and instead spoke of evolved "tacit" understandings (implicit agreements) between herself and her spouse which only sometimes led to an explicit, formalized agreement.

B. A Series of Postponements - "Putting Off"

The typical process of coming to a decision involved a prolonged postponement of childbearing until such time that it was no longer considered desireable at all. Rather than explicitly rejecting motherhood, they described themselves as repeatedly deferring procreation until a more convenient time. Because most wives assumed they would eventualy have children, essentialy what transpired in the interim between marriage and actualy identifying oneself as deliberately childless was a slow process of rationalizing why it wasn't yet convenient to have a family. After a sufficient period of "putting it off" had transpired these wives evidently came to the awareness that there never was going to be a "right time."

159

C. Precipitating Events

Some wives identified a particular precipitating event that resulted in a formalized agreement with their spouse that they forego having children. Evident in their descriptions of various precipitating events (e.g., goals that had caused them to put off having children had come to fruition, health, advancing age, etc.) was the notion that indeed they had been putting off making a commitment to a decision, and had the particular event not occurred, the decision may have been continued to be postponed (at least not in a formalized sense).

D. A Search for Specificity

Noticeable in the reports of how a decision was reached is a lack of clarity as to how or what actually happened. The vagueness surrounding the decision was also apparent to the wives as they tried to relate what led them to their decision. It appeared in their discussions that as a result of their discomfort with such a mystifying lack of insight into that actual events leading to their decisions, they were attempting to fit a linear, organized explanation to a process which had apparently not been reflected on prior to the interview.

Thus, wives were uncomfortable with the vagueness and lack of insight (which they themselves perceived) regarding events leading to their decision. Consequently, their attempts to ameliorate this ambiguity consisted of attempts to outline specific insights or awarenesses they had which played a role in the process leading to the decision. The following represents the generic elements reputedly involved in that process: seductiveness of the lifestyle, observation of the effect of children on their friends' marriages and a recognition that there are no guarantees that should they have children, they would "turn out right."

1. **Seductiveness of the life style.** Although conventional couples may also postpone starting a family until a more convenient time, they eventually reproduce, whereas for many of the wives I interviewed, the postponement period experienced was sufficient enough such that when the opportunity to start a family presented itself, the benefits accruing to the childless lifestyle was perceived as outweighing the

160

perceived benefits which could be derived from having a family. Therefore, in the process of coming to define oneself as voluntarily childless, all wives were in agreement that a major component of the process was the seductive effect of a lifestyle without children. For couples who elect to have children after a substantial postponement, it would appear that any change in their lifestyle should be carefully planned for and its effects anticipated in order that as smooth a transition as possible be implemented.

2. Observing the effect of children on their friends' marriages. Another theme commonly discussed with regard to a decision process is a witnessing of the impact that children have on their friends' marriages. While childless wives are still in the process of "putting off" having children, many of their friends and relatives had become parents. In many cases their children were seen as having a disruptive effect on the marriage, which served to reinforce the advantages accruing to the lifestyle the childless were engaged in.

In addition to children being seen as hampering the quality of the relationships between the parents, five wives described instances where their friends' children, in contrast to the "little bundles of joy" their parents purported them to be, were seen by the childless wives as constantly burdensome.[5] These experiences made having children appear even more undesireable, when coupled with the reinforcing experiences they were having as a function of their "childfree" lifestyle.

3. A recognition that there is no guarantee that their children would "turn out right." In addition to observing (perhaps selectively) that children are a hindrence to the maintenance of a satisfying marriage and that they are "alot of trouble," what I found interesting about several of the discussions of the events that led to identifying oneself as voluntarily childless, were reports of having witnessed children who "turned out screwed up." It appears that the childless wives I interviewed were very aware of the possibility that if they had children, they could just as easily turn into a disappointment as anything else. The notion here is that these women were concerned that despite earnest efforts at good parenting, there could be no guarantee that one's efforts would be

161

successful. This tendency leads me to speculate whether or not parents, prior to having children, were as concerned with this same possibility. In other words, perhaps childless wives were overly concerned with the possibility that their children may prove disappointing.

4. <u>Disassociation from childed couples</u>. As children came to be seen as creating "hassles" and disruptive of social occasions, seven of the wives reported they began to disassociate themselves from their childed friends in an effort to maintain or "protect" their lifestyle which was by now becoming increasingly more attractive relative to their childed friends. Many wives reported that they gradually lost touch with their friends who had children. Other childless couples (or single friends) serve as a support group to which these wives may turn for understanding and validation of their decision, as well as being free to share the same lifestyle. However, the above does not represent the experience of all the wives interviewed. Four of the respondents reported no such tendency to "abandon" friends who became parents. Rather, they reported experiencing no difficulty in accommodating these couples into their social network.

VI. SUMMARY

The decision to remain childless is seen as the outcome of a gradual process, usually characterized by prolonged postponement. General themes of this process included: wives' assumption prior to marriage that she and her husband would eventually have children; the absence of a discussion with their fiancees prior to marriage concerning future plans for childbearing; precipitating events that forced an explicit choice; postponement until a more convenient time (usually unspecified) until finally an implicit understanding was evolved that there was never going to be a more convenient time; a seductive childfree lifestyle which reinforced their postponements; observing (albeit selectively) that children often disrupt marriages; and finally, an awareness or a concern that any children they might have would not necessarily "turn out right."

162

VII. CONCLUSION

This paper has presented a partial look at the process of events leading to a decision to remain childless. No attempt has been made to imply that this is a complete nor representative analysis of that process, rather, the research presented herein was exploratory in nature and there are many more questions which remain to be asked. Certainly any complete analysis of the process of the leading to the decision to parent or not would want to contrast the experiences of childed wives with those who have elected to forego parenthood. Also - such an analysis would probably wish to include husbands - as it is most likely that their own unique perspective would add much to an analysis of such a process.

In conclusion, then, much still can be learned about the process leading to a decision to remain childless.

FOOTNOTES

1. Veevers (1975:475) corroborates my finding that the voluntarily childless tend to hold a number of "unusual" beliefs concerning the attributes of the kinds of persons who become parents.

2. Veevers (1973a:359) also reports that like conventional couples the women in her sample also assumed that they would have one or two children eventually.

3. Veevers (1973a:360) also reports that couples in her sample were at a loss to explain exactly how or when the transition came about, but that they agreed that it was an implicit decision.

4. It is recognized that the lack of such a tendency (on the basis of my sample) may not represent the experience of many deliberately childless women, but rather, may be an artifact of such a small sample.

5. Veevers (1975:477) also observed that when the childless observe parents being hostile toward their children or expressing anger or resentment which they inevitably feel occasionally, they conclude that just as they suspected all along, "they are making the best of a bad situation."

BIBLIOGRAPHY

Cramer, J. C.

1980   "Fertility and female employment: prob-
            lems of causal direction." American
            Sociological Review, 45(2):167-190.

Crane, P.T.

1978   "Processes surrounding a decision to
            remain childless." Unpublished manu-
            script presented at the annual Pacific
            Sociological Association meetings in
            Spokane, Washington (April).

Freshnok, L. and Cutright, P.

1978   "Structural determinants of childlessness:
            A nonrecursive analysis of 1970 U.S.
            rates." Social Biology, 25(3):169-177.

Hunt, S. J. P.

1979   A comparative analysis of childless
            women with low birth expectations.
            Unpublished doctoral dissertation,
            Oregon State University.

Poston, D. L.

1976   "Characteristics of voluntarily and in-
            voluntarily childless wives." Social
            Biology, 23(3):198-209.

U.S. Bureau of the Census

1981   Current Population Reports, Series P-20,
            No. 358, Fertility of American Women:
            June 1979, U.S. Government Printing
            Office, Washington, D.C.

Veevers, J.E.

1972   "Factors in the incidence of childless-
            ness: an analysis of the census data."
            Social Biology 19:266-274.

165

1973a   "Voluntarily child-free wives: an
             exploratory study." Sociology and
             Social Research, 57:356-366.

1973b   "The child-free alternative: rejection
             of the motherhood mystique." Pp. 183-
             199 in Marylee Stephenson (Ed.), Women
             in Canada. Toronto: New Press.

1975   "The moral careers of voluntarily child-
             less wives: notes on the defense of a
             variant world view." The Family Coor-
             dinator (October):473-487.

Wilkie, J. R.

1981   "The trend toward delayed parenthood."
             Journal of Marriage and the Family,
             43(3):583-591

*Department of Behavioral Sciences, California State
Polytechnic University, Pomona, Pomona, California.

CHAPTER 8

THE ONE-CHILD FAMILY: A NEW LIFE-STYLE

Sharryl Hawke and
David Knox*

"How many children do we want?" is a question
most married couples ask.   Current concerns about inflation, population, and the wife's career are causing
young couples to reevaluate commonly held beliefs
about which family size is best (Peck, 1971; Whelan,
1976).   While most couples decide to have two children,
a small but growing number remain childfree.   About
10% choose the third alternative--to have one child
(General Social Science Survey, Note 1; Redding,
1974).

When most couples are asked why they don't consider having an only child, they often reply that
only children are spoiled and lonely and that it takes
at least two children to make a real family.   One
parent of two children declared, "Being an only child
is almost like having a disease--it's not fair to the
child and his/her parents."

Are these beliefs justified?   Does the one-child
family have negative consequences for children and
parents?   As parents who have one child, we sought
answers to these questions.   We surveyed 102 parents
of only children (54 were interviewed; 48 completed a
questionnaire) and 105 only children (53 were interviewed; 52 completed a questionnaire).   These data and
the available literature (mostly dated) revealed a
stark contrast to what is commonly believed about only
children and their parents (Hawke & Knox, 1977).

I.   ADVANTAGES OF THE ONE-CHILD FAMILY

The life-style of the one-child family is significantly different from that of the multi-child family.
But most members of one-child families regard the
differences in positive terms.   The benefits occur for
the child, his/her parents, and the family as a unit.

Advantages for the Child

Ninety-eight percent of the only children surveyed believed that being an only child has its ad-

167

vantages. "I was never compared to a brother or sister," "My life was more private than if I had siblings--I had my own room," and "I got most of the things I wanted like band instruments and my folks took me with them to Europe" were frequent comments made by only children.

But in addition to avoiding sibling rivalry, having more privacy, and enjoying greater affluence, what kind of person is the only child? Several studies have compared the intelligence, school performance, and self-confidence of only children with children who have siblings. In an IQ study involving over seventy thousand children, only children were found to have the highest IQ of any group measured (Thompson, 1950). Regarding language development, only children have larger vocabularies and better verbal skills than children with siblings (Davis, 1937). "Only children use bigger words," recalled an adult only, "because they spend more time around adults."

These early intellectual abilities help throughout the school years. The grades of only children are as good or better than students who have brothers and sisters (Lee & Stewart, 1957). And, more only children who go to college have performance records equal to or superior to children with siblings (Bayer, 1966).

In addition to being bright children and successful students, only children are generally self-confident and resourceful. They are not the "shrinking violets" so often assumed. In general, from preschool through adulthood only children display more self-reliance and self-confidence than their peers with siblings (Guilford & Worchester, 1930; Dyer, 1949; Rosenberg, 1965). "My only will never need a book on assertion," expressed one parent.

And although only children are often thought of as friendless, one researcher found that they are consistently the most popular group among elementary students (Bonney, 1944). "Because I didn't have readymade companions at home," remarked one adult only, "I had to seek out friends. I learned to enjoy meeting new people and to work hard at maintaining friendships."

Although less is known about only children as adults, in general, they are as likely to have successful careers, happy marriages, and good parenting experiences as people who grow up with brothers and sisters (Cutts & Moseley, 1954).

All in all, being an only child seems to provide the climate and experiences which produce successful, self-confident human beings. "I've never considered being an only child a handicap," remarked a young mother. "Only non-onlies think it's a disadvantage." However, it should be kept in mind that in many of the studies on only children, social class is uncontrolled and because a disproportionate number of only children are found in middle and upper class families, their positive attributes are not surprising. Whether or not these positive attributes are characteristic of lower class only children is an issue for subsequent research.

Advantages of Parents

Parents of only children are quick to point out the advantages of the one-child family for themselves. "Being the parent of one child is having the best of two worlds" in the view of one parent. "I can experience the joys and frustrations of being a parent without getting so tied down by parenting responsibilities that I haven't time to pursue my own interests."

In naming more specific advantages of the one-child family for themselves, parents in our survey most often spoke of time. "Kids take a lot of time-- but one kid takes far less than two," reflected the mother of a four-year-old. To further evaluate the time issue, we asked 245 mothers of two children about the differences between having one and two children. Over 60% said that they had less time to themselves since their second child was born. And, only 5% agreed that "two are as easy as one."

Having one child is also related to increased personal and marital happiness when compared to having several. Rossi (1972) concluded that adjustment becomes more difficult with each additional child. And reported marital satisfaction drops with each subsequent child (Feldman, 1971; Knox & Wilson, 1978). "By having an only child you've got some time left for yourself and your spouse," remarked one parent.

In general, the parents in our study were very different from the over-anxious, unfulfilled image so

169

often painted of single-child parents. One-half of the mothers worked outside the home, and often expressed a belief that having one child and working were compatible. One of the mothers said, "Having one child meets my maternal need without 'oversatisfying' it and I've got the time to pursue a meaningful career." Fathers suggested that having one child put less financial pressure on them. "My closest friend is putting three daughters through college and it's about to kill him," expressed the father of an only child. "The advantages to parents to stop with one are obvious," continued this father. "The only hurdle is getting over the fear that something awful will happen to your child if you don't provide a brother or sister."

Advantages for the Family Unit

"The one-child family is a small deck which makes it hard to get lost in the shuffle," observed a teenage only. Since family members continually look to each other for acceptance, fulfillment, and counsel, what kind of family-style is produced by the intense one-child family?

The most noticeable characteristic is the close times among family members. Only children--young and old--believe they have a closer relationship with their parents than people with siblings have with their parents. Parents express the same belief. In a recent study of college students, 40% of the only children reported that their parents were the strongest influence in "making me the person I am today." But only 3% of those students having siblings gave this reply (Falbo, 1976).

In addition to closeness, decision making in a one-child family tends to be more democratic than that in a multi-child family. "When there are several kids, parents often feel they must make the family decisions so that the children will be treated fairly," remarked the parent of one. "In our family we don't have to worry about playing favorites, so we let Marshall participate almost equally in making family decisions." The lines of authority are less clearly drawn in the one-child family and parents seem to relax more in their role (Bossard & Boll, 1956).

170

Another important one-child family advantage is affluence--spending power. The three-person family simply has more money to spend than larger families at the same income level. While money does not buy happiness, it does provide recognized benefits. "Having more money" was an advantage often referred to by both children and parents when describing the one-child family.

"Since children are small and don't eat much," expressed one parent, "it's easy to believe that raising two children isn't much more costly than raising one." The U.S. Commission on Population Growth and the American Future disagrees. A second child cost almost as much as the first. The only savings are in reference to hand-me-down clothes and toys--a small part of the total childrearing expense. In 1972, rearing one child through age eighteen cost about $53,000, while rearing two cost at least $100,000 (Population and the American Future, 1972, p. 81). The words "we can't afford it" are spoken less often in the one-child than in the multi-child family.

The image presented by one-child parents of a close, democratic, affluent family-style is considerably different from the long-admired American portrait of the "Walton" family-style with its tangle of relationships and clear lines of authority. One mother in a one-child family observed that the end results are different. "Parents with several children often seem to view parenting as an all-consuming job. For my husband, daughter, and me, life is more like a three-way adventure."

II. DISADVANTAGES OF THE ONE-CHILD FAMILY

"The one-child family is just like everything else--the bad comes along with the good," remarked the father of an adult daughter. Most parents and their only children agree. Let's examine the negative consequences.

Disadvantages for the Child

From the only child's point of view, the major disadvantage in being a single child is "not getting to experience a brother or sister relationship." Only children speak of missing "a confidant," "someone

171

to help me face the world," "someone to help care for aging parents," or "someone to 'fight' with." In such statements only children are obviously considering only the good side of sibling relationships and are not acknowledging the possibility that a sibling relationship might be apathetic, competitive, or even hostile. "Some of my closest friends have siblings," observed an adult only, "and they have little in common with them and never see them. Having a brother or sister does not guarantee a companion."

In addition to wanting a companion, only children also feel extra pressure on them to succeed. "I'm glad my parents are interested in what I do," said one twelve-year-old, "but I often wish they had another kid to think about so they would get off my back once in a while. I think about my folks as Mama and Papa Bird—each perched on one of my shoulders." But the disadvantage of undivided attention lies not in the attention itself but in the concentrated "dose" received by the only child.

A third disadvantage only children express is a feeling that they have no help in caring for their aging parents. "I know that brothers and sisters seldom contribute equally to the care of their parents," said one daughter of invalid parents, "but I'd give anything to share a little of this load."

Disadvantages for the Parents

One-child parents also recognize disadvantages. "The most difficult concern for me is the thought of my child dying. I can't face being left childless," acknowledged one mother. Another parent believes the biggest drawback is having only one chance to "make good" as a parent. "If you have two kids and the first bombs out, you can always hope the second will redeem the family name," suggests this parent. A third parent adds, "Constant criticism that you are selfish is a disadvantage. You've got to have thick skin or the criticism of your family size will get to you."

But the disadvantage most plaguing to parents of only children is the tightrope they must walk between healthy attention and overindulgence. As suggested earlier, most parents believe it an advantage to have more time, money, and energy for their child, but

172

those resources must be provided in a manner which enriches rather than indulges. "I firmly believe it's not how much you give your child, but how you give it," said one mother. "The problem is knowng when your giving helps and when it hurts."

Disadvantages for the Family Unit

Just as there are disadvantages to the only child and his/her parents, there are disadvantages for the family unit. While most one-child family members enjoy an unusually close parent/child relationship, the three-person group can result in a two-against-one situation. In some instances, one parent and the child align against the other parent. In other instances, at least from the child's perspective, the deck is always stacked two parents against one child.

Finally, there are families in which having only one child leaves members unfulfilled--one child is simply not enough. The risk seems especially high for the mother who has no outside interests; one child is not sufficient to meet her emotional or mothering needs. Similarly, a father strongly wishing for a son may not find contentment in a single daughter. And a child unable to fulfill companionship needs outside the family may feel "wronged" by not having a sibling.

The disadvantages for the only child, his/her parents, and the family unit can result in regret, disappointment, and even guilt about a decision to have one child. A family fearing these outcomes stands little chance of having a healthy, happy experience.

III. CAN THE DISADVANTAGES BE OVERCOME?

How important are the disadvantages of the one-child family? Should they prevent a couple from having an only child? "No" was the answer given by 62% of the one-child parents we surveyed. "Certainly there are disadvantages," says one mother, "But I know of no family size that doesn't have its problems. The trick is to resolve them."

And the parents of only children have some solutions. For example, to overcome an only child's discontent about not having a sibling, parents suggest

173

that the child be encouraged to place more value on friendships. One adult remarked about her experience, "I don't know what having a sister would be like, but I can't imagine having a blood sister more than I do the woman who has been my dear friend for fifteen years."

To combat the problem of excessive attention and indulgence, two remedies were suggested. One was for parents to observe other children their child's age to develop a realistic basis for judging their son's or daughter's behavior and progress. It was also suggested that parents develop personal interests to avoid expecting their child to fulfill their own achievement needs.

The question of an only child's death is diffi-cult, but parents believe it must be put into per-spective. The death of any child is tragic, but another child can never replace the dead child. "To believe that one child can substitute for another is not to value individual life very highly," believes one mother. Similarly, concerns about being criti-cized and having only "one shot at parenting" need perspective. "Once you stop thinking of parenting as a competitive sport, these worries subside," according to a young father.

All parents and children need to be realistic about and plan for the parents' advancing years. For the one-child family it is crucial. Planning that is done before a crisis arises spares both child and parent undue anguish. "We have been saving for over twenty years so that our child will not be finan-cially burdened with us," shared one parent. "And we've already decided that we will use the money to go into a nursing home if necessary before we will intrude in our only's marriage.

As for the possible two-against-one situation, many parents believe just recognizing the potential problem helps. "If you're aware the problem can exist and take steps to prevent it, there is no reason for it to torment the family," expressed one father. "When I saw my daughter and wife began to pair off, I knew that I had to improve my relationship with each of them. That meant not going back to the office at night and listening to rock music with my daughter. It's now the three of us rather than 'them and me.'"

174

In general, one-child parents suggest that disadvantages of the one-child family can be overcome by
positive attitudes and actions. One couple said, "If
you believe the one-child family is healthy and stimulating, you will make it so. If you are guilty or
doubtful about your decision to have one child,
chances are you will let an unhealthy situation
develop." Happy relationships depend on how people
deal with each other--not on how many people there
are.

IV. CONCLUSION

A reconsideration of the one-child family alternative may result in fewer babies being born for the
wrong reasons. One study shows that many parents have
a second child not because they really want it but
because they believe they "must have a second to save
the first" (Solomon, Clare & Westoff, 1956). Other
couples have a second child to satisfy grandparents'
wishes, to try for a child of the opposite sex, or to
conform to the two-child family model so attractively
portrayed by media.

Increasingly, family life specialists are noting
that our world can no longer afford children who are
born for these reasons: The only legitimate reason
for having a second--or a first--child today is wanting that child for himself/herself.

REFERENCE NOTE

1. General Social Science Survey, July 1975. Conducted by the National Opinion Research Center,
Chicago.

B I B L I O G R A P H Y

Bayer, A.E.

1966   "Birth order and college attendance."
            Journal of Marriage and the Family, 23,
            484.

Bonney, M.E.

1944   "Relationships betwen social success,
            family size, socio-economic home back-
            ground, and intelligence among school
            children in grades 3 to 5." Sociometry,
            7, 26-39.

Bossard, J.H.S., &
Boll, E.S.

1956   The large family system: An original
            study in the sociology of family be-
            havior. Philadelphia: University of
            Pennsylvania Press.

Butts, N.E., &
Moseley, N.

1954   The only child. New York: Putnam.

Davis, E.

1937   "The mental and linguistic superiority
            of only girls." Child Development, 8,
            139-143.

Dyer, D.T.

1949   "Are only children different?" Journal
            of Educational Psychology, 36, 297-302.

176

Falbo, T.

1976   "Does the only child grow up miserable?"
            Psychology Today, 9, 65.

Feldman, H.

1971   "The effects of children on the family."
            In Michel (Ed.), Family issues of em-
            ployed women in Europe and America.
            Lieden, The Netherlands: Brill.

Guilford, R.B., &
Worchester, D.A.

1930   "A comparative study of the only and
            non-only child." Journal of Genetic
            Psychology, 38, 411-426.

Hawke, S., &
Knox, D.

1977   One child by choice. Englewood Cliffs,
            New Jersey: Prentice-Hall.

Knox, D., &
Wilson, K.

1978   "The differences between having one and
            two children." The Family Coordinator,
            27, 23-25.

Lee, J.P., &
Stewart, A.H.

1957   "Family or sibship position and scholas-
            tic ability." Sociological Review, 5,94.

Peck, E.

1971   The baby trap. New York: Bernard Geis.

Population and the American Future

1972   Report of the Commission on Population
            and the American Future, Vol. 28, No.
            2.   Washington, D.C.:   U.S. Government
            Printing Office.

Redding, E.

1974   Parents' attitudes and behavior con-
            cerning fertility during postpartum.
            Unpublished doctoral dissertation,
            Oklahoma State University.

Rosenberg, M.

1965   Society and the adolescent self-image.
            Princeton, New Jersey: Princeton
            University Press.

Rossi, A.S.

1972   "Family development in a changing
            world." American Journal of Psychiatry,
            128, 106.

Solomon, E.S., Clare, J.E., &
Westoff, C.F.

1956   "Social and psychological factors
            affecting fertility." Milbank Memorial
            Fund Quarterly, 34, 160-177.

Thompson, G.

1950   "Intelligence and fertility: The
            Scottish 1947 survey." Eugenics Review,
            41, 163-170.

Wheland, E.

1976   A baby. . . maybe? New York: Bobbs-
            Merrill.

*Sharryl Hawke is Staff Associate, Social Science
Education Consortium, 855 Broadway, Boulder,
Colorado 80302.   David Knox is Associate Professor
of Sociology, East Carolina University, Greenville,
North Carolina 27834.

Reprinted from The Family Coordinator, Vol. 27
(July, 1978):215-219. Copyrighted 1978 by the
National Council on Family Relations. Reprinted by
permission.

CHAPTER 9

FACT AND FICTION IN MODERN DIVORCE:
DIMENSIONS AND ISSUES

Douglas B. Gutknecht* and
Barbara L. West*

I. INTRODUCTION

The topic of divorce takes on strategic meaning
because the very survival or viability of the family
unit is brought into question. However, the issue of
the meaning of divorce must be placed within a larger
social and historical context. Furthermore, we cannot ignore the fact that families, choose completely
different ways of interpreting and coping with the
strains and stresses of divorce. Divorce statistics
tell us little about what makes marital life satisfactory or unsatisfactory--thus are not always in
themselves good indicators of marital health or
disruption. Traditional stereotypes and images of
what makes families viable or what effect divorce has
on spouses and children, must be evaluated. The key
issues concern marital expectations, the developmental maturity of partners, the stage of the marriage, the destructiveness of the marital and family
setting, the involvement of children in the divorce
process, the degree of bitterness generated, the
type of custody arranged and the nature of support
systems the family can call upon in time of need.

II. TRENDS IN DIVORCE STATISTICS: PITFALLS OF
    INTERPRETATION

In 1982 there were 2,495,000 marriages and
1,180,00 divorces. The marriage rate per 1,000
population was 10.8 and the divorce rate per 1,000
population was 5.1. The ratio of marriage per 1,000
unmarried women, 15 to 44 years old was 102.6. The
median duration of the marriage was 6.8 years. The
number of children involved in divorces per 1,000
population was 1,174. The number of remarriages per
1,000 for women 14-24 years was 236.4; for women 25-
44 years was 122.8; for women 45-65 years was 30.3.
The divorce rate is declining slightly, while the
marriage rate is increasing slightly. In the U.S.
there is one divorce for every two marriages (Statistical Abstracts of the U.S., 1984).

Additional indications of the extent of the problem are revealed by the ratio of ever-divorced persons to persons who remain in intact marriages and also in statistics of separation. In the former case in 1960 there were 33 divorces per 1000 married whites with spouse present which increased to 83 by 1978; the statistics over the same time period for blacks is 62 to 194. The divorce rates also increased from 32 per 1000 married in 1960 to 59 in 1978. In addition, statistics on separation suggest that the number of women not divorced but separated and heading their household increased 54 percent to 1.5 million from 1970-79 (U.S. Department of Commerce Bureau of Census, 1979). These statistics along with the facts that many younger couples break up after living together and aren't counted as official divorces lead to the possibility that the current statistics on divorce are understated. Further, the idea of desertion, or the poor man's divorce, also contributes to problems of measurement. In addition, trend data indicate that long term divorce rates have risen from near 2% in mid 1850's to about 50% today (Plateris, 1973).

One might define marital dissolution by one of three social categories: separation, desertion, or divorce. Only the latter category is counted in official statistics. Separation may be viewed as a first step, the initial and informal resolve to start the process of disengagement. Although obvious psychological and emotional conflicts and bargaining proceeded this decision, the point is that separation moves the levels of discussion to a new, more serious social plane. We will discuss the stages in a later section. Such a step may provide temporary breathing space and time for reflection, leading to a temporary lessening of conflict and possibly eventual reconciliation. However, without professional assistance in defining why the problems accumulated in the first place, or why old coping strategies failed, a reconciliation often merely delays the final decision. At this point in the process one often hears the refrain that, "at least I tried." Trial separations often provide a necessary measure of confidence on the part of spouses that the right decision was reached. However, for those not convinced that divorce is the only viable and realistic option, separation only seems to prolong the uncertainty and agony of being in a provisional status, creating guilt, fear, and insecurity. One's old life cannot end and

180

and a new beginning tried within the old skins of misery, bitterness, and guilt.

The existence of desertion, often called the "poor man's" divorce is even more disturbing because, unlike separation and divorce, the split is sudden and total. The desertion itself is a rejection of the normative and institutional structure of society and prevents acceptance of any responsibility and the opportunity for the spouse to save face.

These statistics have to be placed in context, however. For example, most divorced persons remarry and the divorced are three times more likely to remarry than never married men are likely to enter their first marriage. Only about 6 percent of all adults over 18 were divorced in 1978 (Statistical abstracts of the U.S., 1980:40). Although the divorce rate has risen sharply during the 1960's and 70's and declined in the early 1980's the yearly percentage of the total population of marrieds divorcing is still relatively small. In addition, two of every three first marriages last a lifetime and about three-fourths of all who divorce remarry. Although 40% of all marriages will someday end in divorce, this statistic results from the fact that 44% of divorced individuals who remarry will divorce again, which pushes up the total percentage of marriages that will end in divorce in the long term. The fact that there is a small but increasing number of couples who marry three or more times adds to the distorted picture. Remember only a small percentage of the total population (e.g., 5 to 6%) actually divorce in any one year.

There are six separate ways that divorce rates can be calculated (Crosby, 1980:51-52). First, the percentage of divorces to weddings, compares the number of marriages (weddings) in a given year to divorces. If there were 100 weddings and 50 divorces, the divorce rate would be 50%. This method implies a high divorce rate and hence problem because of the fact that divorces in a given year result from marriages in previous years and are then compared with only the number of current year weddings. Second, crude divorce rate is the ratio of number of divorces per 1,000 people. Remember that when many more babies are born as during the post World War II baby boom, adding to the total population, the divorce rate goes down. Currently as the number of babies born declines then the divorce rates goes up. Third, a refined divorce rates compares the number of divorces in any year to the number of married women. Fourth, one can compare the number of marriages ending in divorce with those ending because of the death of a spouse. Fifth, age-specific divorce rates compare the number of divorces per 1,000 married women in various age categories. Sixth, a standardized divorce rate summarizes age specific rates and divides this number by the standardized size and multiplies the result by 1,000. The adoption of certain methods of calculating divorce statistics obviously biases our impression of the extent of the problem of marital dissolution.

Using divorce statistics as an indicator of marital crisis or social disorganization also ignores the historical evidence that marriage and family life faced numerous disruptions and crises in the past. For example, in the 19th century early death of a spouse accounted for most marital disruptions and dissolutions. The recent increase in the divorce rate is less important for understanding satisfaction with family life than the reasons that people give for divorce which either "reflects a commitment to the institution or a change to a quite different sort of relationship" (Bane, 1976:22-23). Bane supports the former assertion. The key element in her interpretation is that satisfaction is generally high but spread out over longer years together as a result of an extended family life cycle (Bane, 1976:24). The question of how families readjust and cope with extended years together has created short run strains as a result of new patterns of work, leisure life, health, illness, and the financial strains of retirement. Learning to cope with these crises in the short run may allow a better match between spouses, improved communication, changed sex role responsibilities, and sharing of family tasks in the long run.

Numerous studies document that divorce is not a uniform phenomena; it is distributed unevenly across numerous social, political, and economic categories. Divorce rates vary by regions of the country; they are higher in the Western U.S. where social tolerance reduces the social stigma attached to divorce. Probabilities of divorce after the first marriage increases among men as their age at marriage, education, and income decrease (Glick and Norton, 1971).

The 1980 census indicated that among individuals under age 20 who married between 1901 and 1980, the divorce rate is twice as high as for those who decided to postpone marriage until their late 20's. For women who married before 18, the divorce rate is twice that of women who waited until their early 20's for the first time. In addition, men who earn more money generally have a lower divorce rate and remarry more readily. Women who earn more money often divorce more often and wait for longer periods before they remarry. For females, however, the statistics are less certain because some divorced women, who have a higher personal income, delay or remain unmarried because they are supporting themselves adequately. In addition, marital strain can be felt because some men feel threatened by financially independent women (Bane, 1976:34). Indications are strong that stability of income and employment both better explain stability in marriage than simply the amount of income earned!

> People are more accepting of divorce as a solution to an unsatisfactory marriage. But an increased tendency to end bad marriages probably does not in itself explain the rising divorce rate. The changing role of husbands and wives and new opportunities for women to be employed and independent also seem to contribute to the divorce rate...(Bane, 1976:36).

The larger public trends and social forces actually reinforce marital tensions and conflicts as expectations for self-actualization, personal growth, career plans and new lifestyles put excessive demands on the family (Lasch, 1978). Demands for occupational success and public involvements often compete with needs for a private life and family growth needs. However, the very fact of success in the public sphere of career may create strains in private lives. Individuals with higher levels of education, occupational status, and income may statistically divorce less, but they also establish such high standards that the mundane reality of marriage may create tensions and disappointments. Likewise one may feel that one's attributes and assets can yield better bargains in the growing remarriage market-place, as more individuals divorce.

Divorce trends are made more tangible and real if one finds more divorces occurring in one's network

183

of acquaintances. Abstract statistics can't account
for the brute realities of how people cope with the
influential powers of peers, and close friends, when
interpreting or making sense of the social world.
Escalating divorce rates create a kind of momentum
supporting divorce. The larger available pool of
partners, made available by increasing divorces in
society, tempt one to ask oneself if the grass is
greener on the other side of the bed. Whereas, a
smaller pool of available re-marriage partners might
make one more cautious about one's potential trade-in
value in the marriage market or "flee" market, as the
case may be.

III. DIVORCE AND THE LAW

     Let's examine some of the claims regarding the
increasing number of states with the "easy out" or
"no fault" divorce laws and the apparent increase in
divorce rates. Historically where divorce was legally
more difficult, alternatives to formal legal or dejure
divorce provided an escape hatch--de facto annulments
purchased from church courts for fees; separation, if
fault could be proved; or the poor man or woman's option, desertion. Later, when ecclesiastical courts
lost the unconditional power to grant divorce, civil
courts stepped in to provide grounds--initially adultery, then physical or mental cruelty. Traditionally,
many individuals have stayed together because of economic necessity. However, involuntary separation,
via early death of spouses, created so-called "broken
homes," necessitating orphanages and charity homes for
children (Bane, 1976). The key question, however,
still seems whether or not no fault divorce laws are
the key cause of increasing divorce rates in the U.S.

     No fault divorce laws first became legally bind-
ing in January 1970 in California as a result of the
passage of the California Family Law Act of 1969.
Several states earlier developed aspects of a no
fault law but only California passed a comprehensive
and complete law. In several instances the no fault
grounds only included statutes that specified one
ground for divorce, defined as irretrievably broken
marriages or breakdown of marriage relations. These
grounds prevented the use of the concept of fault in
the proceedings.

     Traditional fault grounds establishing guilt
or innocence included physical cruelty, adultery,

etc. In addition, several states (i.e., Connecticut, Idaho, Rhode Island, New Hampshire, and Texas), added no fault laws to traditional grounds for divorce. In these states fault grounds such as adultery can be used to establish custody rights. In addition to no fault, grounds of incompatibility or irreconcilable differences are still used where no guilt is established.

The idea that permissive no fault laws creates a drastic increase in divorces stems from a set of assumptions embedded in the nature of Anglo-Saxon law. This view recognizes fault as the only grounds for divorce and adversary legal proceedings as the main opportunity to establish fault. The court room becomes a battleground for character assassination and psychological retribution, often creating excessive guilt and lowering the self esteem of the beaten party. In this traditional view of divorce one spouse must be blamed because someone is guilty of disrupting the marriage. Many traditionalists believe that divorce must be made traumatic and difficult in order to protect families from the social disorganization in society (i.e., suicide, crime, mental illness) which comes from high divorce rates. Many family writers have questioned this hypothetical relationship between high divorce rates and social disorganization.

Since 1968 the divorce rate has increased in conjunction with the liberalization of divorce laws by numerous states (i.e., about two-thirds). However, the argument that no fault divorce laws have caused this increase in divorce rates ignores many pertinent issues. Divorce and marital breakups are complex processes. Even when the law is punitive and stringent and the costs high (e.g., cost may include social stigma, loss of reputation, falling out with family, alimony, child support, possibility of resource loss, diminished income or standards of living, loss of social status), it is still the case that punitive laws were not effective in deterring divorce.

The fault argument itself ignores many complex personal and public issues. Any marital relationship has two individuals trying to create intimate emotional bonds and satisfactory communication. The task may sometimes appear impossible in a world of constant disruptions, interruptions, and turmoil. Many parties and social factors are thus involved in the success or failure of their relationship. The

185

idea of fault by only one guilty party ignores both the psychological and social context of the modern family. Divorce, marital conflict, violence, adultery, and other family problems and hassles can be viewed as symptoms of personal and social failure in marriage. Once again we see that family, self, and society are inextricably linked together for better or worse.

There are four reforms needed to change the legal fault system in divorce proceedings beyond the traditional criticisms that overloading the courts wastes essential social resources. The fault or guilt system: (1) ignores the more complex reasons for marital split ups; (2) forces individuals to lie to one another and the court creating additional guilt; (3) frustrates societies' interest in maintaining marital relationships which support stable families; (4) promotes aggressive behavior, bitterness and unforgiving attitudes that might even continue in the custody hearing and ultimate arrangements (Reppy, 1970).

Families may actually suffer by staying together at all costs. Without more adequate understanding of the psychological realities and social pressures that caused the problem in the first place, the climate of bitterness may only increase the living hell for all family members. Accumulated evidence suggests that constant and unresolved conflicts create more damaged children than by making a clean break (Nye, 1957). Since so many remarry successfully (over 50% of second marriages are successful), children of remarried parents do receive adequate care and socialization.

The suggestion that divorce causes other social problems and breakdowns in society results from an inadequate understanding of the problem. Divorce and crime don't correlate highly with easy divorce laws. Broken relationships more often result from poverty, which causes both crime and divorce. It is more accurate to look at larger public issues and structural problems which may cause psychological problems and pressures on individuals. Many families experience financial difficulties during recessions or times of economic instability; but the poor experience these problems constantly, which compounds them into multidimensional problems, affecting numerous spheres of living such as work, family, health, leisure, or lack of it.

186

IV.   EFFECT OF DIVORCE ON CHILDREN

The film, "Kramer vs. Kramer" told the story of a custody fight and the traditional stereotypes associated with standard divorce law, where the mother is assumed to have the inside track as the best parent to guide the child's future. This media portrayal of a dedicated father fighting for custody rights, only publicly establishes what has been found on a mass scale in courts and states, by both men and women, throughout the decade of the 1970's. In the 1970's states like Florida and Kentucky adopted more humane and fair requirements for the situation of fathers in custody cases. In both Iowa and Washington, lawyers are court appointed to represent the interests of minor children on such issues of custody, visitation, and child support. Yet even today several no fault states, like California and Oregon, still consider the issue of spousal misconduct as grounds for custody decisions. However, no fault laws have taken some bitterness out of custody battles and allowed more humane options, like joint custody, to become viable options; one even encouraged by many court attorneys, family counseling services, and expert witnesses.

The question of divorce, although a private matter, obviously disturbs many because of its public ramifications and consequences; particularly those issues which influence the next generation of citizens, today's children. The question of who will socialize and take care of our children and the quality of such care, becomes one of concern to all those interested in the potential negative effects of restructured, blended or bi-nuclear families upon children and society (Scanzoni, 1983).

Current evidence indicates that about 40% of the children born in the mid-1970's will live in one-parent families at least some time before they are eighteen. About 10% of those now living with a two-parent family are living with a step-parent because the remarriage rate for divorced parents is high. The average number of children, including young ones, per divorce has decreased, so by the late 1970's, fifty-two percent of those households headed by divorced or separated women involved no children. One-parent families in 1979 accounted for 13% of all households. The question of the quality of single-parent families certainly requires some reflection. Two out of three children are living with their natural parents as of 1978; 19% are living with one parent and 4% are living with neither parent for a total of 23% not living with two parents (U.S. Dept. of Commerce Bureau of Census, Series P. 20, No. 338, 1979).

The impact of divorce on children is difficult to assess because of the numerous complex variables that affect well-being and development needs at different stages in life. The conventional view and strongest argument against divorce is that children in broken homes will move through life at a disadvantage compared with children from a two-parent intact home. The argument asserts that a child from a broken home will experience reduced psychological well-being, and often inadequate personality development, both essential for coping with life's future stresses. However, the evidence seems to point to the importance of comparing children from broken homes and unbroken homes on factors related to the quality of home life and degree of happiness before the divorce.

When comparisons are made of children from disrupted marriages with children from unhappy but broken homes, the slight disadvantage that broken homes have, when compared to happy intact homes, disappears (Nye, 1957). One-parent homes show no significant difference in school achievement, social adjustment, and delinquent behavior when compared with two-parent families of similar economic status (Murchison, 1974). This research argues against the idea that unhappy marriages need to be retained for the sake of children and supports the idea that good relations are essential in familial life, no matter how many parents are involved. Likewise, such evidence discounts the false idea that liberalized or no fault divorce laws cause bad marriages and problems for children.

The latest research at the Harvard Medical School's Laboratory of Community Psychiatry points up the strengths of children of divorce, separation and widowhood:

"They tend to be more mature, responsible, independent, and self-reliant than kids from two-parent families. They often also have special skills and abiliites unusual for their age, and unusual self-assurance" (Graves, 1982:47).

188

This evidence should not lead us to assume that one-parent families don't experience problems, particularly economic, and that children don't experience some form of initial separation anxiety and distress as a result of parental separation. Bane (1976:112) summarizes the issues that suggest that divorce seems to impact more negatively upon female single parents, creating stress and strain as a result of the following conditions:

loss of economics of scale; greater prevalence of divorce and death among poor families; low and irregular levels of alimony, child support, and public assistance; fewer adult earners, fewer opportunities for female heads of families to work; lower wages than men when they do work.

Weiss (1976:140) calls attention to issues of separation distress even for children who adjust well in the long run to lost attachments:

One list of reactions among children to a loss of a parent includes, among others, rage and protest over loss, maintenance of an intense fantasy relationship with the lost parent, persistent efforts at reunion, anxiety, and a strong sense of narcisstic injury.

While some children actually experience a euphoric increase in self-confidence and self-esteem, the more likely pattern, even for these individuals, were periods of alternating euphoria and separation distress.

Children are more resilient than once thought, although the life of emotions contains many periods of ambivalence and emotional backtracking. We seldom move through fixed emotional stages once and for all without backtracking. Children may move from subordinate role to junior parent or helper role in the new family configuration. Single parents often treat their adolescents as peers and turn to them as a substitute spouse for companionship, understanding, and support (Graves, 1982:47). This new and intense closeness may, however, create paradoxical problems because the child as parental supporter may mature too quickly and feel both sympathy and painful awareness of parental weakness and fallibility. The ambivalence relates to pride in their own maturity and self-reliance, mixed with a wistful emotion that they

189

may have missed some of the fun and luxury of a truly dependent childhood. Such ambivalence may become anger or bitterness in some cases, where one's network of friends all live with two-parent families. Again the importance of support networks and exposure to successful models of alternative family styles may be the most important variable. Likewise, we find today that most children appear more grown up and mature in their attitudes at earlier ages.

V. FACTORS CONTRIBUTING TO DIVORCE

Let's briefly focus on a social-psychological model built upon exchange theory that views the conditions that lead to divorce in order to call attention to factors that couples, even in intact relationships, might reflect upon (Levinger, 1976). This theory asserts that people make choices or exchanges in all areas of life. Exchange theory tries to measure the cost and benefits of behaviors by arguing that behaviors will be continued when benefits outweigh the costs (Heath, 1976).

The exchange perspective applies cost-benefit analysis to divorce--when cohesiveness is strong, then benefits are greater and vice versa. Pair cohesiveness is increased when partners present greater attractions and fewer barriers to each other inside the relationship and more barriers separating one's relationship to outside world. When inducements or benefits to remain in a relationship increase they become attractions or gratifications to remain and not divorce. Likewise, the strength of restraints or barriers for leaving a relationship increases with perceived rewards and decreases in perceived costs. The probability of evaluating rewards and costs thus relates to how we perceive our situation at a given time. Rewards are associated with positive outcomes and might include love, friendship, companionship, status, information, goods, services, money, property, sex, children, support, security, validation of self. Costs might include perceived or real rejection, energy, time, loss of pleasure, lack of sexual variety, vulnerability of ego exposure, or anything that might be defined as an expenditure demanded from staying in the relationship.

Individuals are more likely to stay in a relationship, marital or dating, and reject a divorce or break-up, when the subjective probability of gaining rewards exceeds the costs. Often the objective reality is difficult to measure and one's arbitrary and perceptual calculation becomes our guide to behavior. Individuals divorce or leave, in many cases, when costs exceed rewards from the relationship over a given period of time. Generally longer periods of deprivation or costs lead us to hypothesize the probability of marital or dating disruption. However, numerous factors are often ignored in exchange theories. For example, some additional important variables that are often ignored are self-esteem, understanding the reasons for disruptions of rewards, spouses' ability or potential to change or develop, knowledge of the cycles of disenchantment and life crises, compassion, spiritual and humanistic values. A strict cost benefit analysis oftentimes appears to imply a model of man as a machine devoid of consciousness, intention, sense of community, spirit, values, or history. However, it does provide many pertinent insights into the realities of relationships after the romantic glow of early courtship fades.

There are barriers or restraining forces which can reinforce a relationship and actually keep people together (Levinger, 1976:25): A strong barrier results from a strong commitment to each other, brought about by being of the same religion, sharing the same economic, social, educational, class, or ethnic experiences. Alternative attractions also detract from one's primary relationship. For example, other role-partners, work, friends, former spouse or children, travel schedule, may provide options that make one's perceived relationship less likely of providing inducements.

Alternative attractions demand time and energy which can draw emotional energy away from the primary relationship or marriage. For example, relationships where spouses constantly exclude the other spouse may threaten the bond and create jealousy and increase negative emotions and costs for both parties. However, when both spouses participate in the alternatives as attractions there is less danger of costs exceeding rewards for only one spouse or partner. Again it is the perception of accumulating alternatives as attractions that is most important. For example, relationships outside the primary bond may be attractive but less attractive than a fully functioning, primary relationship. In addition, alternative attractions, like friends, may create a stronger primary bond if a spouse feels more self-esteem and thus provides an added inducement in self-esteem.

The exchange theory of divorce provides an interesting perspective for reflection about one's relationships and how both spouses perceive each other's strengths and weaknesses, costs and rewards. This theory can stimulate some critical analyses and application to each person's own life.

VI. THE PROCESS OF DIVORCE

A divorce is an ending and a new beginning, but it does not end everything about marriage. Although the legal contract is broken, the emotional and psychological relationship between partners often continues. Likewise, an individual may or may not divorce legally, but still experiences the trauma of emotional divorce.

Divorce involves six stages (Bohannan, 1970). First is the emotional divorce, which centers on the important, often traumatic recognition that spouses are no longer nurturing or supporting each other, providing good feedback and building a sense of a common purpose. People emotionally divorce when they grow as individuals yet find no common tasks or projects which allow them to grow interdependently as a team or couple. Second, is legal divorce which means by law. Legal reasons often diverge from the real reasons for divorce, which are often psychological or emotional. Third, is economic divorce which includes the dissolution of the family as an economic unit. Assets must be divided for child support and alimony must be settled. Fourth, is the co-parent divorce in which the issue of custody must be settled. The fifth stage of the divorce process involves a change in status recognized by one's community of friends, neighbors, or family. The sixth and last stage is psychic divorce in which one's autonomy or sense of being as a person is separated from one's partner. The maintenance of autonomy is more difficult when spouses exhibited great dependence on one's mate and the divorce was initiated by the other partner. However, even in such a case where the emotions of loving, even liking may be

192

absent, the sense of attachment proves difficult to eradicate (Weiss, 1976). Such attachments to those we've once cared deeply about point to the emotional complexities of loss and change, divorce and separation.

VII. CUSTODY ISSUES

Divorce itself does not predispose a child to failure or success, it is how it is handled that most influences the outcome. Does divorcing a mate mean at least one parent must divorce the children? How did we get to the point of making divorce into a contest where one parent "wins" or is "awarded" the custody of their own child? Even if it is "uncontested" how has it been decided who will be the "custodial" parent, the primary caretaker whose authority in the child's life will decide issues on education, religious training, medical attention, recreation, discipline, and who will be the one relegated "visitation privileges"?

The history of childhood shows the child as a possession. Around 500 B.C. Roman law structured the paternal role as one of power and authority. The child was the father's property. The legal doctrine of "patria potestas" gave the father the power of life and death over his offspring, as well as complete custody. If before his own death he identified a guardian of his children, that guardian would be appointed custody rather than the mother.

In Victorian England until the middle of the last century, fathers had the right to sell their children into someone else's service. This absolute right was softened by Justice Talfourd's Act in 1839. This act extended the concept of parens patriae to include children under seven years of age. In other words, like the concept of parens patriae giving the state the exclusive power of guardianships over disabled, insane and/or incompetent individuals, it gave the courts the same power over young children. It was not until the end of the 19th century that this right of the courts included all minors.

In agricultural America in the mid-1800s children were valuable economic resources. The divorce rate was four to five percent and with only few exceptions custody was given to the father. However during the Victorian era motherhood became idolized and the pendulum slowly began to swing to the maternal preference. Around the turn of the century the term "tender years" was more often heard. Courts were deciding that the mother was a more appropriate parent to the young child, especially to the child under seven years of age. Not only were psychological theories concerning the importance of a consistent, loving mother shifting society's attitude toward the tender-years doctrine, but also the social changes in the late nineteenth and early twentieth centuries. For example, jobs in the cities took men and women away from the farms; women in significant numbers began working for pay, owning property and exercising their new right to vote. Fewer fathers needed their children's labor. In addition one finds for the first time that fathers without custody had to pay child support and child labor laws became stricter. Children needed to be protected and society began to view the mother's care as of utmost importance to the child's healthy emotional development.

After acceptance of the tender years doctrine, the "best interests of the child" began to appear as early as 1925 in Judge Benjamin Cardozo's New York Court of Appeals. Although this doctrine stressed for the first time that a child has needs and rights which may be different from his parents and must be taken into consideration, judges still favored mothers for many years, except in the most extreme cases.

All of this takes us up to the present, a time in which children's rights are being recognized and custody arrangements are being individualized by family. One-parent custody, also called sole or exclusive, is the preferred arrangement for some. However, more and more fathers are being "awarded" that arrangement. When both parents want to be the sole custodial parent the past history of caring for the children is considered by the court to determine who the principal nurturing parent, both physically and psychologically, has been.

Split or divided custody, which means one or more children live with one parent and the other child or children live with each parent for a portion of the year, is not commonly arranged. But it does

194

exist in special circumstances. Often times it comes about because of the children's preferences or because of the distances of the two households.

Joint custody, also called shared or co-custody, is also on the increase. Early findings present very positive results when both parents cooperate and seem interested in the children's best interests rather than just their own. Prior to 1980 only six states had written shared custody statutes. Now more than half the states have laws regarding joint custody. Some states feel it is a preferred arrangement, while others feel it is an option available only by agreement. Joint custody recognizes that children should have continuing, frequent contact with both parents; that responsibility, decision making, and care should be shared by the parents.

In joint custody a child does not lose a parent, and does not need to experience abandonment or feelings of anxiety because of loyalty conflicts. As earlier stated, divorce itself does not presuppose a child to failure, it is how it is handled that most influences the outcome. Children have the capacity for loving both parents and for having good continuing relationships as long as they are not made to feel guilty or are used as pawns.

Parents in joint custody do not exhibit symptoms of anxiety, loneliness, rootlessness and lower self-esteem as frequently as many noncustodial parents. Perhaps even worse than having those symptoms, joint custody parents are not forced into biological child-snatching, as are many parents in other custodial arrangements.

VIII. BIOLOGICAL CHILDSNATCHING

Think of the words used when couples with children divorce. The process can be "contested," resulting in one parent "winning" or "losing" "custody." Why can't we think of custody as a joint responsibility? Of course "custody" goes along with "visitation rights." However, let's stop and think for a moment-- where else does one have "visitation rights?" In a prison! When a parent "wins custody" he/she is "awarded" his/her offspring. The family is considered "dissolved" or "broken" when in actuality it is restructured, it becomes binuclear, often times, rather

195

than nuclear. The point is, that the words we use paint a very harsh picture, which ultimately forces some individuals into actions they never thought they were capable of. One such action is abducting and/or concealing one's own child or children from the other biological parent.

Many parents have said that they snatched their child because of a loss or potential loss of custody or visitation rights. Other reasons cited are anger over child support payments, especially when excluded from the decision making process in the child's upbringing, as well as jealousy of the ex-spouse remarrying. While some parents snatch their children because they can't bare to drop them off at the other parent's home and they think they can leave all the pain and agony behind by taking the children and fleeing, there are some who are merely carrying out selfish impulses at other people's expense. Some parental childsnatchers just wanted to get even with the other parent and did not even live with the children they snatched. Such parents often leave the children with friends, relatives, and mere acquaintances.

Biological childsnatching is a complex and heart-wrenching result of a win/lose system which encourages exclusive control over children. The individual cases are horrendous. Some of the effects of childsnatching are:[1]

1. Loss of identity due to name changes, perhaps even the color of one's hair; or language, if the family moves to another country.

2. Loss of friendships, old and new. Just at the age when friendships, peer groups, are keenly important, the snatched child has to be cautious in making friends because they will be left behind and/or because the snatching parent makes sure the child does not get too close to anyone to tell them the story.

3. Loss of community ties because most abductors stay on the move so as not to be found. Some sleep in abandoned cars, eating out of dumpsters; some have elaborate plans and move to an entirely new country.

196

4. Feelings of insecurity are common because the child feels he has done something wrong to cause the abrupt change.

5. Feelings of abandonment are common because she has been told the other parent does not want to see her again.

6. Emotional, physical, and/or sexual abuse is common because the parent who abducts a child is under tremendous pressure, causing a low frustration tolerance.

7. Fear of being hurt, killed and/or abandoned by the abducting parent often results in a prisoner's mentality of alignment with the abductor.

8. Preoccupation in replaying their kidnapping is common, especially if they witnessed violence between their parents.

It is hard to believe that society has been so slow in protecting its children from such parental abuse, which in some cases has been caused by our laws (or lack of) and our court system. In 1974 Charles E. Bennett, a Florida Congressman, introduced a bill to amend the Federal Kidnapping Statute, to make parental kidnapping illegal. (The 1934 Lindbergh Law regarding kidnapping was amended by these words: "...except in the case of a minor by the parent thereof.") Agonizing articles began appearing in the media about parents stealing their own child or children. Not only did it only slowly become recognized that every state had its incidences of child abduction but it was estimated that over 100,000 cases per year were accumulating. And it was not even considered a crime! The Justice Department felt that the Federal Government should not be involved in domestic issues. The F.B.I. feared that it would be inundated with child custody cases and many law enforcement officials felt that nobody would want to send a parent to jail for taking his or her own child.

Finally, December 28, 1980, President Jimmy Carter signed into law the Parental Kidnapping Act, which established that all states would be required to give full faith and credit to other states' custody order (jurisdictional standards of the Uniform Child Custody Jurisdiction Act), that the Federal Locator Service would be available for childsnatching cases, and that the Federal Unlawful Flight to Avoid Prosecution Warrants (UFAPS) could be issued by states that had felony provisions for childsnatching.

This is a perfect example of how the law is governed by our behavior rather than it ruling our conduct. And the ultimate pain and sorrow is that because it does not, in fact, rule conduct the horror of childsnatching continues for many families.

IX. REMARRIAGE

Cherlin (1978) argues that remarriage or blended families with children experience more problems than first marriages because the remarriage is an "incomplete institution." The higher divorce rate for remarriages after divorce results from the lack of clear expectations regarding remarriage; remarriage has not been adequately institutionalized. Many problems faced by parents and children in blended families are unique to the new marriage. The institution of the family (in this case the second marriage) does not provide uniform, standard, socially acceptable solutions to the dilemmas of making a reconstituted family work. In contrast, the first marriage is institutionalized; the family unit is supported by institutional standards and controls, in addition to beliefs in the value of consensus and mutual affection:

> In most everyday situations, parents and children base their behavior on social norms: parents know how harshly to discipline their children, and children learn from parents and friends which to protest...the presence of these habitualized patterns directly affects family unity...with choices narrowed, family members face fewer decisions which will cause disagreements and, correspondingly, have less difficulty maintaining family unity (Cherlin, 1978:389).

Ann Goetting (1982) suggests six stations and developmental tasks essential for the remarriage to establish a solid foundation for future success in the face of unclear expectations. First, an emotional remarriage must re-establish the ability to build commitment, trust and love with a member of the opposite sex. Second, a psychic remarriage must allow for the transition in status from individual to new

198

couple. Some autonomy and freedom established during the time of being single must be given to the partnership. Third, a community remarriage reestablishes a couple's world of common or personal friends that recognize the couple. Fourth, the parental remarriage is necessary for integrating all the children of the previous marriages. With more children involved, the task becomes more difficult. Here the lack of institutional guidance regarding stepparent expectations can create many complex problems. Fifth, the economic remarriage establishes the household consumption-production unit, with its division of labor, tasks and responsibilities. Sixth, and finally, is the legal remarriage regarding responsibility toward former spouses and children. Remarriage is here defined by the responsibility for a new family, while continuing to define moral and legal obligations to one's previous family. It is obvious that step families face many challenges.

First, are concerns about love. Today we read so much about the importance of bonding for parents during their child's infancy. Because the stepchild and stepparent more often than not meet past the time the child is an infant there is a deep concern about the possibility of bonding and meeting preconceived notions of parent and child love.

Second, the portrayal of a stepparent in literature is very negative, causing identity and behavioral problems. In addition, recognition of the other biological parent is essential. Leaving him or her out, badmouthing him or her is an affront to the youngster, for children need to identify with both parents. Also, how children are taught to treat the other parent will be a lesson learned about how to eventually treat the educating parent.

Third, discipline is always a big issue in parent-child relationships. Too often portrayed in negative terms, discipline really is guidance with very positive aspects. In the stepfamily unique challenges arise because of mixed feelings about how stepparents should discipline a spouse's biological child. Parents often bring conflicting expectations regarding the tasks of parenting. Even without conflicting expectations because of past history, children are marvelous testers, very capable of trying to get their way with one parent, if the other denies them.

199

Fourth, comparisons can be detrimental. They exist in "real" parent versus stepparent, first spouse versus second spouse, and bond between child and biological parent, which precedes the bond between the new couple. They also exist in favoritism, perceived or otherwise, of his children, her children, and their children. The family tree has been taken over by a family forest.

Fifth, too often stepfamilies come in contact with school systems, therapists, professionals in general, books, and the media which are trying to facilitate coping strategies. Rather than providing needed leadership and nurturance, parents are merely responding, and reacting when they need to be proactive. One cannot enter into a step relationship expecting it to take away the pain, the disappointment of a past relationship. With good communication, and the recognition of spouses' rights, one can enter into a step relationship ready to acknowledge hurt and anger from the past and build a healthy family. Perhaps stepfamilies in struggling with difficult adjustments will help society to be more realistic about our expectations and skills neded for successful family life.

X. CONCLUSIONS

Divorce involves some of the most complex elements in understanding the modern dimensions of marriage and family life. The emotional and psychic aspects are more important than the legal realities. Often we reduce marital problems to arbitrary legal definitions and solutions. Divorce is not an easy process, even though popular manuals speak of the joys of "creative" divorce. Mel Krantzler (1982), author of a book on the process of creative divorce, has since remarried and written a new book on the several stages of marriage called Creative Marriage. Weiss (1976:144) calls our attention to those ambivalent feelings that are part of any divorce:

Ambivalence makes separated individuals uncomfortable with any resolution of their separated state. Reconciliation may result not only in relief at the ending of separation distress, but also in dismay at the return to an unsatisfactory relationship. The decision to divorce may also have mixed implications: not only gratification that freedom appears within grasp but also sorrow that the spouse will be irretrievably lost.

The ambivalent responses of partners to marital disruption is understandable if we view emotions as being important. Psychic disruption and loss or separation is an important dimension of life that individuals often seem unprepared to deal with. Somehow modern men and women assume that breaking bonds of love, friendship, family, community, can be made painless by reliance on rules, contracts, modern attitudes. It is apparent that deep feelings of attachment remind us of our capacity for caring even when our imperfections and the strains of the modern world pull and tug at us. Regardless of our sophistication, the lack of institutional supports give us little emotional help to face an often heartless world.

"Whatever they decide--whether it is to reconcile or to continue their separation, and, perhaps, move on to divorce--they will leave one set of feelings unsatisfied" (Weiss, 1976:146).

REFERENCE NOTES

1. Observations of a chapter coordinator for Chil-
    dren's Rights, Inc., 1977.

BIBLIOGRAPHY

Bane, Mary Jo

    1976   "Marital Disruption and the Lives of
                    Children." Journal of Social Issues,
                    Vol. 32, No. 1

Bohannan, P.

    1970   Divorce and After. New York: Double-
                    day and Co.

Cherlin, Andrew

    1978   "Remarriage as an Incomplete Institu-
                    tion." American Journal of Sociology,
                    Vol. 84, No. 3.

Crosby, P.

    1980   "A Critique of Divorce Statistics and
                    Their Interpretation." Family Rela-
                    tions, Vol. 29, p. 51-58.

Glick, P. &
A. Norton

    1971   "Frequency, Duration and Probability
                    of Marriage and Divorce." Journal of
                    Marriage and the Family, Vol. 33,
                    p. 307-317.

Goetting, Ann

    1982   "The Six Stations of Remarriage:
                    Developmental Tasks of Remarriage
                    After Divorce." Family Relations,
                    23, 31: 213-222.

Graves, P.

1982   "Growing Up Quicker If Not Better:
                 Kids in Single-Parent Families Have
                 Some Advantages." American Health,
                 May/June.

Heath, A.

1976   Rational Choice and Social Exchange,
                 Cambridge, England: Cambridge Univer-
                 sity Press.

Krantzler, Mel

1982   Creative Marriage. New York: McGraw
                 Hill.

Levinger, G.

1976   "A Social Psychological Perspective on
                 Marital Dissolution." Journal of
                 Social Issues, Vol. 32, No. 1.

Murchison, N.

1974   "Illustration of the Difficulties of
                 Some Children in One-Parent Families."
                 In M. Finer (Ed.), Report of the
                 Committee on One-Parent Families,
                 London: Her Majesty's Stationary
                 Office.

Nye, F. I.

1957   "Child Adjustment in Broken and
                 Unhappy Homes." Marriage and Family
                 Living, Vol. 19.

Plateris, A.

1973   "100 Years of Marriage and Divorce
                 Statistics: 1867-1967." U.S. National
                 Center for Health Statistics, Vital
                 and Health Statistics, Series 21,
                 No. 24.

Reppy, Susan

1970   "The End of Innocence: Elimination of
               Fault in California Divorce Law."
               U.C.L.A. Law Review, XVII (June), p.
               1306-1332.

1979   U.S. Dept. of Commerce, Bureau of
               Census, Series P. 20, No. 338,
               Marital States and Living Arrange-
               ments: Manual 1978 (Washington D.C.:
               Government Printing Office.

1984   U.S. Bureau of the Census, Statis-
               tical Abstracts of the U.S., 1984,
               104 (ed.), Washington, D.C.

Scanzoni, John

1983   Shaping Tomorrow's Family: Theory and
               Policy for the 21st Century. Beverly
               Hills, CA: Sage Publications.

Weiss, R.

1976   "The Emotional Impact of Marital
               Separation." Journal of Social
               Issues, Vol. 32, No. 1.

*Department of Sociology, and Human Resource Manage-
ment Development Program, Chapman College, Orange,
California.

CHAPTER 10

ALCOHOL ABUSE AND FAMILY STRUCTURE

Peter M. Nardi*

I. INTRODUCTION

To conceive of the family as a social system is to focus on rules, roles, and relationships. The social structure of a family is its configuration of roles bound together in relationships according to a set of rules evolved by the larger society and by a particular family. For purposes of this discussion, a "family" is any set of people defining themselves as a social, emotional, and economic unit, regardless of legal status, and creating for themselves a set of roles, rules, and relationships. Thus, "family" includes two or more unmarried adults living together with or without children, heterosexual or homosexual, as well as the traditional nuclear family unit of legally married adults and children. It is important to define family this way since alcohol abuse affects all kinds of families without regard to the dominant legal or social norms of a culture.

An analysis of an alcoholic family must, therefore, begin with its structure and the meanings that family creates about alcohol and its use. For every family there exists a set of sociodemographic characteristics which contribute to its social structure and definitions. Socioeconomic status, ethnicity, race, religion, and regional variations (such as urban/rural, north/south, east/west) contribute customs, norms, and rituals to a family's structure. These characteristics are also highly related to customs, norms, and rituals surrounding the definitions and uses of alcohol. For example, a working class Mexican-American Catholic family living in the rural southwest has traditional family rules which stress the power role of the male in decision-making, has religious customs valuing authoritarianism, and has an ethnic tradition of machismo which encourages men to drink heavily. It often becomes difficult, then, for children or wives to confront a problem-drinking father/husband, given the ethnic, class, and religious rules regulating relationships and roles.

In short, the investigation of family structure and alcohol use must begin with an analysis of relevant sociodemographic characteristics and how they relate to that particular family's dynamics and its definitions regarding alcohol use. Most work on families and alcohol use has not done so systematically.

In more general terms, all families develop a set of interlocking roles performing functions necessary for the family unit's emotional, economic, and social survival. Some roles are defined as having higher status (adult roles over children roles) and some roles as having more power (traditionally the males over the females). According to custom, age, and gender, the roles within the family are given meaning and defined. In a healthy functioning family, there exists a reciprocity of power and control; within a problem family, competition for power and control is prevalent and roles begin to shift to accommodate to changes in status and power.

Thus, conceiving the family as a dynamic social system of interlocking roles, defined in part by ascribed characteristics and by the culture's rules, is a useful model when attempting to understand the effects on and dynamics within a family troubled by alcohol abuse. All families change in their definitions of rules, roles, and relationships as members adjust to shifts in age, occupational status, educational level, and economic conditions. But the shifts brought on by alcohol abuse yield effects and produce processes which may lead to the intergenerational transmission of alcohol abuse and related mental health problems. It is this aspect of family structure and dynamics that will be the focus of this chapter.

II. ALCOHOL USE AND FAMILY ROLES

It is estimated (NIAAA, 1981) that about two-thirds of the adult population are consumers of alcohol and that about 10 percent have serious problems with alcohol. Each one of these approximately 15 million alcoholics affects about 5 million other people directly or indirectly. Many of these are family members who rarely receive professional attention or treatment. Growing evidence exists, however, that many of these people also have problems with

206

alcohol or drugs, develop related mental health problems, and may experience family violence and abuse. It is becoming increasingly clear that it is not only the alcoholic who needs treatment but also every member of the family unit. For in order to cope with the alcohol abusing member, others in the family take on roles which appear functionally necessary at the time but often prove to be emotionally and personally dysfunctional in the long term.

Children's Roles

In a traditional, non-problem family, children in our culture usually take on dependent, powerless roles. Decisions and choices are normally structured by adults. Children are expected to be nonresponsible when it comes to making decisions or family policy; they are expected to be dependent on their parents. Children essentially are in compulsory relationships with parents while a spouse is in a volitional one (Greenleaf, 1981).

In the alcoholic family, however, role reversal is a common event (Nardi, 1981). As the family system accommodates to shifts in parental drinking patterns, children's roles alter. Children of alcoholic parents often take on roles of responsibility in which they become the parent to the alcoholic who is acting like a child (i.e., non-responsible, dependent, and powerless). These children sometimes care for younger siblings, cook and clean, run household errands, and even balance checking accounts, all above and beyond the normally expected sharing of family tasks. These children increasingly adopt adult-type roles of responsibility within the family system, thus leading to changes in relationships between adults and children.

In other families, children cope with family role disruption by adopting placating and adjuster roles (Black, 1980). They begin to act as mediators between arguing parents or they learn consistently to give in to situational demands and to others' feelings. In these situations, children of alcoholics have received a clear message that it is not important to discuss their own feelings, but to spend the time dealing with their alcoholic parent's problems and, in many cases, with their non-alcoholic parent's needs. It is not uncommon to find children in surrogate spouse roles in addition to surrogate parent roles.

In some families, children of alcoholics become scapegoats, receiving the message that they are the cause of their parent's drinking problems (Seixas, 1977). Often this is exhibited by physical and emotional neglect or by physical and sexual abuse (NIAAA, 1981). Some of these children cope by acting out and taking on delinquent roles.

In Cork's (1969) study of children of alcoholics, the alcoholic family appears to be characterized by shame, resentment, anger, and inconsistency. Children were often confused about the rules and their role expectations. They were isolated, lacking in self-confidence, anxious, and ashamed. Their relationship with the non-alcoholic parent was also strained and tense.

In short, when alcohol problems produce dysfunctioning parental roles, children often adopt functional parental roles in order to cope with the family problems and to fulfill necessary family tasks. While learning to be more responsible and adult-like, these children also receive a message that their feelings are secondary. As these overly responsible children (and those who become scapegoats, adjusters, placators, or were abused or neglected) become adults, they carry with them into their adult relationships (at home and work) the anger, resentment, guilt, lack of trust, and low self-esteem they developed as children. They also reaelize that the roles they took on to cope with shifts in the family system are no longer functional in adult relationships. Not dealing with one's own feelings, consistently doing other people's work, rescuing other people from their problems, and constantly doing what one thinks the other wants are not mentally and physically healthy behaviors in adulthood. Children of alcoholics, as adults, have failed to learn how to identify their own feelings and to deal with them once discovered. They continue to be overly responsible and to conceal the mental and physical scars of abuse and neglect. It is when they turn to some form of compulsive behavior, such as excessive alcohol use, that the outcomes of growing up in an alcoholic family become evident.

Shifts in children's roles to accommodate alcohol problems in the family system, while positive and necessary at the time, may later in life lead to continuation of alcohol abuse unless identified and treated early on. Hence the need to focus on the entire family system and the changing rules, roles, and relationships that accompany disruption of the family structure. By understanding alcoholism as a family problem and by viewing the family as a system of shifting roles and relationships, the intergenerational transmission of alcohol abuse may begin to be halted.

It is also important for specialists involved with family problems to look at the positive outcomes that may result from growing up in an alcoholic family. Not all children of alcoholics are delinquent or alcohol abusers. Many enter helping professions and service-oriented occupations. Anecdotal evidence suggests that some become good listeners, altruistic, and empathetic. In other words, many children of alcoholics may have adoapted coping roles which demonstrate healthy adjustment and positive outcomes. No research has yet focused on this dimension.

Whatever the effects may be, there is a necessity to differentiate impact of alcoholic parents on child-rearing according to variations that exist among families and the other social systems of which they are a part. As mentioned in the Introduction, family dynamics are also a function of such demographic characteristics as ethnicity and race, religious traits, family size, socioeconomic status, and regionality. For example, it is difficult for children raised in authoritarian families (often related to religiosity and ethnicity) to confront their parent's drinking problems, for lower income families to afford extra support services (such as housekeepers and private mental health programs) or for one-parent families to cope in as smooth a way as a two-parent family might.

Little research exists that focuses on the mediating effects sociodemographic variables may have on the outcomes of growing up in an alcoholic family. Yet it is likely that these variables will contribute something to how a family defines the problems in the first place and to how it responds by changing the rules, roles, and relationships of ther system.

Significant Others' Roles

Whether the alcoholic's partner in a close relationship is the legal spouse, a same-sex or opposite sex lover, or simply a roommate, that person must learn to adjust to the alcoholic's problems and the disruption of the family system. Within such a system, the rules, roles, and relationships between a significant other and the alcoholic shift to accommodate the new disruptive behaviors. The responses the significant other makes not only affect the alcoholic's behavior and feelings, but also contribute to those of the significant other. Like children in the family system, partners take on roles to meet family tasks and adopt relationships which may seem situationally functional but may prove in the long run to be mentally and physically unhealthy for everyone within the family system.

Jackson (1954) has argued that wives of male alcoholics go through seven stages in adjusting to the alcoholic situation. Initially, attempts are made to deny the problem and to create the illusion of a normal relationship. While concern is expressed about excessive drinking, both partners avoid the strains and issues related to drinking. In stage 2, attempts are made to eliminate the problem when the family begins to experience social isolation due to drinking incidents. The wife begins to feel self-pity, a loss of self-confidence, and inadequate. Yet attempts are made to cover up and to maintain the family structure of roles and relationships. Disorganization characterizes stage 3 when the family gives up attempts to control alcohol use. The duties and responsibilities of family roles are no longer being enacted by appropriate persons. The alcoholic's spouse has lost almost all self-assurance and experiences guilt and a further loss of self-respect. Violence, role reversals, and role conflict can occur at this stage. In stage 4, attempts are begun to reorganize the family system in response to a crisis situation. The spouse has taken over the alcoholic's roles and the alcoholic is increasingly viewed as a dependent child. For the woman of a male alcoholic, this usually signifies a gain of status and power in a traditional family system of male dominance. By bringing some order and stability back to the system, the spouse begins to regain self-esteem and assurance. For many, however, leaving the family system or developing an alcohol problem signifies stage 5. Some begin to depend on alcohol as the only apparently viable means to cope with the alcoholic partner and the concomitant chaos while others have found the newly acquired self-confidence and power roles comfortable enough to believe they can make it on their own and leave the disruptive situation.

In stage 6, the family reorganizes, often without
the alcoholic spouse. At times the alcoholic makes
attempts to return to the family system by playing on
guilt feelings. Stage 7 is the reorganization of the
entire family if the alcoholic returns having achieved
sobriety. Problems usually occur when attempting to
alter roles and relationships once again. For the
woman, newly achieved power and control become difficult to relinquish and some tension exists in accommodating to a sober husband's revitalized roles. Slowly the family system adjusts to include a recovering
alcoholic and some degree of stability is achieved.

Recently, the term "co-alcoholic" has been developed to describe the non-alcoholic significant
other. It incorporates the concept of the partner
evolving in similar ways to the alcoholic. That is,
it emphasizes the idea that the significant other
goes through stages similar to the development in an
alcoholic: denial, loss of trust, diminishing sexual
interaction, low self-esteem, low self-confidence,
and helplessness. In other words, the non-alcoholic
partner begins to share the problems and loss of control the alcoholic experiences.

Often the non-alcoholic partner inadvertently
enables the alcoholic to continue drinking. As the
significant other increasingly enacts the duties of
the alcoholic's roles and takes control of the family
system, the alcoholic is alleviated from responsibilities and shielded from the problems due to alcohol
abuse. This results in the family members becoming
accustomed to the newe roles, rules, and relationships, often enabling the alcoholic to continue
drinking without further serious consequences (Hanson
& Estes, 1977).

In same-sex relationships (lovers or roommates)
other issues may emerge. Power is potentially distributed more equally in these relationships, unlike
traditional heterosexual ones in which power is distributed according to gender differences. When alcohol problems are introduced in same-sex relationships,
shifts in power between two potential equals create
added tensions (Nardi, 1982a). Homosexual "families"
must also deal with the values of significant others
who make up an extended family of close gay friends.
Confronting the positive meanings of alcohol and
drinking within the gay community, gays and lesbians
must reconcile their problem drinking patterns with

their extended family's emphasis on social drinking. The role of such family systems and significant others takes on added meaning for gay people since they require these communities to maintain and legitimate their identities in the context of an often hostile society (Nardi, 1982b).

In sum, regardless of the nature of the family system, alcoholics influence the emotional and physical lives of their significant others (spouses, lovers, partners, or extended families of close friends). The violence which may occur, the tensions and arguments which do occur, and the concomitant feelings of guilt, fear, despair, low self-esteem, and low self-assurance need to be addressed. As members of a family social system, the significant others are continuously modifying their roles and relationships to accommodate to shifts in the alcoholic's behavior. While the attention is focused on the problem drinker, the partner is developing undetected his or her own problems and mechanisms for coping. Some take on new power and control, some develop denial and enabling techniques, and others begin to cope as the alcoholic has done--with alcohol.

As with children of alcoholics, the significant others do not emerge from a dysfunctioning family system untouched. Reaching out to them and giving them more positive and less destructive ways to cope with the problem drinker and their own feelings of inadequacy and fear become the goals of family-oriented treatment.

III. TREATMENT IMPLICATIONS

Viewing the family as a social system of interlocking roles, rules, and relationships and recognizing that reorganization occurs in times of problems lead to important treatment and prevention strategies. Wolin, Bennett, Noonan, and Teitelbaum (1980) have discovered that family rituals enacted in the family system have salient implications for tretment and prevention of alcohol abuse. Family rituals (symbolic forms of communication repeatedly acted out in systematic fashion over time) "contribute significantly to the establishment and preservation of a family's collective sense of itself" (Wolin, et al., 1980:201). Rituals clarify roles, delineate relationships, and define rules for a particular family system. The researchers found that in those families in which

212

rituals were substantially altered during times of heaviest parental drinking, the transmission of alcohol problems to the children's generation occurred. During such rituals as family dinners, holidays, and weekends, the alcoholic parent in these families usually drank and got drunk while the families accepted this behavior by failing to respond to it.

In those families in which family rituals remained relatively unchanged during periods of heaviest parental drinking, there existed a lack of transmission of alcohol problems to the children's generation. These families rejected the alcoholic parent's drunken behavior by confronting the parent or by talking negatively about it among themselves. They tended to keep their holiday rituals intact.

This research indicates the importance of maintaining a structure to the family system and the relevancy of focusing on all the members in prevention and treatment programs. Many programs emphasize the interactional and communication patterns of the family, not simply the problem drinking (NIAAA, 1981). Treatment programs usually work with the alcoholic alone and in family sessions. Yet, despite the growing recognition of family dynamics influencing individual alcohol behavior, relatively few alcoholics are treated in family therapy (NIAAA, 1981).

When family treatment does occur, the first stage is to identify how the alcoholism is perpetuating the family system. In what ways does the family accommodate to the changes in roles, rules, and relationships brought on by the problem drinking? Once the dynamics and interactions among the partners and children are identified, treatment can begin with each family member individually and then together. It is important to allow situations in which the children can discuss their feelings without their parents being present and for the significant others to express their issues without their alcoholic partner. Then, it becomes therapeutically relevant to bring the family members together in a group session to work out the dysfunctional ways they may be using to cope with the problem and to learn better methods in dealing with it.

As Janzen (1978:139) states,

Regardless of who the patient is, the important thing in treatment is to clarify the nature of the interaction among the dyads and triads in

213

the family group. In this way, previously
established destructive patterns can be inter-
rupted and changed. Since conflict in a family
is to be expected, the goal of therapy is to
help family members find new ways of resolving
such conflict.

IV. CONCLUSIONS

If there is one way of summarizing the dynamics
of alcoholism and the system of family roles, it is
with the concepts of power and control. It should be
recognized that the struggles for control within a
relationship may lead to alcohol problems as well as
be the results of alcohol abuse. The relationship
between the alcoholic and other family members is a
competitive struggle among people driven by strong
dependency needs and who usually seek to maintain
drinking patterns in order to continue control
(Shapiro, 1977). The request for help by the alcoholic (a statement of loss of control) is answered
by the partner and children who attempt to control
the alcoholic's drinking and to maintain family
stability. By taking on new roles and relationships
of power and control, family members often find
themselves liking these new positions of responsibility and develop a need to maintain control even
when the alcoholic achieves sobriety. Herein lies
the struggle for power and control and the dynamics
of enabling and cover-up behaviors.

The struggle for power and control is also
exhibited in the alcoholic's attempts not to lose
control and to maintain power in the family system.
While announcing the need for help, the alcoholic
is simultaneously asserting the reluctance to be
helped. This contradiction and the helpless, inadequate feelings this engenders in non-alcoholic family
members can lead to unhealthy coping devices adopted
by partners and children.

By focusing on the family as a system in which
control and power shift and in which struggles to
maintain stability are common, we can learn much
about the dynamics of families in general and about
the unique dimensions that accompany family suffering
from the disruptions brought on by problems of alcohol
abuse. We can also develop better techniques and
strategies more specifically geared to the treatment
of alcohol problems and to the prevention of the
intergenerational transmission of alcoholism.

BIBLIOGRAPHY

Black, Claudia

    1979   "Children of Alcoholics." <u>Alcohol Health and Research World</u>, 4, pp. 23-37.

Cork, Margaret

    1969   <u>The Forgotten Children</u>. Don Mills, Canada: Paperjacks.

Greenleaf, Jael

    1981   "Co-Alcoholic/Para-Alcoholic: Who's Who and What's the Difference." Presented at National Council on Alcoholism annual forum, New Orleans.

Hanson, Kathye &
Nada Estes

    1977   "Dynamics of Alcoholic Families." In Nada Estes and Edith Heinemann (Eds.), <u>Alcoholism</u>, pp. 67-75. St. Louis: Mosby.

Jackson, Joan

    1954   "The Adjustment of the Family to the Crisis of Alcoholism." <u>Quarterly Journal of Studies on Alcohol</u>. 15:4, December, pp. 562-586.

Janzen, Curtis

    1978   "Family Treatment for Alcoholism: A Review." <u>Social Work</u>, March, pp. 135-141.

Nardi, Peter M.

    1981   "Children of Alcoholics: A Role Theoretical Perspective." <u>Journal of Social Psychology</u>, 115, pp. 237-245.

Nardi, Peter M.

1982a   "Alcohol Treatment and the Non-Tradi-
               tional Family Structures of Gays and
               Lesbians." Journal of Alcohol and
               Drug Education, 27:2, Winter.

1982b   "Alcoholism and Homosexuality: A
               Theoretical Perspective." Journal of
               Homosexuality, 7:4, Summer.

National Institute on
Alcohol Abuse and
Alcoholism (NIAA)

1981   Fourth Special Report to the US Con-
               gress on Alcohol and Health. Re-
               printed in Alcohol Health and Research
               World, 5:3, Spring, pp. 2-65.

Seixas, Judith

1977   "Children from Alcoholic Families."
               In N. Estes and E. Heinemann (Eds.),
               Alcoholism, pp. 153-161. St. Louis:
               Mosby.

Shapiro, Rodney

1977   "A Family Therapy Approach to Alco-
               holism." Journal of Marriage and
               Family Counseling, 3:4, October,
               pp. 71-78.

Wolin, Steven, Linda Bennett,
Denise Noonan, Martha Teitelbaum

1980   "Disrupted Family Rituals: A Factor
               in the Intergenerational Transmission
               of Alcoholism." Journal of Studies on
               Alcohol, 41:3, pp. 199-214.

*Peter M. Nardi, Department of Sociology, Pitzer
College, Claremont, California 91711.

SECTION III

WORK, STRESS AND PERSONAL LIFE:
MANAGING BOUNDARIES AND COORDINATING ROLES

Douglas B. Gutknecht*

Families today are undergoing numerous pressures and stresses brought about by social and economic changes that pose new problems and opportunities for learning how to manage boundaries between public work and personal lives. Individuals in their personal and family life are subject to numerous, often competing exchanges and interactions. In this section, we will explore the topic of stress and conflict both at work and in the family or private life. We will explore the impact of work on family life -- how the family itself interprets, shapes, manages and copes with the demands of work, careers and employment status -- and the impact of family life on work -- in both family run businesses and corporations. In addition, we must recognize the work that is not measured by traditional, economic standards -- work performed for personal growth or mastery skills. Finally, new forms of work in the home is an emerging trend. Here we can explore the emerging electronic cottage and the potentials of computers and other media like television to alter the very definition of work, homelife, play, and leisure.

The topic of work, stress and personal life requires us to evaluate not just the negative interrelationships but the complementary ones as well. In fact, the quality of home life may prove in the long run a better prediction of job satisfaction than the work environment itself (Bersoff and Crosby, 1984:79-83).

All families experience conflicts, stresses, and burnout at various times throughout their life cycles. Some of these stresses are expected or normal because they result from developmental stages and tasks that most families must face -- birth of children, children beginning school, empty nest, retirement and death of a spouse. However, even recognizable and predictable seasons and changes in our lives impact family members in different ways. The family system also reacts as a result of its unique patterns of roles, interaction styles, communication skills and support networks. In addition, each family faces the episodic and unpre-

217

dictable stresses, conflicts and crises that overwhelm
their coping ability -- divorce, illnesses, affairs,
loss of job, etc.

I. DEFINING STRESS

    Girdano and Everly (1969:3) define stress as a
"fairly predictable arousal of psycho-physiological
(mind-body) systems which, if prolonged, can fatigue
or damage the system to the point of malfunction and
disease." Stressors are the causes of stress -- physical, social or psychological conditions or situations
that trigger a stress reaction or response.

    Stress outcomes are either psysiological or psy-
chological. Girdano and Everly (1979:11-12) called
the former, a "psychogenic or psychosomatic" disorder,
which includes emotionally caused physical disorders
such as backache, skin disorders, peptic ulcers, mi-
graine headaches, respiratory disorders; and the latter
"somato-genetic" disorder where anxiety, anger, fear
and frustration actually increase body's vulnerability
to organic diseases. The former involve organ damage
but not infection or degeneration, the latter include
the nature of infection and degeneration. The com-
bined meaning of both disorders is what may be generally defined as psychosomatic disorders.

    Stress is the body's nonspecific response to any
demand placed upon it, whether pleasant or unpleasant
(Seyles, 1954). Stress is a fact of life and can add
to our pleasures and enjoyment of life. Our goal in
life should not be to try to completely avoid or eliminate stress but to learn to recognize our typical re-
ponse patterns and whether they are causing us problems.   If we observe negative stress patterns, we
should try to change them.

II. PHYSIOLOGICAL CHANGES AND THE STRESS RESPONSE

    What happens to our bodies when we encounter
stressors. The physical reaction is rather simple,
although variations in the strength and effect of
hormonal reactions vary. The activator stressors signals the hypothalamus, in the mid-brain. It is yet
uncertain whether the signal comes from frontal or
cortex or elsewhere. The hypothalamus activates the
interior pituitary or master gland in the adrenal
cortex and the sympathetic or automatic nervous system
including the adrenal glands on top of the kidneys,

which regulates catechamines, adrenaline (epinephrine) and nonadrenaline (nonepinephrinic).

People under stress feel a wide variety of subjective states and behave in many ways that indicate stress. Some people look, feel, and act agitated, nervous, hyperactive, fidgety or shakey. Others feel depleted, enervated, drained and depressed. Many feel uncertain and look different to us as they squint their eyes and grind their teeth without even knowing it. Many react with anger and often feel like they are out of control or sinking into oblivion. Others find the sensations and moods difficult to pin down or label but they know one thing - they feel different than usual.

Seyle (1954) contrasted distress with eustress. Seyle believed a certain amount of stress or "eustress" is good for everyone. Stress can provide energy, motivation and enthusiasm for well-being, challenge, contentment and enjoyment. Without stress we might suffer from boredom and loneliness; from reduced social contacts. Distress is actually the negative or more chronic type of stress. Distress, disease, suffering and malfunction arise when either stressors become too numerous, or our coping strategies fail us. Everyone experiences some degree of stress, most of the time. If we truly experience no stress, we would probably be dead. Stress is unavoidable but it is also costly to our personal and social well-being.

Seyle (1954) believed that since stress is the body's nonspecific response, individual patterns of great activity, by itself, cannot account for negative outcomes like Coronary Heart Disease (CHD). For example, he believed that two types of human beings, "race horses" and "turtles" respond to stressors in different ways. A race horse thrives on stress, and the need for a fast-paced, active, lifestyle. Inactivity, routine and a slow pace would bore a race horse, producing negative stress and outcomes. In contrast, a "turtle" often requires a quiet, relaxed and leisurely paced life. Too much activity produces frustration and strain in the turtle. Seyle believes that the dangers of overwork and excessive striving for the Type A personality are exaggerated, arousing unnecessary anxiety. However, people must not mistake their capabilities and push themselves beyond their normal stress endurance level.

What is "too much stress" or what length of time is too long depends on the individual and his or her capacity to cope. One person may be able to handle large amounts of long-term stress before developing problems, whereas another individual may manifest symptoms after only a short time period. How stress is experienced, again, depends on the capacity of the individual to adapt.

Two cardiologists, Meyer Friedman and Ray Rosenman (1974) began noticing some recurring behaviors among their cardiology patients, especially in relation to their way of dealing with time. They noticed an extreme anxiousness of the patients in their waiting room, and the fact that their conversations constantly centered around time, work and achievement. From their 8-1/2 year contact with coronary patients, they formulated a construct of action-emotion behavior patterns like competitive, excessively involved with their work, always racing the clock, that seemed to surround the coronary-prone individual. They labeled this type of behavior "Type A Personality". Studies known as the Western Collaborative Studies, showed that Type A behavior preceded the development of coronary heart disease in 72 to 85 percent of the 3,411 men tested!

Research efforts in the early 1960s by Holmes and Rahe (1967) were conducted to see if change had major effects on health. They concentrated on generic change that resulted in either positive or negative consequences. From their work they developed the Social Readjustment Rating Scale (SRRS).

This scale listed 43 specific life events occurring within the past 12 months, each carrying a weight dependent upon the amount of stress. These units were called life Change Units (LCU's). The most heavily weighted event was the death of a spouse (100 LCU): the lowest being a minor violation of the law (11 LCU). Surprisingly, outstanding personal achievement is rated 28 LCU, only one point less than trouble with in-laws. This points to an important aspect of the study of life events--it concentrates on generic change, a force which causes stress through the destruction of homeostasis. They found the higher the score an individual had on the SRRS, the more that individual was suscep-tible to disease. The word susceptible was used be-cause the rate of incidence of disease could also depend on the individual's ability to adapt to certain situations.

The problem with Holmes-Rahe's research is that it overemphasizes major personal crisis and life-event changes. Overdoing the idea that stress only comes in big doses, caused Holmes-Rahe to look at the effects of major illnesses, traumatic events like deaths of spouse or close family, trouble at work, detention in jail, foreclosure of mortgage, pregnancy, sexual difficulties, etc. Such emphasis on major events requiring adjustment downplays the realities of our daily work and life experience. Each of our daily lives is filled with little assults upon our self worth. These little problems add up. Each of us can construct our own hassle index and determine the toll upon our own health and well-being. Try listing all those hassles that seem to really bother you and make you feel and think that your well-being, satisfaction and enjoyment of life is being seriously impaired. Each small stress bruises our psyche and causes stress. We live in a disposable throwaway society with increasing stress each day as a result of widespread and complex changes.

Adams (1978:166-168) has identified four major categories of things that create stress in our lives. First, there are work related major changes such as job change, increased work hours, major reorganization in organization structure, or change in pace of work or your activity level. Second, are nonwork related major life changes already discussed. Both categories from Holmes and Rahe's social readjustment scale. Third are daily pressures on the job such as limited feedback, poor communication with boss, unclear job responsibilities. Fourth, are pressures away from work such as pollution, noise, concern over economy, anxiety about family life. A fifth category might be minor hassles which do add up.

Adams stress model also offers a view of how stress breeds and leads to psyciological and psychological problems such as hypertension, elevated cholesterol, low HDL (high density lippoproteins) anxiety, depression. Stress breeds in our unique personal circumstances such as adjusting to families, job, school, illness, lifestyle changes, aging, midlife crisis; to changes in our society and social expectations regarding proper behavior, success, work performance; unhealthy lifestyles, scripts and roles which put our minds, psyche and bodies out of their natural balance and harmony.

Sailer, et al. (1982:35) lists manifestations of
five types of reactions: 1) subjective, including
anxiety and low self-esteem; 2) behavioral, such as
accident proneness, excessive eating and impulsive
behavior; 3) cognitive, including the inability to
concentrate and make decisions, forgetfullness and
hypersensitivity to criticism; 4) psysiological, including increased blood and urine catecholamisms and
corticosteroids, increased blood glucose levels, increased heart rate blood pressure, dizziness, diar-
rhea, ulcers; 5) organizational, including absentee-
ism, poor productivity, high turnover, job dissatisfaction, high accident rates and low morale.

III. STRESSES IN FAMILY LIFE

        Family stresses left unattended can lead to many
different problems, crises, and consequences. The
individual and the family in the modern world, as
we've seen, is subject to many stresses in its internal and external relationships. These stresses
threaten to impair individual family members and the
family unit's ability to promote its own welfare and
happiness. A short list of family stresses include:

1. Disordered relationships, patterns of communica-
    tion and nurturing.

2. Acquisition of a stigmatized member through birth,
    illness, marriage, remarriage or even adoption.

3. Acquisition of excess family members, which places
    a strain by adaptive resources (internal and ex-
    ternal) of parents and the family system. Too
    many children, relatives or parents can become
    dysfunctional in a society that relies upon out-
    side employment. However, in certain situations,
    utilizing all family members to assist the family
    unit might decrease certain stresses, like finan-
    cial difficulties, while increasing stresses on
    individual family members who would have to give
    up free-time or school, in order to go to work.

4. Severely limited coping or adaptive capacity
    (insufficient income, school or personality handi-
    caps, resources, time, support groups, extended
    family).

5. Loss of a family member through separation, di-
    vorce, desertion, death, mental problems, physi-
    cal illness, prisoner of war.

6. Normal developmental stress or crises that overwhelm a families adaptive capacity or ability to
   cope -- birth of a child, or an additional child,
   child starting school, moving residences, adolescence, children departing home (empty nest), midlife crises, death of parents and friends, retirement, death of spouse.

The family, in our view, is a uniquely flexible,
primary social organization; an open system subject to
stress from its environment, depending upon the nature
of the event, how it is perceived, and the resources
available for anticipation and positive coping versus
reacting, defense or negative coping.

Families must learn to anticipate, manage, and
transform their patterns of internal relationships
and external interactions. These evolving patterns,
scripts and negotiations provide a stable context for
both personal growth and change for all family members.
In summary, we must identify four sources for family
stress and conflict: 1) internal adjustments to a
growing number of extra-familial forces and institutional actors or stakeholders; 2) individual member
adjustments to internal family system dynamics and
forces; 3) transitional points in the normative developmental family life cycle; 4) and idiosyncrastic
strains of stresses which hit us at unpredictable
moments.

IV. THE SOCIAL CONTEXT

Our society today puts great pressures on individuals and families while offering fewer social
supports than in the past (Bensman and Lilenfeld,
1979). We are caught between private and public
roles, between our deepest individual needs and public
demands as citizens of a complex and interdependent
world. We constantly face dilemmas and stresses in a
society that paradoxically requires the repression of
deepest being for the sake of individual success.

Too often when we speak about the increasing
stress and strain effecting our lives, we forget that
stresses operate at all system levels. Somehow we must
develop skills that allow us to move between system
levels and see the consequences of our actions. If we
remain stuck in only one level, we will become short-
sighted and ill-informed about the requirements for
reducing stress. Looking at stress from a system perspective allows us the opportunity to fashion a more

strategic, systematic and integrated view of the causes of stress and stress management for our personal and work lives.

Life is a constant process of managing and deciding how to solve problems which create stress. We search for information and identify problems out of curiosity to explore the possible consequences of troublesome situations. Then we must decide how to implement a strategy, program, or solution to the potential or current problem. Solving social and relationship problems which create much stress requires much experience, information, awareness and ongoing, longterm learning strategies and social skills. The inability to solve our problems, or at least to reasonably manage them, creates much stress in our lives. Individuals and family members must become better problem identifiers and decision makers. Every individual can learn to solve problems with the right information. When we fail to solve problems by always attacking them impulsively, we end up feeling even more anxiety, insecurity, uncertainity, frustration and ultimately low self-esteem. Our low self-esteem is thus tied to our weakened intellectual grasp of our social situation and our increasing fear of social failure. Stress decreases as a result of our ability to interpret, organize and solve life's social and intellectual problems.

Tension and worry are actually often part of problem identification and decision-making activities. However, excessive worry can prolong stress and contribute to the failure of our problem solving strategies. Muscle tensions are actually locked into problem solving strategies, because we utilize mental images in our memory to reconstruct the problem situation. Since our bodies and mind are linked, so do our mental and actual physical images become linked through memories of the problem situation. Mental images allow the mind to scan the world for emerging gestalts or whole patterns of information. Humans utilize such information for trial and error learning, dreaming, daydreaming, fantasy, hoping or worrying. Excessive muscle tension can be produced by negative images of problem solving, when insufficient information, low self-esteem or confidence, and few social and cognitive skill strategies appear available. The individual's tension level increases as the images of failure become more vivid in the mind, as a product of thought or cognition. The mind then becomes fixated or preoccupied with sensations of uncertainity and failure, creating even more physiological stress and accelerating the disease process. Left unattended this stress incubates and attacts the body daily. The long-term results have already been mentioned.

Stress is truly a product of our mind-body link. However it begins in our minds with our hopes and dreams of enjoyment, satisfaction, stability, friendship, success, etc. How we interpret opportunities, risks and obstacles can challenge us to perform or overwhelm us with the consequences of stress. Stress is the legacy of each individual and becomes dysfunctional only as each of us define its meaning, as we decide certain circumstances are interfering with our hopes and dreams. But we still don't know why certain things are stressful at one time and not stressful at another.

My theory of the answer to this unresolved question lies in the acquisition of informational, cognitive and other social skill strategies which bolster our sense of self-esteem and mastery of modern, complex situations. The basis is intellectual or cognitive curiosity. The curious person has an engaged or activated intellect which tries to organize, make sense of, order, and cope with anything that is unfamiliar and interesting in his/her environment. The curious intellect is poised to always explore the unfamiliar in order to determine how to restore harmony, reestablish meaningful events, and modify expectations of perceptions, hopes, desires, beliefs to a more real sense of the situations. The key is thus intellectual curiority, meaningful social perception, and social and cognitive skills, which thrive upon the process of long-term exploring and learning, not just makeshift and short-term outcomes.

V. FAMILY LIFE, STRESS, AND THE CHANGING NATURE OF WORK

Statistics indicate that drastic changes are occuring in the make up of the traditional family. The traditional family of working husband, and housewife mom, with two or three children, is declining. We now have families of single parents, childless couples, older adults living together, adult children living with parents, more single adults with adopted kids.

The diversity of family forms has resulted from many social and economic trends -- like the increasing divorce rates which increases single-parent families, recession, structural unemployment, and more permissive sexual attitudes, among many factors. But the largest single factor behind the emerging diversity of family forms is the emergence of women in the workplace. Implications of this revolutionary change will be documented in this section. In addition, individuals and families can learn to cope with these changes. However, we must keep the focus on work and family issues, and not let them become defined solely as "women's problems" or "women and work issues."

It is important to underscore the fact that work and family life effect each other. The traditional, functionalist argument has fostered a view of the family as promoting separate worlds for the male breadwinner and female housewife. In addition, the topics of work and family have been viewed as unrelated topics with fairly complete segmentation -- events in one arena were believed to be unimportant to the other arena. For some men and women such segmented functions and roles reinforced their stereotypes. However, as social and economic trends began to change more rapidly in the 1960's, the interconnection became more evident. The old patterns in the family and work division of labor created new stresses and required new adjustments and problem solving strategies. Today it is necessary to document the trends more comprehensively and truly study the topics of work and family together.

Payson (1984:50) has documented several trends in the involvement of women today in the work world, particularly in the service sector:

1. Most of the white and pink collar, middle and lower occupational classifications are dominated by women, and in the next decade one-half of all available jobs will be in this designation.

2. In 1983, over 45 million women were working. In 1984, there were 51 million women working; by 1990, 58 million, and by 1995, 61 million.

3. 1982 marked a year when growing numbers of children lived in homes with a working mother -- 25% lived in families with a father absent or out of the labor force; 50% of all children under 18 have mothers who are in the work force.

4. In 1983, 45% of all working women were single, widowers, divorced or separated.

5. Last year, 25 million American women worked full-time, year around. Women's participation rates are increasing at a more rapid pace than men's -- there are 18 million more women in the work force today than 1970, but 11 million of them are there because of their greater participation rates.

Every society creates its own social memory, social endowment or legacy of trust and caring, which individuals can draw upon in times of need, disharmony, failure or illness. Traditionally women have provided free labor to this legacy. The functionalist position is based upon the assumption that as the household production function declined, the household consumption function took its place. Thus, the home as a separate consumption unit became separated from an external work location or job. Pleck (1976:30) suggests this functionalist assumption is wrong, because production in the home declined only gradually. In addition we find modern home economists and econometricians challenging the rigid distinction between production and consumption:

> This perspective on work deemphasizes wage-earning, suggesting a much broader definition of 'work' which includes non-market labor, most of which was (and is) performed by women.

The economic or production value of caring work is a social resource. It has continually been downplayed. Now, however, the caring pool of women nurturers is declining. The current situation is demanding a response to this decline of the caring resource pool. The use of nonemployed women is decreasing, and so are the number of available individuals capable of assisting in-laws, joining service clubs, associations or volunteer groups. In fact this is one reason we hear so much talk of stresses on families trying to cope and the need for new social or public policies to support day-care, flex-time or flexible work hours, cafeteria-style benefit packages, and longer maternity leaves.

Many today are calling upon both government and business to develop better family policies, and corporate employee benefits. Although there are limits to using public institutions to solve family problems and stresses, new partnerships between institutions

227

and social supports can lessen the burden -- community partnerships between local parent-teacher associations, church groups, business, volunteer groups, colleges and government agencies can unite in addressing the issues of caring for future generations. The stresses facing modern families are not the result of women working, but the changing nature of employment which requires more support services to assist families. Without social supports, stresses on families, spouses and children will increase. In this view making a living itself becomes one of the greatest stresses in the lives of families. Beyond work itself many new sources of stress must be managed by modern families using such resources as media and computers.

VII. THE CHAPTERS AHEAD

Gutknecht probes the impact of television upon youth and family life in Chapter 11. This chapter views television as a potentially powerful tool for active family involvement, parenting, and enhanced family communication, if used with sensitivity and awareness. Parents, however, must be educated to bring out these potentially valuable uses of this intriguing electronic medium. The chapter explores the following topics: first, several critical, yet suggestive, social critics set the context for the discussion; second, research regarding television and child literacy development and potential for violence; third, many active family strategies for utilizing television to enhance socialization, learning, communication, and family wellness.

Reitz in Chapter 12 offers an exploratory assessment of the various trends and forces that computers have exerted upon family life today and directions for the future. He discusses the following arenas where computers will have an impact upon the family; recreational, educational, and financial. But the most important dimensions will probably be in the area of telecommuting and the electronic cottage.

Kepner in Chapter 13 explores the family and the firm using a co-evolutionary perspective. This provocative and innovative chapter explores family relations within the family firm using family therapy and coevolutionary insights. Within family firm the study of the family system is so tightly interwoven with those of the business system that they cannot be disentangled without seriously disrupting one or both systems. Here we learn much about family systems, and social supports can lessen the burden -- community partnerships between local parent-teacher associations, church groups, business, volunteer groups, colleges and government agencies can unite in addressing the issues of caring for future generations. The stresses facing modern families are not the result of women working, but the changing nature of employment which requires more support services to assist families. Without social supports, stresses on families, spouses and children will increase. In this view making a living itself becomes one of the greatest stresses in the lives of families. Beyond work itself many new sources of stress must be managed by modern families using such resources as media and computers.

VII. THE CHAPTERS AHEAD

     Gutknecht probes the impact of television upon youth and family life in Chapter 11. This chapter views television as a potentially powerful tool for active family involvement, parenting, and enhanced family communication, if used with sensitivity and awareness. Parents, however, must be educated to bring out these potentially valuable uses of this intriguing electronic medium. The chapter explores the following topics: first, several critical, yet suggestive, social critics set the context for the discussion; second, research regarding television and child literary development and potential for violence; third, many active family strategies for utilizing television to enhance socialization, learning, communication, and family wellness.

     Reitz in Chapter 12 offers an exploratory assessment of the various trends and forces that computers have exerted upon family life today and directions for the future. He discusses the following arenas where computers will have an impact upon the family; recreational, educational, and financial. But the most important dimensions will probably be in the area of telecommuting and the electronic cottage.

     Kepner in Chapter 13 explores the family and the firm using a co-evolutionary perspective. This provocative and innovative chapter explores family relations within the family firm using family therapy and coevolutionary insights. Within family firm the study of the family system is so tightly interwoven with those of the business system that they cannot be disentangled without seriously disrupting one or both systems. Here we learn much about family systems, family therapy, small business firms which resemble families, the value of family therapy for consulting in business settings, and how to promote change through information and awareness.

Vayoanoff in Chapter 14 discusses the impact of several work stresses in corporate families -- employment insecurity and career mobility, job content and satisfaction, amount and scheduling of work at home, geographic mobility and the corporate wife role. All of these factors impact the family system and create stress, role and identity confusion. These stresses present themselves in life events as acute changes and somewhat enduring situations which require behavioral problem-solving and advanced coping strategies. The precipitating circumstances are -- father gone from home for long durations; father bringing home too much work which occupies a great deal of his time; father unable to leave the tensions of work behind and displacing hostility upon the spouse and children. The impact of corporate stress often produces a loss or lack of self esteem for both husband and wife and the failure of individual family members to support each others growth needs. The problem faced by the wives involves how to get them functioning to assist and understand their often absent spouse and begin to reincorporate their husbands into the family and parental system -- they must relearn how to work as a team.

In this sytem, if gone unchecked, the corporate family is in grave trouble. Two important avenues of assistance are available. First the family can seek outside assistance for their difficulties. This is the common avenue pursued by most families seeking help. In addition, a growing positive approach to managing the problems of corporate families is "peer support." In these situations, the corporate family is able to share common concerns, problems and especially strategies with people in like situations. Peer support groups have proven to be quite beneficial for families that suffer from the stresses of corporate life.

Skinner reviews the literature of family stress and coping in Chapter 15. Sources of dual-career strain are discussed along with the coping patterns employed. Although dual-career living is stressful, most participants defined the life style positively. The prime task for such families is achieving a balance between the advantages and disadvantages of dual-career lifestyles.

230

BIBLIOGRAPHY

Adams, John D.

1980   Understanding and Managing Stress.
                San Diego: University Associates,
                Inc.

Bensman, O., &
R. G. Lilenfeld

1979   Between Public and Private: Lost
                Boundaries of the Self. New York:
                The Free Press, Inc.

Bersoff, David, &
Faye Crosby

1984   "Job Satisfaction and Family Status."
                Personality and Social Psychology
                Bulletin, Vol. 10, no. 3, March: 79-83.

Friedman, Meyer, &
Ray Rosenman

1974   Type A Behavior and Your Heart. New
                York: Alfred A. Knopf, Inc.

Girdano, Daniel, &
George Everly

1979   Controlling Stress and Tension: A
                Holistic Approach. New Jersey:
                Prentice-Hall.

Holmes, Thomas, &
Richard H. Raye

1967   "The Social Readjustment Rating Scale."
                Journal of Psychosomatic Research,
                Vol. II: 213-218.

Payson, Martin F.

1984   "Wooing the Pinkcollar Work Force."
                Personnel Journal, January: 48-53.

231

Pleck, Elizabeth H.

1976   "Two Worlds in One: Work and Family."
              Journal of Social History, Winter.

Sailer, Heather R.,
John Schlacter, &
Maaler Edwards

1982   "Stress: Causes, Consequences and
              Coping Strategies." Personal, July-
              August: 35-48.

Seyle, Hans

1954   The Stresses of Life. New York:
              McGraw Hill, Inc.

CHAPTER 11

EXPLORING THE IMPACT OF TELEVISION UPON YOUTH
AND FAMILY LIFE: CHALLENGES AND OPPORTUNITIES

Douglas B. Gutknecht*

Do we really understand this complex electronic
evolving communication medium called television (Ellis,
1983; Greenfield; 1984)? Some call it names like the
"boob tube" or "idiot box" which reveals much about our
relationship with TV. While I will try to present a
more balanced picture of the positive and negative
consequences of television for the American family, my
own bias is toward caution when examining the effect of
TV upon our individual and family lives.

We will first explore some insightful and critical
views of TV; second, examine the research on TV and
child literary development and potential for violence
and aggression; third, explore active family strategies
for utilizing TV in a more productive and educational
manner.

I. EXPLORING TELEVISION: CRITICAL VIEWS

Postman (1982; 81-97) associates the influence of
TV with the disappearance of childhood. The argument
suggests that television supports a distinctive form
of egalitarian communication; everyone regardless of
age, sex, level of education receives the same information. Television eliminates important adult-child distinctions, particularly social contacts which support
cognitive development. Adulthood is taking over more
territory from childhood, creating what Postman (1984:
94) calls the "adult-child". The adult-child is overly
dependent upon television for information and socialization. The requirements of mature and literate adulthood, in contrast, are the product of print media and
literary culture. There is the need for:

> ...the capacity for self-restraint, a tolerance
> for delayed gratification, a sophisticated ability
> to think conceptually and sequentially, a preoc-
> cupation with both historical continuity and the
> future, a high valuation of reason and hierarchi-
> cal order (Postman, 1982: 99).

Postman argues that the key distinction between
adult and child is destroyed by television. Adult

233

knowledge is based upon logic, literacy, authority in cognitive evaluation and reason, while the world of childhood necessitates a certain amount of awe, mystery, secrets, and shame. The adult world and its contradictions, violence and tragedy should not be allowed to easily enter the sheltered and priviledged world of childhood secrets:

> ...electronic media find it impossible to withhold any secrets. Without secrets, of course, there can be no such thing as childhood (Postman 1982: 80).

Television is called the "total disclosure medium" by Postman because it brings the whole culture out of the closet for the eyes of every viewer. Much television thrives upon the constant supply of novel, surprise-filled information; undifferentiated information that requires only the perception of pattern recognition, and not conception, linguistic or logical rigor. Thus, television destroys boundaries, breaks cultural taboos, and instantly reveals intimate secrets that should be learned in controlled doses, as one developmentally matures. Homosexuality, incest, abuse, murder, sadism, become as familiar to children as Saturday morning cartoons. Children appear as little adults, and Gary Coleman clones thrive. The cult of youthful adults, seen on commericals and television dramas, pressures child-adults to look like the highest paid 12- and 13-year-old models; mothers to look no older than their daughters or daughters to look as old as their youthful mothers. All distinctions between ages and developmental stages are reduced to a fake, exploitive, and transparent egalitarianism.

Postman, a media ecologist from New York University, is primarily interested in the general cognitive and social consequences of media, and ignores the debate in the research literature. In fact, the real debate over the potential of television is just beginning. David Marc (1984: 35-36) speaks intelligently to some issues ignored by Postman:

> The distinction between taking television on one's own terms and taking it the way it presents itself is of critical importance. It is the difference between activity and passivity. It is what saves TV from becoming the homogenizing, monolithic, authoritarian tool that doomsday critics claim it is...TV is culture. The more one watches, the more relationships develop among the shows and

234

between the shows and the world. To rip the shows out of their context and judge them against the standards of other media and other cultural traditions is to ignore their American origins and identity.

The key for Marc is to overcome the arrogance of "high" or purely literary culture, in order to appreciate the cultural vitality and creativity inherent in a popular cultural medium like TV. The problem with the medium is not the medium itself but the way it is often used by network conglomerates. Marc (1984: 39) argues that the rise of marketing products, demographic trends and profiles helped destroy the early creativity of television:

> The fall of the genre took place amid increasing demand for a 'product' as opposed to a 'show' in the growing television industry. As the prime-time status rocketed upward, sponsors, agencies, and networks became less tolerant of the inevitable ups and downs of star-centered presentational comedy. The sitcom and other forms of representative drama offer relatively rigid shooting scripts that make 'quality control' easier to impose.

The potential of television to enlarge the imaginative, and creative foundation of learning has been eroded by the marketing surge. Networks select programs based upon demographic information regarding potential consumers of commodities. The true potential of television lies ahead in cable TV, interactive video, and adventurous producers who create programs like SCTV "the first television program to demand of its viewers a knowledge of the traditions of TV, a self-conscious awareness of cultural history" (Marc, 1984: 44). Television viewing thus has the potential to become an imaginative and active reconstruction of our culture and history:

> The greater imaginative adventure of movements through time, space and culture take precedence over the flimsy mimesis that seems to be the intention of the scripts. Their whole fast-food smorgasbord of American culture is laid out for consumption...Instead of masscult ripping off highcult, we have art being fashioned from the junk pile...Experience is re-formed and recontextualized, reclaimed from chaos. Television offers many opportunities of this kind...If demography is an attack on the individual, then the resilience of the human spirit must welcome the test.

235

II. EVALUATING THE RESEARCH ON TELEVISION AND LITERACY

Television is such a pervasive, social phenomenon that it is often difficult to study. We know it impacts our behavior, perceptions, leisure, consumption styles, values and ultimately the health and well-being of our families and children. Good research, however sparce, is fortunately increasing. Most studies fall victim to the temptation to overgeneralize. Pervasive social topics often tax the resources of social scientists trying to link relevant theory and research to a more socially useful and rigorous public policy. The issue of TV and academic achievement is one of the complex questions that demands better research than now available.

Briller and Miller (1984: 6) attack an important study entitled "Student Achievement in California Schools." They claim that a strong relationship exists between heavy viewing time and lower test scores. Briller and Miller suggest that the major influences upon test scores are socioeconomic variables: children of white collar and professional parents do best on academic tests, regardless of amount of TV viewing time. They criticize the Department of Education study for relying upon self-report data, which often understates the amount of TV viewing by higher socioeconomic groups. Briller and Miller (1984: 8-9) conclude the evaluation by citing the positive contribution of TV, particularly instructional TV, to potential literary and academic achievement:

> TV thus helps to broaden their experience by exposing them to situations and events to which they might not otherwise have access. Stricker and Farr claim that 'instructional television programs can increase the range of language experiences that children have in school and can be highly motivating'. The quest of educators should be for more and better ways to capitalize on the useful aspects of the child's viewing experience.

Gerbner et al. (1984) disagrees with this view. The issue, according to this research, is not one of blaming TV for the cause of declining academic performance but the unresolved question:

> Does television viewing exert an independent influence on academic achievement, and if so, for whom, under what conditions and which direction (Gerbner, et al.; 1984: 10)?

236

The key to the controversy, according to Gerbner et al. (1984: 10), is the nature of interpretation and inferences drawn regarding the size of predicted relationships. Small statistical effects can produce great consequences, if we are considering the population of youth in the entire nation or subsamples of vulnerable groups. In addition, weak statistical correlations with small samples of children, might prove significant with larger samples and lead to opposite conclusions. Controlling for background variables like I.Q. and social class will allow research to discount spurious relationships and, also, provide better statistical correlations across sub samples. In the former case, controlling for I.Q. or social class can highlight the possibility that either of these factors, not amount of viewing, is responsible for an apparent relationship between television viewing and achievement. In the latter case, such controls will allow researchers to specify important relationships in different population subgroups.

Many variables (social class, I.Q., religion, leisure time, personal activities, communication, quality of family interaction, English fluency) mediate or influence relationships between viewing and achievement. The relationships are complex; TV viewing is not the only cause of declining literacy, SAT or reading test scores. However, Gerbner et al. (1984: 13), cites evidence which supports the argument, "that those who spend more time watching television will get lower scores, and that some groups of students are more vulnerable."

Newman (1984: 14-15) documents some indirect effects of TV upon children's reading performance, without supporting the simplified argument that TV replaces reading activities, thus contributing to declining SAT scores. Newman doesn't feel the relationship between number of TV viewing hours, and scores on reading achievement tests is an adequate measurement of the complex relationship between TV and a child's reading performance. The important point is the relationship between television viewing and the process of developing reading maturity:

I found that after controlling for sex, socioeconomic status, intelligence quotient and reading achievement scores, those students who were inclined to watch a good deal of television (three or more hours per day) and read little (less than two books per month), chose books of significantly

lower quality than others in the sample. The
scores of students who were heavy TV viewers and
heavy readers were not differentiable from those
who did not choose to watch TV. Again, factors
other than media patterns appear to influence
reading behavior, including such variables as home
environment, role models, and personality characteristics such as energy and perseverance (Newman,
1984: 14-15).

Fetler (1984: 104) also investigated the importance of such mediating variables as study habits,
characteristics of the home environment, and social
class upon the school achievement (reading, mathematic
and written expression) of sixth-grade students. His
research discovered the following:

1) Students who viewed more than six hours of
   television per day had sharply lower achievement scores on all three context areas (Fetler, 1984: 11).

2) Students watching relatively moderate amounts
   of television have higher achievement scores
   than those who report watching less...One can
   speculate, however, that television offers
   some information that is relevant to success
   in school. This information would most plau-
   sibly relate to vocabulary and English language usage...(Fetler, 1984: 111-112).

3) The suggestion that students who would otherwise do well by virtue of aptitude or environment seem to be the most adversely affected by
   increased viewing is born out here (Fetler,
   1984: 113).

4) The profile of heavy viewers suggests that
   viewers habits are characterisic of the family
   unit not the individual...(Fetler, 1984: 115).

5) There appears to be a 'threshhold' amount of
   viewing beyond which television has a striking
   negative association with achievement which is
   not easily explained by other variables (Fetler, 1984: 116).

Fetler (1984: 117) also calls our attention to
weakness in many studies. He observes that they fail
to demonstrate a casual relationship between variables;
to establish random assignment of subjects to both

treatment and control groups; to utilize statistical controls for all relevant backgrounds variables; and to address the limitations of artifical experimental situations.

These research weaknesses regarding TV and children's literacy add to complex problems of trying to understand the impact of TV upon our society and families. Another theory of importance is the relationship of TV and violence, the topic we will now address.

III. EVALUATING THE RESEARCH ON TELEVISION AND VIOLENCE

Definitions of violence are difficult to agree upon. We will follow Wertzel and Lometti (1984: 24) usage by defining the terms violence and aggression interchangeably as:

The purposeful, antisocial infliction of pain for personal gain or gratification that is intended to harm the victim and is accomplished in spite of societal sanctions against it.

Wertzel and Lometti (1984: 24) maintain that "problems involved with arriving at a definition of violence are many because violence is not obvious or clear-cut:

The circumstances under which action occurs, the acceptability of the action by a culture's norms and mores...are all examples which can radically alter whether or not an action is considered violent.

Wertzel and Lometti (1984: 24-25) also reveal some prevalent weaknesses in studies of television and violence:

...Of equal importance--and equally controversial-- is the way which scientists attempt to measure violent or aggressor behavior...The crucial question of course, is whether or not exposure to television violence causes its occurance in real life...the point is correlation can never tell us anything about causation...A correlation between viewing television violence and aggressive behavior could be produced by any of the following: (1) viewing violence leads to aggression; (2) aggressive behavior leads to viewing violence; (3) both viewing violence and aggressive behavior are the product of a third condition or set of conditions such as

239

age, sex, income or family socioeconomic level.
Some of these third variables include the level
of aggressivity among peers, parental behavior
(aggressivity, anger, etc.) parent-child interaction (ways children are punished, nurtured,
etc.) demographic factors and intelligence.

Pearl (1984: 18) argues that a large body of
empirical evidence supports the correlation of television violence and later aggressive behavior in children. Four processes which produce violent behavior
in children watching TV are identified as: 1) observational learning; 2) attitude change; 3) physiological
arousal; 4) justification processes.

Accumulated research points to the importance of
observational learning in children's violent behavior.
Children learn to behave aggressively by watching significant adult or peer role models. Also, children
more often imitate the aggressive behavior they observe, when the opportunity arises immediately after
they've observed it. Somehow the passage of time seems
to extinguish the strength of observational learning.

Secondly, children learn attitudes of aggression,
mistrust, and fear from TV. Violent programs penetrate
the attitudes of young children, and make them more
prone to accept and practice aggression and violence.
However adults can change children's potentially violent attitudes by immediately processing TV shows --
discussion provides a contrast or meaningful framework
for critical evaluation and understanding.

Physiological arousal processes lead to the following effects:

> One is desensitization. For example, boys who
> regularly looked at violent programs showed less
> physiological arousal when they looked at new
> violent programs. Another possibility is that
> merely the increase of general arousal level will
> boost aggressiveness. Another alternative sug-
> gests that people seek an optimal level of arous-
> al; aggressive behavior is arousing, and the per-
> sons who are desensitized may act aggressively to
> raise this level of arousal (Pearl, 1984: 20).

Justification theory argues that already violent
people will view violent TV programs, or enjoy episodes
of violence, because they can rationalize or justify
their past aggressive behavior. If they are merely

imitating their favorite violent hero, then their actions are justified. Imagination and reality become blurred; after all they are only following the example of someone important. In this view TV violence only becomes a pretense and reinforcer of already learned patterns of violence.

The situation of potentially harmful consequences for millions of young children is a significant social issue. The debate over correlation versus causation merely obscures the facts that "television is an influential teacher of children and adults. Ironically the networks have pursued, and used the concept of positive programming in defense of some of their children's productions" (Chaffee, et al., 1984: 31). It is important that we consider the socialization and learning effects of TV's view of the world upon the values, attitudes, perceptions and behavior of our young children and impressionable adolescents. The context of sanctioned violence on TV can create an environment of tolerance toward violence in general. But the impact upon the troubled, nonsupervised, autistic or violence prone child is more acute, and demands a more vigorous and immediate response.

Salamon and Leigh (1984: 119) note that children's preconceptions about the effort needed to comprehend or understand material presented on television influences the effort and eventual success with which they process information and gain something of intellectual value. Children learn what to expect from TV from their family contact, peer advice, observations, formal education and cultural sterotypes. These beliefs, norms and expectations regarding the limited intellectual relevance of television programming, sets the context for interpreting how much intellectual effort the individual will expend to gain information from TV. Expectations, thus, can cause youth to activate less mental effort on TV progarams than they may, in fact, require.

Decoding or processing TV information is not viewed as an important mode of learning and, hence, less cognitive effort is given to processing information. Children and adolescents make few distinctions regarding the type and level of programing difficulty, or potential knowledge content. Cultural sterotypes and social pressure detract from teaching children that they must often expend more effort to benefit from the educational use of TV and other media sources.

Students with higher education levels and from families where TV is not utilized as a source of knowledge or information, fail to see the possible learning potential of the best quality TV programs (Salamon and Leigh, 1984: 134). In order to better utilize TV for increasing literacy, we must begin to change student's learned expectations regarding the amount of cognitive effort needed to process relevant information, encode ideas, and form hypotheses from TV programs. Using TV as a learning tool requires parents to become actively involved in creating an interactive, exploratory and questioning environment. TV can function as one component of a holistic educational environment, if used cautiously and creatively.

IV. FAMILY MEDIA MANAGEMENT STRATEGIES

We must finally address the components of healthy and active family media utilization. The family system must interact actively with external electronic, informational and media systems. Although this view does not support a simplistic view of the "dominating media" and "passive family," the external media system does often influence children's viewing habits, cognitive picture of the world, consumption decisions, reading ability, intellectual habits, educational achievement, and leisure time choices. The influence of the media, though sometimes bordering on domination, is both pervasive and subtle in its effects. This chapter argues that families must better articulate their own needs and interests and evaluate the type, source, reliability, and amount of media information they receive.

The family must function as a social and political force in order to pressure media to recognize the family's legitimate role in selecting and evaluating diverse media experiences. Such a view doesn't sanction a censorship position but acknowledges that bargaining and pressure can be exerted by those interested in evaluating and managing the negative impacts of unconstrained electronic media.

Family media management is based upon the expansion of opportunities for families and communities to evaluate and utilize media information efficiently and productively, in order to enhance family and individual informational needs for personal and social well-being. Such a view places primary emphasis on both media education and healthy family communication. Every family should become involved in supporting media awareness

242

campaigns and educational programs that allow for a more interactive, open, critical, and interrogative use of the media. Each family must explore what it can do for itself, rather than only what the media does to it.

The key element in this process view is developing cognitive-information skills. The family system that is capable of a more critical assessment of information will be more healthy and vital. Thus, families who can maximize good communication, within and between systems, have more good or relevant information, and thus can better meet their own and their communities' needs, goals, and interests. Highly interactive and informed families, as well as political action groups, create a more viable and responsive democracy. Media concentration, without responsive intermediate institutions like strong churches, families, communities or volunteer groups, results in more dependent and passive citizens.

Media involvement and critical evaluation should be a family project. Establishing lifelong developmental skills and techniques is essential for strong families. We lose the ability to critically scan and responsibly select the sources and amount of information as we become habituated to passively turning on the TV, or other electronic media, without asking ourselves what we expect to gain from participating in this media experience. Watching TV should be active and based upon dialog and interaction. This means actively discussing media presentations before, often during, and definitely after their completion.

Media saturation, i.e., too much viewing, often promotes habitual, passive viewing and the inability to feel in control of our lives. We lose control over our ability to feel we can cope with information. Saturation or overload results from: (a) too much information that is not readily assimilated, therefore becoming noise, and (b) too few media skills on the part of the viewer or user of media. This situation produces "media ignorance" and "media burnout," which prevent children from utilizing TV in a positive manner. In addition to personal and family stress, anxiety, and feelings of powerlessness, information overload leaves media users more susceptible to manipulation.

The family must become a highly interactive and participating unit, which evaluates, critically, all types of electronic media presentations. The family must learn those roles and skills which help them to actively evaluate and confront the potentials of electronic media for expanding cognitive skills and relevant information. New roles must be formulated to enable the family to assimilate vital, relevant information, which, then, can be used as a resource in family decision-making.

A highly interactive family environment facilitates lifelong education. This view supports the concept that personal learning is a family project; frequent family interaction actually increases possibilities for exploring diverse new opportunities for learning and involvement in the lives of others (Marks, 1977: 192-196; Spretzer, et al., 1979).

In contrast to passive family viewing, families can actively facilitate a responsive relationship with TV and other media: (1) The TV set is a voluntaristic object, i.e., it has an "off button" and families should keep account of the time spent on TV watching and gradually reduce that time until it reaches zero and then start a maintenance program of selective viewing; (2) Responsible viewing entails consulting a viewing guide to insure discriminative choices; (3) Public television stations offer unique and varied programming, plus subscriptions to viewing guides, supplementary reading and reference materials and textbooks. Such supplements further enhance the interactive and participatory experience of public television; (4) Cable stations offer a variety of locally oriented and relevant programs. In addition, interactive viewing programs present issues in formats that promote debates, dialog and examination of content by voting, either electronically or by phone; (5) Home video recording devices and computers have recently become affordable to the average family and offer an incredible combination of viewing and learning opportunities. Outstanding software and video programs can be chosen by parents for both their entertainment and educational values.

Although novel as it may seem to most parents, watching television with the children offers parents valuabe opportunities for shaping and modifying the socialization they receive from media. For example, after the program the family can discuss examples of cooperation, affection, or sharing that stood out for them. The family could play games such as "re-write the script" which invites family members to improve upon or humanize the program they just viewed, to make the characters interact in more positive ways.

Educational media programs often facilitate humanistic and informative guidance towards more worthwhile media viewing by providing means to increase viewer discussion and analysis. Parents and children, themselves, can learn to create categories for evaluating films and TV programs. Keeping score cards on programs can increase awareness and become a fun family game, allowing family members to examine the relative merits of the program, characters, script or themes. This approach invites learning, sharing, growth, openness and trust.

The message is clear: parents must be encouraged to use media as a tool for family socialization, not as an electronic baby sitter. We must encourage parents to take an active approach in using media as a resource for healthy and participatory socialization, family communication, social awareness and active involvement with the world.

BIBLIOGRAPHY

Briller, Bert &
Steven Miller

    1984   "Television at the Crossroads: Assessing
Academic Achievement." Society, September-
October, pp. 6-9.

Chaffee, Steven H.,
George Gerbner, Beatrix A. Hamburg,
Eli A. Rubenstien, Alberta E. Siegel
& Jerome L. Singer

    1984   "Defending the Indefensible." Society,
SeptemberOctober, pp. 30-35.

Ellis, Godrey (Ed.)

    1983   "Television and the Family." (Special
Issue) Journal of Family Issues, June
4(2).

Fetler, Mark,

    1984   "Television Viewing and School Achieve-
ment." Journal of Communications,
Spring, pp. 104-118.

Gerbner, George,
Larry Gross, Michael Morgan
& Nancy Signorielli

    1984   "Television at the Crossroads: Facts,
Fantasies and Schools." Society,
September-October, pp. 9-13.

Greenfield, Patricia Marks

    1984   Mind and Media: The Effects of Tele-
vision, Video Games and Computers.
Cambridge, Mass: Harvard University
Press.

Marc, David

    1984   "Understanding Television." The Atlantic
Monthly, August, pp. 33-44.

246

Mander, Jerry

1978   4 Arguments for the Abolition of Tele-
                vision. New York: Morrow & Co.

Marks, S.

1977   "Multiple Roles and Role Strain: Some
                Notes on Human Energy, Time Commitment."
                American Sociological Review, December,
                42, 921-936.

Newman, Susan B.

1984   "Television at the Crossroads: Reading
                Performance." Society, September-
                October, pp. 14-15.

Pearl, David,

1984   "Television at the Crossroads: Violence
                and Aggression." Society, September-
                October, pp. 17-22.

Postman, Neil

1982   The Disappearance of Childhood.   New
                York: Dell Publishing Co.

Salamon, Gabriel &
Tamar Leigh,

1984   "Predisposition about Learning from
                Print and Television." Journal of Com-
                munication, Spring, 119-135.

Spreitzer, E.,
Snyder, E., &
Larson, D.

1979   "Multiple Roles and Psychological Well-
                Being." Sociological Focus, 12(2),
                1241-148.

Wentzer, Alan &
Guy Lometti,

1984   "Researching Television ?" Society,
                September-October, 22-30.

CHAPTER 12

HOME COMPUTERS AND THE FAMILY

Karl P. Reitz*

I. INTRODUCTION

When Thomas Edison invented the light bulb, he started a process that has made electricity an almost indispensible product in the home. It is certain that he did not anticipate the hundreds of ways in which we use electricity in our daily life at home. The light bulb itself was only a device which did not serve any new purpose but only replaced more cumbersome and less esthetic forms of lighting. No one imagined that in only a few short years, a variation on the light bulb would make the new worlds of radio and television possible.

The invention of the microchip is also sure to be an event which is going to bring about vast changes in the way in which we and future generations go about our daily lives. It has been less than fifteen yers since the introduction of the microchip to the general con sumer in the form of simple calculators. Since then, the microchip has not only become more complicated, but also much less expensive. The first hand-held calcu- lator with no memory and only simple arithmetic func- tions cost something in excess of $300. Considering the alternatives available at the time, it was an in- expensive device. Slide rulers, volumes of mathemati- cal tables and bulky mechanical calculating machines were standard fair to those who needed to do extensive calculations. For the same cost as that first calcu- lator, it is now possible to purchase a general purpose computer with thousands of bytes of memory and program- mable in standard computer languages. It is hard to even comprehend the rapidity of this change let alone its consequences.

The first widely purchased computer specifically designed for home use was the Apple. It has been fol- lowed by a large number of products manufactured by an increasingly diverse set of companies. These de- vices have also increased more rapidly in terms of complexity. This change in technology certainly had social consequences, yet the form of these consequences is just recently beginning to be assesed. This assessment is unfortunately doomed to obsolesence almost before being completed.

The large number of computers already in American homes indicates a substantial need, either real or simply perceived. The industry which has virtually mushroomed into being is continuing to foster its own growth by feeding on parents' anxiety over the educational needs of their children. It is possible that the promise of computers as depicted by the advertising agencies of some computer manufacturers will not be met. Yet it is certain that many people have already had their lives changed by computers and are living differently because of the possibilities which the computer has made available.

Among those who have felt the impact of the computer most positively have been the handicapped. The blind are no longer dependent on having sighted people translate the written word into audible speech or braille text. The paralyzed individual has been given moth communication abilities as well as mobility. But they no doubt appreciate most the independence and self respect gained through being able to provide for themselves and to contribute to society. If these consequences of the computer age are the only ones forthcoming then it even now has been a blessing beyond measure. But the computer age is only beginning and there are sure to be more changes both positive and negative.

In this chapter we want to explore the changes which have been brought about by the home computer. We will be particularly interested in the changes which have occured in people's interactions with their families. We will speculate on what consequences these changes may have in the future. The chapter will be divided into sections which pertain to the different ways in which home computers have already been used.

II. ENTERTAINMENT

The largest use of home computers has been for entertainment. Electronic video games were the first products using the microchip technology that were purchased in large numbers for home use. These products featured paddle games with only a few variations. However, the sophistication of these video games began to grow rapidly along with an intense competition between manufacturers. It was not long before the names of these companies became household words, like

Atari, Commodore, Coleco, and others. When it became apparent that general purpose computers like Apple could play games as well as be used for a vast variety of other purposes, the products that could be used only for playing games fell on hard times. Those companies which had committed themselves to producing video games exclusively were hard pressed until they were able to produce inexpensive general purpose computers which would play the games for which they had previously been known as well as the other functions of which a computer is capable. Now, instead of electronic products which only play games, the market is filled with general purpose home computers.

Even though these computers have the capability of doing a wide variety of tasks, they are used mainly for entertainment. The time that people spend on their home computers must come from time spent on other activities. According to one study, this time comes mainly from time spent watching TV. That means that time spent on a passive form of entertainment has been replaced with a less passive form of entertainment.

Although the first games on the home computer were games that required only good reflexes and eye hand coordination. They were soon replaced by more sophisticated games which were borrowed from the electronic arcades. One of the first and most popular of these games is Pac-Man. Pac-Man requires more than coordination from the serious player. It requires the recognition of complex patterns in the movement of ghosts which the player must avoid. It did not take long before the market was filled with a very large and varied collection of home computer games. These included even some of the worlds most sophisticated games such as chess. These games have increased in complexity and can require finely honed cognitive skills. The games which are simple translations of non computer games have not achieved the popularity of those games which utilize the unique features of the computer. They involve fast moving action, a constant changing environment and even a story line. One of the games that has some of these features is the highly popular Zork.

Another significant feature of the popular home computer game is the fact that they are almost always played by just one person in competition only with themselves of the computer. The fact that this solo activity is an important feature of the use of home computers as entertainment is supported by the above

mentioned study which also indicated that one of the
areas in which more rather then less time was spent
was in being alone. Other studies have indicated that
one of the motivations for playing video games is to
be alone. This result contradicted the researchers
expectation that the video arcade was a place for
social gathering as much as for game playing.

Although the video arcade is not the same as a
home computer, its' use in terms of players and their
motivations is paralleled in a short time by versions
of these games on the home computer. The way in which
the video arcade player interacts with the arcade
games is indicative of similar behavior at home with
the home computer. The electronic arcade games have
been on the cutting edge of computer technology. They
have enjoyed a huge success, and have been the margin
of profit for many small businesses which have included them in their establishments. Although several
researchers have suggested that the video arcades serve
the purpose of being a social gathering place, the
evidence indicates differently. Although there is considerable social interaction in a crowded video arcade
most individuals are totally intent on their interaction with their particular game. Social interaction
occurs mainly between those who are waiting in line for
a particularly popular game.

That these video arcade games are an important
source of revenue for the establishments which house
them, is evidenced by the large amounts of money which
are spent on them by the players. Since the same kinds
of skills which are used in playing these games can
also be employed and exercised in non-computer games
such as baseball, basketball, card games, and other
mainly free games, it remains an open question as to
why players prefer the more expensive video arcade
games. The answer may be suggested by the above discussed individualized competition. Few video games
involve inter-human competition. Even if such competition is an option with a particular game, those
options are rarely exercised. On the other hand, the
other games mentioned above almost always involve
inter-human competition. This is supported by the
players of these games in response to question regarding their motives for playing the games. One of the
most significant motivations was to be alone. We may
be witnessing a reaction to the American ideal of
competition. For growing young boys, the American
ideal is one who competes intensely in sports. The
introduction of games which require complex skills,

yet can be played with only the individual being in competition with him or herself, may offer a refuge from the predominance of competition elsewhere. That males in our society are socialized to be competitive may also explain why the predominate sex of the video arcade player is male.

It is interesting sociologically, that one of the main uses of the microchip technology by common people is in the form of entertainment. The major feature of this use are that these games are 1) highly complex and interactive, 2) not inter-human competitive, and 3) usually played alone. Games are a part of every culture and they usually reflect the skills important in that culture. Games are usually played by all the members of a society. Only in our own culture are a substantial number of individuals left out of the major sports because only the best get any reward for their skills. Computer games are designed to reward the player at any level. The more sophisticated a computer game is the more popular it is. This indicates that the players want to be extended to their limits in terms of the number and extent of their skills. That these games are played alone is not as easily explained. Given that humans are intensely social creatures, it would seem that games which involve only one person would not be popular but such is not the case. Early electronic game makers designed their games to be interhuman competitive. But it soon became apparant that the most popular games were those that could be played alone. Most games still allow a two player competition, however that option is rarely exercised. It is probable that this lack of social interaction in video and computer games is an interaction effect with the third feature. The alternate forms of skill using games available to a young male are always intensely interhuman competitive. For those who have not been particularly successful at those competitive pursuits or who simply don't care to be competitive, video and computer games come as a challenging way in which their skills can be exercised.

This hypothesis could be tested by comparing two sets of individuals. The one group would consist of individuals attracted to those sports where individual skills are emphasized (such as baseball or swimming), and the second would be those individuals who prefer participation in games which are more team oriented and which require large amounts of cooperation like basketball. These two groups could be compared in terms of the amount of time playing video and computer games.

III. EDUCATIONAL

The scene opens with a downcast schoolboy handing his obviously poor report card to his distressed father with a concerned mother talking to a knowledgeable and understanding authority. This figure explains that one way in which the parents' child might be helped is by buying him a computer. The following scene shows the now enthusiastic boy working at a computer with an approving father standing behind. The last scene is again like the first, but now the obviously proud and happy boy is showing his report card to delighted parents.

The ad described above is one of many which attempt to give the message to parents that without the advantage of a home computer, today's child cannot hope to compete in the educational world. The purpose of the ad is of course to sell more home computers, but whether the message of the ad is factual is indeed questionable. The ad does reflect the growing interest in computers as assistants in the educational process.

Educational software is probably the second leading seller in the software field. Research on its effectiveness is very mixed. But this is not to say that computers cannot be effective tools in the learning process. Even if computers are not effective as some would like us to believe, it is clear that advances in hardware and software are making them more effective. This means that if computers have not already changed the educational world, they will.

The choice of which computer to buy is not the most difficult choice faced by the computer-buying public. The number of computers available are small compared to the extensive choices available in terms of software. Because this is true the most popular features of magazines published for home computer users are reviews of software. One such review was published in **Psychology Today** with the title "Programs Which Really do Help Children." This title alone indicates some of the cynicism with respect to the computer's efficacy as an educational aid. The most revealing aspect of this review is not in the reviews themselves but in the types of programs which were termed "helpful". Of the 20 programs reviewed, eight had to do with teaching mathematics and most often with counting. Four had to do with language techniques such as spelling, word processing, and reading. Five others had to do with art and music.

From this list it is apparent that programs dealing with mathematical concepts are the leading form
of educational software. That is not too surprising
considering that mathematical computation is the thing
that computers do best. Secondly, the ease with which
one can make corrections in the process of writing,
makes word processing probably the single most used
serious function of the home computer. These two functions together represent the large majority of computer
educational programs. They of course only scratch the
surface of the world of knowledge and skills which are
a part of any child's school experience.

Both math and writing skills are exceedingly important although in different ways. Both are forms
of communication, both involve rules of grammar, and
both contain a fair number of facts which need to be
memorized. Traditional math, however, has been highly
concerned with the processes or techniques with which
one can find the answer to simple numerical operations.
Enormous amounts of school time are used to the end
that after five years of elementary school the typical
student can add, subtract, and divide integer and deci-
mal numbers. These are tasks that the simplest and
least expensive calculators can do. Certainly computers can help in the task of giving students the
practice, and immediate feedback that makes the tedious
task of learning these techniques somewhat easier. But
even more importantly, the computer will allow more
time to be spent on the useful task of learning why and
how these mathematical techniques can be applied.

There are few programs which help teach social
skills, music appreciation, cultural values, creative
expression, and other less structured learning experiences. The increased sophistication of both hardware
and software is making computer aided instruction more
valuable in many areas. However, computers are still a
long way from being of any great help in the teaching
of less structured materials. Probably the best educational software packages available today are those
written by software firms which teach the learner how
to use their particular software packages.

What does this mean from a sociological point of
view? Educational software is not now at a level which
significantly impacts present educational processes.
Schools will continue to operate in at least the near
future similarly to their present operations. However,
the change in software and hardware will mean a sharp
increase in the use of computers as educational aids.

Since computers are not limited to in-school use, more and more educational tasks can and will take place in the home. Because the home computer as opposed to those at school can be used at all hours by all members of the family in a variety of tasks, families will be more willing to spend the money for their own computers rather than contributing money voluntarily or non-voluntarily (in the form of taxes) for school computers. This means that more time at home will be spent in educational pursuits and consequently less time may be spent away at school. An even more important consequence is the ability of children in remote locations to benefit from master teachers who are now designing educational software.

Textbook writers are hampered by their inability to give immediate feedback to their readers. Such is not the case for the software writer. Because of the computer's ability to give immediate feedback to the user, the softerware writer can motivate the student as well as present material. The software materials produced by master writers and educators will be valuable property. The amount of time and therefore money needed to produce good software will probably prevent individuals alone from being significantly involved in producing such material. It will be the large textbook publishers who have the capital to invest in the development of educational software. But once developed it can be mass marketed. Students can learn from well developed software without the help of a teacher, this is something a textbook could never do. This means that students no longer need be in a classroom environment in order for significant learning to take place. It will be like being able to hire the very best tutors at a fraction of the cost. The cost will not be insignificant. Both the best hardware and best software will be afforded by those economically well off.

Economic barriers will increase as the less economically advantaged are less able to afford the constantly changing hardware technologies which will be used. Computers also break the present gread advantage that the public sector has in providing educational opportunities by putting the efforts of skilled educators into the hands of the homecomputer user, not just in the form of the written word but in an interactive mode. Computers also allow for a great deal of individualization. If our collective forms of education are to survive, they will have to recognize their purpose not as means of instilling skills and techniques but as the major socializing institutions of our society. Movement in just the opposite direction has been the trend for public education recently. This prognosis might be mitigated by the fact that the cost of home computers has dropped so dramatically. We may see the day in which it becomes public policy to see that all children will either be given a home computer or at least have unlimited access to computers and good software.

Home computers will therefore make it possible for more of the educational process to take place in the home. At the same time the learning that can be most easily assisted by the home computer will be made less important. It is likely that the kinds of learning experiences which are not as easily transferred by computer may enjoy an increased share of children's time, with the net result that the amount of time spent by children away from home is left unchanged.

IV. ECONOMICS

The increased complexities of the modern home economy have made the home computer a useful device in the management of that complexity. Multiple mortgages, varieties of bank accounts, complex tax shelters, credit card accounts, and other such economic devices all require good record keeping. This is something which the home computer can do very well. Other than word processing programs, the best selling software packages have been those that are called data management programs or spread sheet programs. Although these are two distinct forms of software, their use is almost always economic. They are particularly popular among small businesses. As more individuals learn how to use these programs and as they become more available to home computers, these software packages will find their way into home use.

Recognizing that more families will have home computers, banks are preparing to allow home computers to "talk" to their own computers. Rather than mailing statements to account holders, the home computer owner will be able to inquire about his or her account without leaving home and at any point in time. The account holder will be able to pay their bills and to make transfers between accounts simply by directing his bank's computer to carry out the transaction. At this writing there is only a very small amount of this type of remote banking transactions taking place. However, the use of bank terminals for use by after hours business is on the increase and yet has become increasingly dangerous as criminals take advantage of the unprotected terminal user. Except as cash dispensing machines, automatic tellers provided by banks at remote sites are nothing more than remote terminals. The ability to execute banking duties in the safety of one's home will be an attractive alternative.

Modems which are devices which allow a home computer to "talk" over telephone lines to other computers make it possible for home computers to be used as terminals to larger computers. This development will decrease the amount of mail which is composed of bills. Billing in paper form will no longer be necessary. Bills are only hard copy forms of computer records. Transferring these records to the home electronically could mean substantial savings in energy. If hard copy form of these records were desired by the account owner he or she could simply have their own computer print such a copy. All of the trips made by a consumer to the bank to deposit their payroll checks, to the postoffice to buy stamps, and by the postal personnel to deliver bills and payment checks could be eliminated. This shift from a paper economy of checks moving from place to place to an electronic economy where electronic information will move from place to place will be an even greater shift than the shift from a money economy to a paper economy.

Since economic transactions will increasingly take place through one's own home computer, the task of entering these transactions into the computer for record keeping purposes will no longer be necessary. The banks records of one's account may be automatically transferred to one's own records. This will make data management and budget type programs for the home even more useful. It will allow the home computer user the capability of quick graphic representations of one's own budget processes. Such budget awareness could change people's economic priorities. For example, the fastest growing sector of the American economy is in services. People may become aware that their own jobs provide services to others who are in turn providing services to others who finally provide services to those at the start who need services provided them because they are out working to provide services and so on. This specialization of services has made service work increasingly sterile and uninteresting. People's awareness of this fact and the amounts they pay for services may give them the courage to provide their own services, and which will in turn reduce their own dependence, their boredom, and their vulnerability to exploitation.

258

It is hard to assess the consequences of the move to an electronic economy. There are some who believe that such a move increases the risk of a "Big Brother" type government. Since telecommunication can be monitored easily, an electronic economy makes the privacy of one's own financial dealings difficult to protect. From a bankers point of view, we are already in an electronic economy since most bank records are in computer form and electronic transfers between banks a reality. These records can be monitored and subpoenaed in legal proceedings. The risk of "Big Brother" occuring is scarcely increased by giving individuals the same capability.

There are also those who feel that financial transactions via telecommunication make them more vulnerable to fraud as exemplified by the rise in credit card fraud. Whether this is because credit cards are more vulnerable to criminal activity or because credit cards are being used more is open to question. Criminal activity will no doubt keep up with the best technology. Technology can also be used to increase the security in electronic finances. For example, there is some research taking place which might result in the replacement of the signature with an image of one's retina as the means of identification.

The home computer has had an impact in home financial matters mainly in terms of record keeping. This is going to change in the very near future. Already several companies are test marketing services in which customers can tie their computers into their bank's computers in order to request transfers of money from account to account, to pay bills, and to determine balances. The same services allow the customer to shop and order items from selected stores. All of this can be done without leaving one's home.

V. TELECOMMUTING

The way in which home computers are likely to have their greatest impact is via the ability of workers to do their work at home. A growing proportion of people today are employed not in production of hard goods but in "paper pushing." Paper pushing is the processing of information. This processing is increasingly being done not on paper but in an electronic format. In most companies, clerks and secretaries need to be in close proximity to each other and to the file cabinets which are the storage media for paper documents. This necessity for workers prox-

259

imity to these paper storage devices is to facilitate the physical movement of each single item, which collectively forms an emmense flow of paper in a typical office building. If each piece had to be moved any substantial distance, the costs in terms of time and energy would be prohibitive.

If however, a company's "file cabinets" were electronic mass storage devices which could be accessed via telephone lines, the need to move the clerk each day into close proximity to the "file cabinets" would be eliminated. Now the employee could reach into the file cabinet from his or her own home. A number of companies already have realized that it makes sense to allow workers to do their job in their own homes. They save money by not having to provide these workers with office space, cafeterias, air conditioning, parking spaces, day care centers, and the other amenities of the modern office complex. All the worker needs to have is a terminal or better yet a computer at home and a telephone line to the companies computers.

One company which has employees working at home is Blue Cross/Blue Shield of Washington D.C. These workers enter insurance claims into the companies computers via terminals and telephones from their own homes. They are paid by the number of claims they process. Many of them are women with children. By working at home they can care for their children and attend to their needs and at the same time be earning a living. According to Electronic Services Unlimited, as many as 10,000 employees in the United States are similarly earning their livings staying at home and yet working for companies located elsewhere. They accomplish this by "telecommuting."

Telecommuting will not establish itself as a major work pattern overnight. The implications that telecommuting has for the traditional work place are immense. The changes that telecommuting entail are going to make companies very wary in adopting it as the norm. Traditional lines of authority will be impossible. Traditional ways of monitoring work habits will have to be replaced. Loyalty to the company and identification with it will no doubt drastically decrease. At the same time, actual production in terms of documents produced, and time spent can be accurately assessed and monitored for each employee. Because the usual ways of monitoring an employee's performance will not be production. This will no doubt lead to piece rate pay as in the example above. If workers are plentiful, such a trend would be profitable to employers. It would be similar to the situation occuring in the garment industry where women are paid piece rates for sewing garments in their homes. Since these workers are usually not organized, their wages are often quite low.

Workers have usually won higher pay by organizing. In the past this has meant that they have had to meet and discuss face to face matters of common interest. Telecommuting would tend to make such meetings difficult if not impossible. However, the same technology which makes telecommuting possible also makes teleconferencing possible. Telecommuters in a particular industry could easily organize themselves into a teleconference in which they could discuss again their common interests without leaving their homes. This type of conferencing would be most likely among higher skilled workers, who at the same time would be in greater demand.

Another change that telecommuting makes possible is that workers would no longer need to live within east regular commuting distance from their place of work. The technology which makes possible really fast data transmission over standard phone lines has been rapidly improving. This means that it is no longer necessary to tie up an expensive phone line for any length of time in order to telecommute. An entire day's worth of data entry could be burst over a phone line in a very short period of time. This means that a worker could almost live anywhere in the country and still communicate relatively inexpensively with his or her companies computers. Employees will choose to live where they want to live, not where their jobs dictate they live.

In a time when both members of a married couple are pursuing careers and are facing decisions about how to change jobs without uprooting the other member, these consequences of telecommuting will be most welcome. There have probably been a large number of couples who have separated or divorced because job transfers or career advancements by one of the members of the couple have necessitated moves which the other member was unwilling to make. The breakup of the extended kinship networks in the move from rural areas to urban areas in the search of jobs has long been noted. A long term consequence of telecommuting may in fact mean a reduction in the number of kinship separations and may precipitate a return of the extended family.

The home computer now used mainly for games, may in the future be the key to the solution to some of society's most pressing problems. The breakup of the nuclea family as well as the extended family has been pinpointed as one of the major sources of difficulties in our society. Drug use, crime, poor educational performance, lack of moral training, child abuse, and many others have been associated with a breakdown of the family. Computers may ease some of the pressures which have caused this breakdown. The involvement of both parents in childrearing may also be a consequence. Societies in which such dual sex childrearing is the norm have been shown to be among a world with less violence, they will indeed have become a positive force.

Telecommuting may also ease the rate at which the world is gobbling up its nonrenewable resources. If it is no longer necessary to move the masses of people from home to job and back again each day, huge savings in energy would result. World tensions which are caused by the need for these resources would be eased. For these reasons alone it would seem that telecommuting should be encouraged at all levels.

VI. SOCIAL IMPLICATIONS

We have already indicated that the advent of the computer and its introduction into the home will have major implications for the future and the ways in which we live our lives. Many of these implications will be in the social realm. There has been a tendency among those who have given social concerns precedence in their lives to view computers with some trepidation. This fear has not been unjustified. Those who own home computers have been shown to spend less time with their families, more time alone and more time at work. On the face of this evidence, it would seem apparent that computers at home increase the alienation which has already plagued the American household.

These negative first results however are a consequence of the fact that our major institutions have as yet not really come to grips with the possibilities raised by the computer age. As has been already pointed out, the possibilities educationally and in work related ways make for an individualization and flexibility in terms of place as well as time and rate

262

that heretofore was impossible. Neither schools nor companies have really recognized or taken advantage of these possibilities. Therefore early users of the home computer have been doing so on top of the time they already spend at work or at school. The fact that they are probably mastering their work or their learning at a faster rate than their coworkers, has probably not occurred to their teachers or supervisors. When educators and managers begin recognizing that progress and production can indeed take place at home, changes will be forthcoming. Until then, workers who wish to learn the full capabilities of their computers will have to do it to the detriment of some of their other optional activities.

Not until the immense possibilities of the personal computer have been fully explored by our educational and industrial institutions, will there be much in the way of major social impact. But when (not if) that happens, some major changes in our social world will be apparent. Probably the single most important change will be that both parents will be the major sources of influence in a child's life. Similarly as people are free to choose where they live instead of having their jobs dictate their residence, kin will again be of major importance. Personal lifestyles will also not likely be dictated by companies. Since company directors and managers will have little in the way of direct contact with their employees, workers will tend to live in nonhomogeneous ways. One could imagine a man with long hair and a beard, sitting under a tree overlooking a small lake, with his cabin nearby. His children are playing around him, he has a portable computer on his lap, and is in the middle of his day's work for IBM.

*Karl P. Reitz, Department of Social Relations and Department of Computer Science, Chapman College, Orange, California.

CHAPTER 13

THE FAMILY AND THE FIRM:
A COEVOLUTIONARY PERSPECTIVE

Elaine Kepner*

The unique nature of the family-owned firm has presented dilemmas and frustrations to those who manage, work in, and consult with such firms. Organizational theorists have found it difficult to apply their taskoriented, competency-based models to a business in which the boundaries between task and kinship considerations overlap. Practitioners who work with such organizations find that the types of interventions successful in other situations are likely to be rejected or to be found inadequate in dealing with the particular complexities involved. Founders are called on to make choices that put them in "no win" double-bind situations. If they base their decisions on what the firm needs, kinship bonds may be disrupted and damaged; if they choose to honor family bonds, the business is likely to suffer.

I. THE UNIQUE PROBLEMS OF THE FAMILY FIRM

What can be done to understand this unique form of organization and respond to the types of crises that seem to be inherent in it? Early practitioners in the art of working with family firms attempted to identify the primary sources of the problems that plague them from a linear-causal perspective. The most salient causes identified include the nature of the entrepreneurial personality, disturbances in the father-son relationship, nepotism, and the influence of family dynamics on executive and management decisions.

Recently, new perspectives based on an "open systems" approach have emerged. While they differ in many repects from each other, the various perspectives all regard the family and firm as sub-systems of a metasystem in which boundary conditions are overly diffuse and permeable, resulting in a high degree of mutual influence that is dysfunctional when viewed from the firm's perspective. Intervention strategies are designed to strengthen and regulate the boundary conditions of each system to prevent spillover of family agendas into executive and management decisions.

However, a view of the family firm as a total system has yet to be fully developed. All of the

265

literature on the family-owned business has been written from the firm's perspective. Although it does acknowledge that family dynamics intrude on the rational functioning of the business, little or no attention has been given to that other part of this complex system: the family as a system. The firm's perspective is structured by its primary consideration: the adaptation and effective functioning of the business. Yet this view fails to take into account the fact that the tightly interwoven strands of family and firm may not be disentangled without seriously disrupting one or both systems. The firm's dualistic perspective focuses on one system at the price of the other: One gets the impression that the family is still something of a scapegoat in the family-firm system. This dualism ultimately sets the family and the firm at loggerheads with each other.

An alternative view of the family firm would transform this dualistic view into a comprehensive one that would violate neither family nor firm as systems. From a systems perspective, one cannot consider the family firm without assuming that the behavior of any one part of a system will influence and be influenced by all other parts of the system. The family may act upon and influence the firm but, at the same time, it is influenced by the communications it receives from the firm.

When the maintenance of the family's integrity and cohesiveness is a consideration, as the chief executive often makes it, we need to begin to ask a different set of questions. For example:

°What is the nature of the interactive relationship between the family and the firm?

°How do events in one subsystem affect the other, leading to a crisis in the system as a whole?

°Given the interpretation of these sub-systems, how can one go about unraveling the complex of intertwined strands so that the fabric of each system is not irreparably damaged?

This chapter attempts to expose the complexity of relational patterns between the firm and the family, and within the family itself. The ecology of the family firm as a whole system cannot be comprehended unless the more neglected half of the system is, for the moment, placed in the foreground.

266

II. THE COEVOLUTION OF FAMILY AND FIRM

At the founding stage of the family firm, those in each of the respective systems perceive the other as being distinct, separate, and well-bounded. The relationship between family and firm is not considered problematic. The founder usually creates and develops the enterprise at the same time that he or she creates a marriage and has a family. The founder is not trying to build a family business but is driven by a need to actualize an idea or set of values, with a preference for controlling the destiny of that which is created. The spouse is usually occupied with developing skills as parent and homemaker, and as the creator of a social and extended-family network. The mission of each of these systems is sufficiently different and compelling that the illusion of separateness can be maintained for many years, even though each subsystem is developing a force field of its own with respect to the other.

The purpose of the business is to make money. Even though people development may be a widely held value, the firm must produce goods and/or services at a profit, or it cannot survive. This goal is explicit and commonly understood. To support this, the firm develops structures, processes, and control mechanisms on the basis of "rationally" derived management models or empirically tested practices, which are also explicitly labeled. Whatever the model, authority and responsibility are distributed hierarchically; there is a clear division of labor and function, and activities are coordinated in a planned manner. Because an organization is fundamentally a pattern of roles and a blueprint for their coordination, it exists independently of particular people and can survive in spite of 100 percent turnover of membership.

On the other hand, a family is in the business of caring for and developing people; its boundaries are sustained by face-to-face contact, and membership in that system is by blood, not through criteria of competence. How a particular family interprets its goals and carries them out is highly variable, depending on culture, social class, values, and personal idiosyncracies. But both the goals and the manner in which the family operationalizes them are rarely explicitly labeled. Instead, it is necessary to infer norms, operating procedures, roles, and decision-making processes from the family's behaviors and communication patterns. Furthermore, such tangible criteria as profit-and-loss statements give a business a decided

267

barometer of its success. The criteria used to measure success in a family are loose and intangible terms, such as the level of each member's self-esteem, the members' ability to function as responsible and autonomous human beings in an age-appropriate manner and, finally, the experience of affectional ties and a sense of loyalty upon which the system as a whole depends.

Let us now focus on the family as a system before elaborating further on the co-evolution of family and firm and the interactive effects of one upon the other.

III. THE FAMILY SYSTEM

In this section, I will be providing a context for understanding family systems in general, their purpose as satisfiers of certain universal human needs, the way they are organized to perform their functions, and the cultural dimensions by which they regulate themselves and their development. Under each of these topics, I will describe the ways in which the family's organization and culture are influenced by its relationship with a firm.

The family is a social system endorsed by law and custom to take care of its members' needs. The glue that holds it together through the vicissitudes of its lifecycle transitions and the intricate, complicated interpersonal linkages are the emotional bondings and affectionate ties that develop between and among its members, as well as a sense of responsibility and loyalty to the family as a system.

The family functions as a whole system. Actions of one family member affect and influence the actions of all other members and the system as an entity. For example, the wife who wants to return to school or to her former career introduces shifts that affect the homeostasis of the system. All members will feel the impact. If this shift is supported and maintained, the system's rules and norms will change, and other individuals will experience the stress of new norms as they take on different responsibilities and roles. If this shift is not supported, the system becomes dysfunctional in terms of its purpose: One or more family members will carry the symptoms of dysfunction—in this case, probably the couple in terms of an increased emotional distance between husband and wife.

IV. PURPOSE OF THE FAMILY

In addition to providing for the economic security of its members, the family must satisfy deep social and emotional needs for belonging, affection, and intimacy, and it must provide a sense of identity that includes experiencing one's self as a source of influence and power.

Belonging Needs. All of us need to feel that we belong to and can be accepted as a member of a group. To be included gives us a sense of our self-worth.

Intimacy Needs. Intimate attachments are not baseed on one's dependency needs alone. Instead, they are predicated on valuing and cherishing the other for who the person is, rather than for what the person could or should be. This attachment can be depended on over time and through changing circumstances; it survives through periods of conflict and separation. What the family provides, as no other institution can, is an orderly access to intimacy.

Identity and autonomy needs. Just as we are drawn toward others to share and to connect, so do we need to pull apart and differentiate ourselves from the herd. It is through separating that we find out who we are: Our identity is a process of distinguishing ourselves from everyone else. We discover our unique qualities, capabilities, and values by experienceing our differences. To do this, we must be able to say "no," to exert influence on others and the flow of events that sometimes threaten to engulf us, and to feel that we have the power to make our own chocies and to take responsibility for their consequences.

This inherent rhythm that pulls people together and pushes them apart is a polarity that every family must manage. If there is too much individuation, with each person doing his or her own thing, the system suffers. On the other hand, too much unity and merging causes the individual to become so enmeshed in the family that he or she cannot separate and become an autonomous and competent adult.

V. THE ORGANIZATION OF THE FAMILY

To satisfy and manage the needs of belonging, intimacy, and identity, the family organizes itself by dividing labor and allocating responsibility into different parts, or subsystems. The obvious categories are the couple, the parents, and the children. Each of these subsystems performs certain specialized functions for the family, and each of them maintains a boundary between itself and the other subsystems.

The spouse subsystem has a two-fold function: to meet the personal and interpersonal needs of the husband and wife and to carry the leadership dimension for the system as a whole. It must maintain certain separate activities and privacy boundaries to differentiate itself from the rest of the system. As a policy-making body, it decides on such things as the way family resources will be used, where and when family members will go on vacation, who will manage the finances, how the family will relate to their in-laws, who will be included in the extended family and social network, how aging parents will be cared for, and so forth.

As soon as they marry, couples begin to work out the rules about who is to take charge of which area and under what circumstances. There are three basic modes of relating with respect to leadership in the spouse system: Symmetrical, complementary, and reciprocal.

A symmetrical relationship is a competitive one in which each spouse needs to prove to the other that he or she is just as good, powerful, skillful, and intelligent as the other. It is a relationship in which each one is simultaneously indicating a wish to determine the rules and to have equal control. A status struggle begins, and once such a behavioral sequence starts it often spreads and becomes pervasive.

A complementary relationship is one in which one spouse is in charge of certain areas while the other spouse has different areas of control. Traditionally, roles and responsibilities were differentiated along gender lines: The husband, who provided the major financial income, made the decisions involving allocation of resources; the wife ran the household as she wished, disciplined and supervised the children, and spent whatever funds she deemed necessary to care for the family. However, today's age of affluence and egalitarian values has led to a general loosening of the traditional role definitions and to increasingly complex marital relationships.

Today, the mode of many marriages is a reciprocal relationship in which spouses alternate between symmetrical and complementary modes of relating, depending on the nature of the situation to be managed and their respective talents and resources.

The parenting subsystem evolves as the couple have children and begin to raise a family. As parents, the couple work out ways of managing the education and upbringing of their children. Whether or not they discuss these matters and consciously decide how they will do this, their behavioral interactions with the children determine the way in which conflicts among the siblings will be managed and the way in which attention, nurturance, support, and limit setting will be handled for each child.

The sibling subsystem is a peer learning group. Siblings relate to each other for mutual support, and for some caretaking and care-giving functions. It is the environment in which social and educational skills and competencies are acquired; it is also the arena in which competitiveness and assertiveness are developed and sometimes honed to a fine edge as they compete for the love, attention, and approval of their parents. Their existence as a subsystem provides a sense of mission for the parents and can be a transformative and transpersonal developmental experience for the parents.

Triangling

When spouses are unable to meet each other's needs for affection and companionship or unable to resolve the inevitable differences and conflicts between them, they may make an alliance with one or more of the children and draw that child into the spouse subsystem as a third member. The child becomes overly involved or enmeshed with that parent, and the usual generational boundaries are breached. Such triangles develop in a number of ways: The parent becomes the child's protector, and the child becomes the parent's protector. Sometimes the parent may draw one child in for support in a conflict with the other marital partner; thus the child may become either (1) a judge or advocate in the spouse system or (2) the scapegoat of the system by being the symptom bearer (getting ill, failing in school, or engaging in delinquent behavior). This forces the parents to align themselves with each other to deal with the "sick child."

Other sets of people or entities that are outside the nuclear family may be "triangled" into the spouse subsystem. These may not be physically present, but they exist in the hearts and heads of one or both of the spouses. These may be one or more members of the family of origin, one or both spouses' careers, or the family business. In a first-generation family business, the interloper may be the founder's "kitchen cabinet"-- people who are like a second family to him or her. As one founding entrepreneur labeled it after analyzing a dream he had after a consultation on succession, "I realized that my trusted and valuable colleagues in the firm are my symbolic 'mistress'." For the family involved with a firm, the business may be experienced as a shadowy but nonetheless potent third party to their family life.

VI.   DIMENSIONS OF FAMILY CULTURE

According to Edgar Schein, "culture" is a human invention; it is a way of perceiving and thinking--of judging, evaluating, and feeling; it is a way of acting in relation to others and a way of doing things and solving problems. Culture deals with the problems of internal integration and social survival and, as such, it tends to be passed on as a preferred set of solutions to successive generations. The pattern of culture that has been adopted or inherited serves to reduce anxiety by providing a set of guidelines as a basis for action; it gives purpose, value, and meaning to what might otherwise be experienced as overwhelming or confusing events. Families develop rules to enforce their cul- ture; these rules are usually covert, but can be in- ferred from behavior and communications.

Families can be described in cultural terms by the way in which they manage differences and conflicts, individuation, emotional expressiveness, the congruence of their perception of reality, and separation and loss.

Management of Conflicts

Management of conflicts refers to the way in which a family system deals with differences between and among its members. Some differences are prefer- ences, the resolution of which is arrived at by a pro- cess of "give and take." Other differences may be pro- found: Differences in values and in perceptions about the system's goals and purposes are not so easily re- solved. They may be dilemmas that must be managed rather than problems that can be solved. Some families believe that differences are dangerous. They suppress acknowledgement of them and discourage attempts by anyone in the system to bring them into awareness. But these conflicts do not go away; they simply go underground and are expressed indirectly through simple withdrawal or through passive-aggressive behavior.

The spouse relationship usually prescribes the way in which differences will be managed in the family system. Symmetrical couple relationships are likely to produce families in which differences are expressed spontaneously, continually, and in an escalating fashion--without benefit of a direct encounter and conflict negotiation about the differences. These relationships breed a "no-win" situation. Complementary families, in which parental roles are well differentiated and the leadership style is authoritarian tend to apply rigid rules about what is right and wrong and reject influences that would compromise these rules. Reciprocal families would be more likely to listen to different points of view, encourage discussion and negotiation, and try to come to a resolution that, if not perfect, can be lived with. They are also likely to have some healing mechanisms or rituals that validate the person and support their self-esteem during and after the battles.

Obviously, the way differences are managed affects the kind of influence that people can wield and their individual sense of power as an influencer.

Individuation

Individuation may be nonacceptable, tolerated, or encouraged in families. Pressure may be brought to bear so that everyone thinks and feels alike, and differentiation is actively discouraged. In families where nondifferentiation is extreme, the identity of one person becomes fused or enmeshed with that of another; parent-child relationships are symbiotic, and each cannot, or will not, get along without the other. A little further along the continuum are families that permit a type of individuation that is consistent with the rules, range, and norms of their culture. Criticisms of deviant behavior are frequent, either by discrediting, blaming, or scapegoating (that is, seeing the problem as a fault or basic inadequacy in the individual). In other families a high degree of individuation and autonomy is fostered, and children are listened to and have appropriate influence on family decisions.

Emotional Expressiveness

Feelings and emotions are some of the resources that we, as human beings, are born with and develop. They give us information about what makes us feel good, how we want to relate to others, and what we want to do with our lives. Feelings enable us to be affectionate, to say no or yes, to be empathetic, and to care for others as well as ourselves. Some family cultures are based on the assumption that feelings are unreliable, embarrassing, and not to be trusted, so that the members never learn to accurately label and differentiate between one set of feelings and another. The expression of feeling is either very subdued, inhibited, or ritualistic. Some families are more comfortable with the expression of negative feelings and the quality of their empathy is somewhat strained. By contrast, some family cultures can encompass and value both negative and positive feelings, and encourage the expression of feelings that are appropriate to the context. Negative emotions are accepted as information, and the members are quick to pick up the feelings of others and to approach problems with directness and with a lack of defensiveness.

Acceptance of Change, Separation and Loss

A number of critical transition periods in the family life cycle, beginning with the marriage, impact on the family as a system: the birth of the first child; the early years of raising and educating the the children; management of teenagers struggling to be autonomous and free, the process of becoming a launching center for the next generation while maintaining a suportive home base, maintenance of ties with children and grandchildren, revitalization of the marriage in the middle years, and adjustment to age and retirement. Each of these transitions is marked by progressive increases in the degree of separation, and the feelings of loss that the separation entails may be painfully intense during certain transition periods.

In families, major transitions occur every five to seven years; so within a given time period, it has had more practice in managing transitions than have such larger social systems as organizations, whose life cycle spans a longer time frame. The capacity to accept separation and loss--to grieve and then let go and move on--is at the heart of the skill repertoire needed for healthy family adaptation. In a sense, a competent family of origin "self-destructs," and

274

families vary in their ability to deal with this. However, whatever the degree of competency the family has developed to deal with separation and loss, the stress is compounded when transitions in the family life cycle coincide with transition crises in the life cycle of the firm. At these times (for example, during the succession-planning process) each system is concerned about maintaining the integrity of its own system boundaries and is more resistant to differentiation and separation. The major symptoms of dysfunction in the family/firm relationship are likely to occur during the periods of simultaneous transition stress in each of the systems.

VII. PERCEPTION OF REALITY AND FAMILY MYTHS

Families' cultures are based on certain beliefs and assumptions that create a matrix of shared meaning and a perception of reality that is experienced by all system members. This can be influenced, for example, by parental attitudes about the meaning of life.

Some parents take their children as they are and go with the flow of their unique developmental process. The meaning the child makes out of this is that life is a fluid dance; errors in form and performance are part of living and the dancer can trust his or her own feelings and perceptions to take him or her through the next series of steps. Other parents, who feel that there are things one does to guarantee success in life, mold their offspring to fit a particular pattern: if life is a dance, it is a highly formalized waltz. This child's view of reality is that there is a fixed path one must tread, that there are right and wrong "steps" to make, and that one must discern the correct moves to make.

Among the many facets of a family's shared perceptions, two stand out as significant: the myths held by a family and the way these myths are a set of well-integrated beliefs; they form the group's inner image of itself, allowing a positive perception to be maintained despite flagrant evidence to the contrary. Take, for example, parents who have had a relatively easy time raising young children; they still see themselves as a happy, untroubled family even though one adolescent son has a drinking problem and the daughter has just run away from home for the fourth time. Family myths also refer to fixed-role perceptions, as illustrated by the family members who continue to treat the eldest daughter, who was a rebellious child, as the

275

"bad, irresponsible child," even though she has earned a Ph.D. and raised a family. The child who was the "late bloomer" is still seen as a slow learner by the family despite later success in academia and business.

Family myths are often internalized by the individuals involved; although they are distortions of present reality and needs, they continue to operate in the roles these individuals play out in their adult lives, including those they take in the family firm. The eldest son who has been the responsible child becomes the guardian of the family assets; the aggresive one in the family takes over the business.

VIII. THE FIRM'S EFFECTS ON THE FAMILY

The particular way in which the family's cultural dynamics are influenced by their relationship with a firm will vary depending on such factors as the management model adopted by the firm (which may be a royalist, competency-based, or mixed model), the clarity with which boundaries and opportunities presented by the firm to family members are communicated, and the particular family culture that develops independent of the firm's influences. Given these qualifications, there are certain influences the firm will have on the family dynamics because the firm is a part of the psychological if not the actual environment of the family. It is always a "third party" that is carried around in the minds of people in the family system. The health of both the individual and the system is affected more by how it manages and adapts to forces that impinge on it rather than by what it has to manage. The conditions I will be describing do not necessarily produce unmanageable stress; they simply represent a different set of dilemmas for the families involved in a firm situation.

I would like to look at some of the interactions within the family and between family and firm that affect the family as a while system--its subsystems and the family culture. These family dynamics then bleed over into the firm and back to the family in a circular, cybernetic pattern.

IX. EFFECTS ON THE FAMILY SYSTEM

The family as a system derives some of its sense of belonging, influence, and social identity from being related to a successful enterprise and a successful entrepreneur. This is a mixed blessing because certain

276

costs and consequences--for example, a heavy social and travel calendar in the service of the firm--may put time and energy constraints on the intimate relationships in the system. The famly may feel responsible for protecting and projecting their image of being a well-functioning and cohesive family, and masking or ignoring the ordinary conflicts and strains of family life.

The effects of this are illustrated by the reminiscences of a 32-year-old founder's son in the business for five years:

> Growing up in this family was like being a member of a royal family. A lot of people knew me and treated me well just because my father had an important business in the community. It had its good points, though. I always knew what I could do when I grew up, and I had a lot of advantages other kids didn't have, like trips to Europe every summer and the best bike on the block. But my parents made a federal case out of every mistake I made. When I goofed off at school or got into some minor scrapes as a teenager, they'd blast me about what that would do to the family's image in the community. Well, "Blast the business," I thought at that time. Now that I'm in the business and slated to take over when Dad retires, I worry about whether I'll ever be able to fit into the old man's shoes. It's a bit more than I expected or bargained for.

X. EFFECTS ON SPOUSE AND PARENTING SUBSYSTEMS

The social demands of the business may seriously intrude on the energy and time available to the couple for time alone. In the traditional family business in which the founder is the male head of the family, the typical family relational pattern is a "complementary one"; he is in charge of the economic security for the family, and she is in charge of the home, child rearing, and social and community responsibilities. Basically, the wife accomodates to support the husband's demanding career. While this life structure may be eminently satisfying to many women, it does constrain and limit her choices. Many younger wives today find this situation not entirely satisfactory. But it is difficult to push the system's existing boundaries when the financial and social benefits that flow from the business through the husband are so pleasurable. And it is an onerous task to move into a more challenging

stance when the husband is such an important authority
figure in the family system and is, moreover, perceived
by those who are outside the family as such a powerful
and important person.

For the father in such families, the dilemmas are
also painful and exhausting. Whether the message is
given directly or indirectly by the parents, by the
time the children are grown up and enter the business
as second-generation leaders, they know they will inherit the business assets in some way. Along with
the firm's executives, they experience themselves as
stakeholders in the business. They have a special
interest in how the business will be managed and/or the
way in which the assets will be distributed, and perhaps they confuse the differences between management
and ownership--possibly because they have seen their
father, the first-generation founder, being successful
in both roles. In any event, the children's attempts
to exert influence on father as they come into the
business, or as he is getting ready to retire, may make
him appear more resistant to retirement than ever.

As one owner said:

I didn't develop this business to create a safe
nest for my family. I was simply carrying out
my mission in the world--creating an extension
of myself and my values. Of course, I'm very
pleased that I will leave my wife and children
with an assured income because they will inherit
the stock ownership. But now I'm getting ready
to retire and I find myself feeling resentful
toward my children because they take for granted
what I fought for and finally achieved. They
and the executives in the business, whom I also
brought up, so to speak, are squabbling about
"their" rights! Sometimes I want to shout "A
plague on both your houses" and sell this damn
thing to the highest bidder!

XI.   EFFECTS ON SIBLING SUBSYSTEMS

It is a universal and normal phenomenon for children to compete with each other for preferential treatment from parents. From the child's perspective, there
are always inequities and injustices, some of them inherent in their birth order. Younger children envy the
capabilities and privileges enjoyed by the older ones;
the older ones resent that the younger ones are babied
and allowed "to get away with murder." Female children

278

resent the roles and rewards conferred on their brothers, and frequently vice versa. Middle children, sandwiched between their sibings, have their own axes to grind. All of them try to compete for the love, care, approval, and attention of the parents, no matter how hard they try to be fair.

Sibling rivalries begin as soon as the second child is born into a family, and frequently these hostilities continue throughout their lives. During adolescence, however, as the children begin to leave home, they bond with peer groups and develop outside love relationships, and the rivalries begin to dissipate. As the children separate from the family of origin and establish lives and careers of their own, they may even begin to regard their siblings as people for whom they have some real fondness. In a family firm, on the other hand, it is easy to transfer childhood feuds into the business arena. Furthermore, the roles and rewards conferred by the father on the children who come into the business are experienced as symbols of the father's love, regard, and preference--which exacerbates the original rivalries even further.

From a normal developmental perspective, the father-son relationship is fraught with ambivalences on both sides, and is a difficult one to manage. Usually the son both (1) identifies with father and wants to be like him and (2) competes with him for the mother's attention. When the son enters the business and the father becomes his supervisor, the problems are compounded. One owner of a successful business of his own and the son of an entrepreneurial founder tells this somewhat poignant story.

> I'm the son of a founder, but I went out on my own after working for Dad for eight years; I'm happy to report that I now own a thriving business of my own. I just couldn't take it anymore--working in Dad's business. It was ruining me and tearing the two of us farther apart. Now my sons are in college and I've already told them there will be no place for them in my business. It's hard enough to build a decent father-son relationship, and it just gets too damned complicated when father becomes boss or teacher. My sons, of course, think I'm just being arbitrary and stingy. I guess you just can't win in a situation like this.

279

If one of the sons becomes the wife's favorite, she may promote him for leadership in the firm--which further alienates father from son. This will be acted out as the father introduces and manages the son's career in the firm.

The father-daughter relationship and the daughter's development is also more complicated than usual. Family businesses usually operate on the principle of primogeniture; the mantle of leadership is passed on to the males in the family--usually to the first-born son. With some rare exceptions, the daughters are not considered in the line for succession. Growing up in such a situation creates subtle but powerful reinforcements for already existing cultural stereotypes.

Sometimes the father is ambivalent about the role of daughters in the business--a situation that creates a double-bind situation for the daughters. The case of an empire-building entrepreneur illustrates the rebound effects of this on the firm, the daughters, and the family. Father had encouraged her to major in economics in college and to earn a Master's degree in business administration. Because she demonstrated competence in the business as a vice-president in charge of financial planning for six years, she expected to be chosen as one of the inner circle in the succession plans. Her father died unexpectedly one month after her younger brother, the heir apparent, had graduated from college. She relates:

> The succession plan my father left turned over the leadership to my brother and a small group of nonfamily professionals, with no mention or provision for me at all. I felt betrayed and humiliated by my father. I've always been very close to my brother, but now I can't look him in the eye without wanting to scream. I'm sorely tempted to cash in my stock--although I know that would create havoc with the business right now-- and go to work for one of our competitors!

Daughters who do not choose to enter the business may fall back on the time-honored option for women of exerting their influence vicariously--for example, by promoting their husband's career in the family business to protect their interests. When conflict develops between her husband and father, or her husband and her brothers, she finds herself in a dilemma. She may be forced to choose between loyalty to her own nuclear family and her family of origin. Daughters who do enter the business, on the other hand, must deal with the usual array of subtle and overt resistance in what has been a predominantly male domain, with the added burden of being the boss's daughter.

XII. EFFECTS OF THE FAMILY SYSTEM'S CULTURAL DIMENSIONS

Of the five separate but interrelated family culture dimensions previously discussed, the ones most likely to be influenced by the family's relationshp to the firm are those dealing with management of conflict, individuation, and perception of reality.

Management of Conflict

Willingness to acknowledge difference and appreciate deviance from cultural norms varies, of course, from family to family, but the pressure on a family-firm family to maintain an image of cohesiveness may suppress family conflicts. Furthermore, the economic interdependence between family and firm makes it difficult for people to tell each other when their needs for belonging, influence, and intimacy are not being met. Although the business may be perceived as an intrusive "third party" in the family's life, it is problematic to bite the hand that feeds you. Furthermore, the family frequently views father as a powerful or heroic larger-than-life figure. The children may find the normal testing of authority boundaries as too threatening. With these factors operating in the system, the family may not provide itself with an opportunity to learn healthy conflict-negotiation skills or to develop healing rituals and mechanisms.

Individuation

Individuation may be harder for family members to achieve; at least it will be a different process than that of the average person, whose psychological dependence on the family diminishes when he or she becomes economically independent and establishes a career outside the boundaries of family influence. Sons of founders usually find it more difficult to test out and gain a sense of their own competency under their father's shadow. Whatever their role in the family firm, they are simply more visible than others. They are being appraised as a replacement for father, and their "mistakes" are being judged by different criteria than those applied to nonfamily managers or executives. Because of family myths about father and firm, many sons burden themselves with the belief that they must

281

be "just like dad" to be a successful leader in the business. In realty, they are entering a business that is in a new and different stage in its developmental life cycle, a period in which the business is becoming more differentiated and structured. New control mechanisms and integrating and executive functions are required to manage a more complex enterprise; whatever the son's role in the business, it will not be as encompassing as that of the father.

Perception of Reality

Knowledge about the external environment--the "real world"--may be expanded for the family through their contacts with people and events that cross into the boundaries of family life through father and the firm. However, their perception of reality is influenced by their identificaiton with the firm as a source of social power and prestige, and they may develop a bloated sense of their own importance. Furthermore, the firm's myths and culture may be different from those of the family even though father is central to both systems. Family members entering the firm may go through a period of culture shock and resocialization to adapt to the firm's myths and culture.

As we have seen, myths are perpetuated by "time binding," a way of denying the passage of time. While such denial alleviates pain, it can lead only to denial of other realities and eventually to dysfunctional symptoms. The succession issue is one that tests the ability of the family system to deal with the pain of loss, separtion, and change in the inevitable process of growth and development, aging, and death. Obviously, change is inevitable with the passage of time. The distress it creates also opens up the possibility of wisdom, which comes with acknowledgement and acceptance.

XIII.   THE PROCESS OF CHANGE

All change in living systems involves a conflict between two opposing tendencies: the pull to remain the same and defend the status quo and the push to change its processes and structures and move on to a new level of differentiation and integration. Maintenance of the status quo is comfortable; it is supported by well established, semi-automatic, and dependable behavior patterns requiring minimal effort and low risk. Change, on the other hand, is energizing but challenging. Because there is always the risk of failure, change is experienced both as a danger and as an opportunity and thus is approached with ambivalence. Equilibrium is destabilized and, temporarily, the system seems to regress or function in a less than optimal fashion. Transitions involve new and different problems that must be solved and new skills that must be learned. Some of the previously adaptive attitudes, beliefs, and behaviors must be given up before a new gestalt or configuration can emerge.

Some of the changes associated with the developmental life cycle of the family in relationship with the firm are first-order changes--that is, they are responses to minor fluctuations and do not require any major changes in the ground rules by which the family operates. For example, both firm and family make only minor shifts when the eldest son is employed in the firm during summer vacations. Some changes are second-order changes, requiring a major shift in orientation and expectations and the creation of new boundaries and rules. Two such second-order crises occur for the family when the firm's organization develops in size and complexity and outsiders or professional managers are brought in, or when company stock is placed on the public market.

Anyone who tries to answer the question, "What can be done to reduce the tension and uproar that can occur between the family and the firm at these critical times?" is bound to sound simplistic and prescriptive in a situation that requires a profound appreciation for the singularity and uniqueness of the families and the firm in their interactional relationship with each other. However, there are some concepts that can serve as guidelines in developing preventive interventions that might head off some of the more serious problems.

Information

The first of these concepts has to do with information. In social systems, information is a type of energy that leads to reduction of uncertainty. Lack of information leads to uncertainty, and uncertainty is a fertile breeding ground for projections and political maneuvers.

To avoid human beings' natural tendancy to fill in the information vacuum with illusions and false expectations, the founder can prevent the tensions between family and firm from developing into serious symptoms by communicating his or her thoughts or de-

cisions as early as possible to the family and the firm
on these issues:

Who will be considered for what roles in the
firm: Sons? Daughters? In-laws?

What are the criteria of competence required for
positions in the firm, and what are the criteria used
to assess this competence?

How will the inherited assets be distributed and
managed?

The founder can do this by informing them per-
suading them, consulting with them, or collaborating
with them in the decisions that lead to a resolution
of these questions. Formal or informal mechanisms can
be evolved in the family's life to learn about the
business and to develop an informed understanding of
the whole system of which they are a part and on which
they depend.

Awareness

The second of these guideline concepts has to do
with awareness. Utilizing the leadership of the spouse
subsystem, the family as a system can become aware of
the additional layers of complexity with which they
must all deal in being matrixed with a firm. This
awareness itself may be curative. They can pay more
attention to the satisfactions for belonging, identity,
and intimacy in the family system and build protective
boundaries to prevent encroachment by the firm. If the
family can develop an appreciation for difference,
divergence, and conflict and understand its members'
needs for influence or participation, they will be able
to create processes and mechanisms to inform, influence,
negotiate, and heal.

If access to information about what is happening
in the firm is not contingent on being a member of the
firm, some of the problems arising between firm and
family may be alleviated.

B I B L I O G R A P H Y

The author is indebted to the growing body of literature on the theory and practice of family therapy for the concepts expressed in this paper. Notable sources are the following: Lynn Hoffman's <u>Foundations of Family Therapy</u> (Basic Books, Inc. 1981); William Lederer's and Don Jackson's <u>The Mirages of Marriage</u> (W. W. Norton & Company, 1968); <u>No Single Thread: Psychological Health in Family Systems</u>, edited by Jerry M. Lewis (Brunner/Mazel, 1976). Two papers on the co-evolutionary perspective have been particularly useful; Penny Penn's "Circular Questioning" (<u>Family Process</u>, September 1982), and Lynn Hoffman's "A Co-evolutionary Framework for Systemic Family Therapy." which is a chapter 2 of <u>Family Diagnosis and Assessment</u> (Aspen Publishing Company, 1982).

*Elain Kepner currently serves on the faculty of two graduate professional education institutions: the Gestalt Institute of Cleveland -- where she is on the staff of the organizational and systems development program -- and the Fielding Institute, an external degree program in psychology. She also lectures at Teachers College, Columbia University in the organizational psychology program.

She received a B.A. and Ph.D. from Case Western Reserve University and was a professor in the clinical psychology department there for a number of years.

She is a partner in Richard Beckhard Associates and coconsults with Mr. Beckard on succession planning for family firms.

CHAPTER 14

WORK ROLES AS STRESSORS IN CORPORATE FAMILIES

Patricia Voydanoff*

There is a growing interest in examining the impacts of executive work roles in corporate families in spite of a general tendency on the part of corporations and executives to ignore or deny the relatedness of work and family roles. This position, referred to by Kanter (1977b) as the denial of connections, has been supported by a strong allegiance to the protestant ethic among corporate executives which includes high priority on work roles, strong dedication to achievement and advancement, and loyalty to the corporation. Executives have been expected to be "good family men" without having family obligations infringe upon work role responsibilities.[1]

Recent work indicates that there are several characteristics of executive employment that serve as family stressors which are related to low levels of marital satisfaction and family cohesion and to difficulties in performing family roles. Stressors are defined as problems requiring solutions or situations to which the family must adapt in order to maintain the functioning of the family system. Stressors can be of two types: (a) life events or acute changes affecting the family, and (b) relatively enduring situations requiring problem solving behavior or coping strategies (Moen, Note 1; Pearlin, Note 2). Several aspects of executive work roles function as chronic stressors in relation to the family, e.g., routine husband-father absence resulting from long hours and frequent travel, work-related stress associated with time pressure and mobility aspirations, and the tendency for a divergence of interests to develop between husband and wife. In addition to these relatively enduring stressors, more actue life-event stressors occur including geographic mobility and job transfers, nonroutine husband-father absence resulting from long-term travel assignments, and acute stress associated with status changes such as promotions.

I. SOCIOECONOMIC STATUS AND OCCUPATIONAL SUCCESS

The literature on the relation between socioeconomic status and family life is extensive and the findings are quite consistent. Socioeconomic status is related to patterns of family behavior including division of labor, marital power and decision-making, and socialization practices and values. In addition, positive relations between socioeconomic status and marital happiness, cohesion and stability are reported from most research. Scanzoni (1970) has developed a model of family cohesion which places major explanatory power on the husband's success in the occupational sphere as measured by socioeconomic status. However, it has been reported recently that the relation between occupational success and marital happiness and cohesion is curvilinear with less satisfactory marital relationships being more prevalent among those who are most and least successful in the occupational world (Aldous, Osmond, & Hicks, 1979). This contrasts with Scanzoni's hypothesis of a direct relation between occupational success and marital happiness and cohesion. Aldous et al. (1979) supported their hypothesis by specifying some of the correlations reported by Scanzone (1970) and Blood and Wolfe (1960) that indicated a leveling off or decrease in happiness and cohesion among those in higher occupational and income categories. They also cited Dizard (1968) who reported that, in his study of middle-class couples, those who were most successful in their occupations were most likely to have marital relationships deteriorate over time. He explained this finding by suggesting that a gulf develops between the husband and wife because of different life situation requirements.

It has been reported in other literature that a minimum level of income and employment stability are necessary for family stability and cohesion (Furstenberg, 1974). Beyond this minimum the family's subjective perception of adequacy becomes relatively more important in relation to happiness and cohesion (Oppenheimer, 1979; Scanzoni, 1970). Men with middle-level incomes and occupational status may be best able to combine work and family roles whereas those at the lower end have too few economic resources and those at the upper end have difficulty performing family roles (Aldous, 1969; Aldous et al., 1979; Kanter, 1977b). The evidence for this hypothesis is not conclusive; the hypothesis is quite provocative when viewed in the context of the analysis of executive work role stressors.

II. EXECUTIVE WORK ROLE STRESSORS

Job Security and Career Mobility

It has been noted in the recent business literature that executive employment is becoming increasingly insecure due to top-heavy managements, depressed industries, automation and computers, and managerial upheavals. It involves a greater likelihood of unemployment among all levels of management as well as decreasing opportunities for promotion into higher levels of management as well as decreasing opportunities for promotion into higher levels of management. Reactions to unemployment among the middle-class are relatively severe in terms of status loss and self-esteem; impacts on the family have not been studied (Braginsky & Braginsky, 1975; Briar, 1978; Elder, 1974; Goodchilds & Smith, 1963; Powell & Driscoll, 1973). Fineman (1979) reported that stress accompanies unemployment among managers in situations where managers are highly involved in their work, where unemployment coincides with family problems, and where repeated job-seeking attempts fail. Stress is lower among manaagers where job satisfaction and job involvement have been low, where managers interpret job loss as a challenge to meet or a problem to solve, and where they feel confident about their abilities to meet the challenge.

The highest rates of unemployment and economic uncertainty are still found within the lower and working classes. However, strong economic striving and desire for mobility among the middle class may have effects on the family comparable in some ways to the effects of job insecurity and fear of unemployment. In addition, those executives not meeting their achievement aspirations must adjust to the discrepancy between aspirations and accomplishments. Mizruchi (1964) saw the strain associated with this disparity as a major source of anomia in the middle class. Following Durkheim, he referred to this type of anomia as boundlessness. Part of the midlife crisis among executives centers on the need for middle-aged executives to come to terms with the discrepancy between current achievements and aspirations set earlier in their careers. Problems associated with mobility striving and gaps between achievement and aspirations have not been studied in relation to the family except perhaps for Blood and Wolfe (1960) who found that the wives of occupational strivers are less satisfied with their marriages than other wives with husbands in high status occupations.

Job Content and Satisfaction

It has been suggested that the content or requirements of the work roles of successful executives lead
to or are accompanied by the development of personality
traits or attributes that are inconsistent with successful family life. This incongruence is found on two
levels. First, the personal traits needed for a happy
family life are not necessarily compatible with those
needed to become a successful executive (Bartolomé,
1972; Maccoby, 1976; Zaleznik, Note 3). Managerial
careers stress the development of the "head" at the
expense of the "heart" (Maccoby, 1976). Second, the
husband and wife may grow apart psychologically and
develop different interests as the husband grows in
his career (Dizard, 1968; Foote, 1963; Levinson, 1964;
Seidenberg, 1973). This is especially true if the wife
is not employed outside the home.

Research on job satisfaction and the family com-
plements the analysis of occupational success discussed
above because job satisfaction may be positively related to family role participation and marital happiness except for those with the highest levels of job
satisfaction, i.e., a curvilinear relation may exist
(Aldous et al., 1979). Bailyn (1970) found a positive
relation between job satisfaction and marital happiness
for couples in which the husband was family oriented.
However, she found a negative relation between husband's job satisfaction and couple happiness for those
couples in which the husband was career oriented and
the wife family oriented. Thus, the Aldous et al.
(1979) hypothesis that high levels of job satisfaction
can hinder marital satisfaction is supported among the
couples fitting the general orientation of many corporate families, i.e., a career-oriented husband and a
family-oriented wife.

Amount and Scheduling of Time

Executives tend to work long hours and to take
work home frequently. Findings on the impact of number of hours spent working on family roles are not
conclusive. Time spent working is related to family
strain (Mortimer, Note 4); however, the number of hours
worked does not significantly influence the performance
of family roles except for recreation (Clark, Nye, &
Gecas, 1978). Pleck (1977) has suggested that attitudes toward family role performance are more important
than work time, i.e., executives can choose to spend
their off-work time, limited though it may be, either

in family activities or other leisure-oriented pursuits.

It may be that the timing of work role activities has a greater effect on the family than the number of hours worked. Those who travel extensively or work evenings and weekends may find it difficult to fulfill some aspects of family roles including companionship with spouse and children, attendance at family and school functions, and participation in household duties (Culter & Renshaw, 1972; Kanter, 1977b; Renshaw, 1976; Young & Willmott, 1973).

Geographic Mobility

Frequent transfers have been considered an integral part of moving up the corporate ladder for executives. In recent years, however, some executives and some corporations have been reexamining the costs and benefits associated with corporate transfers. Increasing, though still small, numbers of executives are refusing transfers (Costello, 1976). Personal and family considerations top the reasons for refusal. Corporations are beginning to seek ways to ease the strain of transfers for their employees and their families.

A wide range of family responses to frequent moves has been reported in the literature. In some situations these moves have been found to be stressful for all family members (Tiger, 1974); in others, families have little difficulty adjusting (Jones, 1973; McAllister, Butler & Kaiser, 1973). It is necessary to consider the conditions under which moving is stressful. Factors making a difference in adjustment include the number and timing of moves, degree of family cohesion and integration, ages of children, and the extent to which the wife has difficulty making new friends and transferring her credentials and contacts (Margolis, 1979; Portner, 1978; Renshaw, 1976; Jones, Note 5). After many moves some corporate wives give up trying to become part of yet another community and become isolated and depressed (Seidenberg, 1973).

Role of the Corporate Wife

The executive role has been analyzed as one example of the two-person career, i.e., an occupation in which the wife has well defined duties that are an integral part of the husband's occupational role (Papanek, 1973). These include supporting the husband in his work, taking care of the home so that the husband can

291

spend more time at work and be able to relax when at home, participating in volunteer work to develop business contacts, entertaining work associates, and attending work related social functions (Kanter, 1977a, 1977b). The role also is associated with several problematic characteristics--frequent moves, lack of personal identity development, difficulty in integrating the husband into family activities, lack of parallel growth between husband and wife, and myriad psychological disturbances such as depression and alcoholism (Kanter, 1977a, 1977b; Seidenberg, 1973; Vandervelde, 1979). Information on the prevalence of these problems is limited; most of the data come from corporate wives in clinical settings.

Corporate wives are less likely to be employed than other women partly because their husbands' work roles impose constraints on their employment (Mortimer, Hall, & Hill, 1978). In spite of these constraints, however, wife employment is increasing among women with high educational levels because of changes in sex role orientation and increased occupational opportunities. If the wife also has a career, she is likely to experience role overload because she may continue to fulfill traditional family responsibilities in addition to full-time employment (Holmstrom, 1972).

III. COPING STRATEGIES AND SUPPORTS

Within the limits of the current literature, several relations between executive work role stressors, family roles, and cohesion have been documented. Within the context of current employment practices it is important to examine coping strategies and supports used by corporate families to moderate the impact of work stressors.

Boss, McCubbin, and Lester (1979) have outlined three coping strategies used by corporate wives in dealing with husband-father absence: fitting into the corporate life style, developing self and interpersonal relationships, and estabishing independence and self-sufficiency. A related study of the wives of Navy servicemen revealed five coping patterns--maintaining family integrity, developing interpersonal relationships and social support, managing psychological tension and strain, believing in the value of spouse's profession and maintaining an optimistic definition of the situation, and developing self reliance and self-esteem (McCubbin, Boss, Wilson, & Lester, Note 6). Mortimer (Note 7) has shown the importance of the wife's support of the husband's work in mediating the relation between job-induced strain and marital satisfaction. Burke and Weir (1975, 1977) also reported that satisfaction with the husband-wife helping relationship effectively mediated between job and life stress and several measures of well-being including job, marital, and life satisfaction and mental and physical well-being. This work suggests the importance of coping strategies and supports within the family itself for limiting the impacts of work role stressors.

Several organizations are attempting to deal with stress in corporate families by holding "executive seminars." In these seminars, the strains and pressure of corporate life are discussed. Executives and their wives are helped to develop personal and family resources to handle their problems. The Harvard Business School offers a course for married students and their spouses on how executives can meet the demands of both work and family responsibilities (Greiff, 1976). The Menninger Clinic seminars on midlife transitions among executives deal with psychological resource development and the integration of work and family roles (Rice, 1979). Others bring together husbands and wives to discuss issues relating to corporate life and marriage (Becerra, 1975). Seminars also have been held to deal with the stresses associated with business travel (Culbert & Renshaw, 1972).

The reduction of work and family stress is also dealt with in the literature for corporate executives and their wives. The American Management Association recently published a "how to" book for executives who want to achieve success in both marriage and corporate careers (Ogden, 1979). Hall and Hall (1979) have developed many practical suggestions for dealing with stress and role overload among two-career couples. The literature written for corporate wives is also changing. Earlier writings stressed the importance of the corporate wife in smoothly handling family life so that her husband could devote himself to his work. A recent book tells corporate wives how they may become more independent without hurting their husbands' careers (Vandervelde, 1979).

Much more needs to be done to develop coping strategies and supports for corporate families. This work should progress on several levels--encouraging the development of internal coping strategies for family units and individual family members; providing group supports for families and individual members,

293

e.g., seminars of various types; and developing community supports for corporate families, e.g., child
care for two-career families. Based on McCubbin (1979)
these strategies and supports need to be oriented
toward both chronic and acute stressors.

REFERENCE NOTES

[1] In this paper analysis is limited to male executives and their families. More research is needed to determine the extent to which the findings and conclusions apply to female executives and their families.

1. Moen, P. Patterns of family stress across the life cycle. Paper presented at the Annual Meeting of the National Council on Family Relations, Boston, 1979.

2. Pearlin, L. I. The life cycle and life strain. Paper presented at the Annual Meeting of the American Sociological Association, Boston, 1979.

3. Zaleznik, A. D. C. S. Isolation and control in the family and work. Paper presented at the Symposium on the Family: Setting Priorities, Washington, DC, 1978.

4. Jones, S. Corporate policy on the transferring of employees: Sociological considerations. Paper presented at the Annual Meeting of the North Central Sociological Association, Louisville, 1976.

5. McCubbin, H. I., Boss, P. G., Wilson, L. F., & Lester, G. R. Developing family invulnerability to stress: Coping patterns and strategies wives employ in managing family separations. Paper presented at the 9th World Congress of the International Sociological Association, Uppsala, Sweden, 1978.

6. Mortimer, J. T. Work-family linkages as perceived by men in the early stages of professional and managerial careers.

BIBLIOGRAPHY

Aldous, J.

    1969   "Occupational characteristics and males'
                    role performance in the family." Journal
                    of Marriage and the Family, 31, 707-712.

Aldous, J., Osmond, M., &
Hicks, M.

    1979   "Men's work and men's families." In
                    W. Burr, R. Hill, I. Reiss, & F. I. Nye
                    (Eds.), Contemporary theories about the
                    family. New York: Free Press.

Bailyn, L.

    1970   "Career and family orientations of hus-
                    bands and wives in relation to marital
                    happiness." Human Relations, 23, 97-113.

Bartolomé, F.

    1972   "Executives as human beings." Harvard
                    Business Review, 50, 62-69.

Becerra, M.

    1975   "Marriage and the corporation." Nation's
                    Business, 63, March, 82-84.

Blood, R. O., &
Wolf, D. M.

    1960   Husbands and wives. New York: Free Press.

Boss, P. G., McCubbin, H. I., &
Lester, G.

    1979   "The corporate executive wife's coping
                    patterns in response to routine husband-
                    father absence." Family Process, 18,
                    79-86.

Braginsky, D. D., &
Braginsky, B. M.

    1975   "Surplus people." Psychology Today, 9,
                    68-72.

Briar, K. H.

1978   The effect of long-term unemployment
on workers and their families. Palo
Alto: R & E Research Associates.

Burke, R. J., &
Weir, T.

1975   "The husband-wife relationship." The
Business Quarterly, 40, 62-67.

Burke, R. J., &
Weir, T.

1977   "Marital helping relationships." The
Journal of Psychology, 95, 121-130.

Clark, R. A., Nye, F. I., &
Gecas, V.

1978   "Husbands' work involvement and marital
role performance. Journal of Marriage
and the Family, 40, 9-21.

Costello, J.

1976   "Why more managers are refusing transfers." Nation's Business, 64, October,
4-5.

Culbert, S. A., &
Renshaw, J. R.

1972   "Coping with the stresses of travel as
an opportunity for improving the quality
of work and family life. Family Process,
11, 321-337.

Dizard, J.

1968   Social change in the family. Chicago:
University of Chicago Press.

Elder, G. H.

1974.   Children of the great depression.
Chicago: University of Chicago Press.

Fineman, S.

1979   "A psychosocial model of stress and its
        application to managerial unemployment.
        Human Relations, 32, 323-345.

Foote, N. N.

1963   "Matching of husband and wife in phases
        of development." In M. B. Sussman (Ed.),
        Sourcebook in marriage and the family.
        Boston: Houghton Mifflin.

Furstenberg, F.

1974   "Work experience and family life." In
        J. O'Toole (Ed.), Work and the quality
        of life. Cambridge: MIT Press.

Goodchilds, J. D., &
Smith, E. E.

1963   "The effects of unemployment as mediated
        by social status." Sociometry, 26,
        287-293.

Greiff, B. S.   "The executive family seminar: A course
                 for graduate married business students."
                 American College Health Association, 24,
                 227-231.

Hall, F. S., &
Hall, D. T.

1979   The two-career couple. Reading, MA:
        Addison-Wesley.

Holmstrom, L.
1972   The two-career family. Cambridge:
        Schenkman.

Jones, S. B.

1973   "Geographic mobility as seen by the wife
        and mother. Journal of Marriage and the
        Family, 35, 210-218.

Kanter, R. M.

1977a   Men and women of the corporation. New
        York: Basic.

Kanter, R. M.

    1977b   Work and family in the United States:
                A critical review and agenda for research
                and policy. New York: Sage.

Levinson, H.

    1964   Emotional problems in the world of work.
                New York: Harper.

Maccoby, M.

    1976   "The corporate climber has to find his
                heart." Fortune, December, pp. 98-108.

Margolis, D.

    1979   The managers. New York: Morrow.

McAllister, R., Butler, E., &
Kaiser, E.

    1973   "The adjustment of women to residential
                mobility." Journal of Marriage and the
                Family, 35, 197-204.

McCubbin, H. I.

    1979   "Interating coping behavior in family
                stress theory." Journal of Marriage and
                the Family, 41, 237-244.

Mizruchi, E.

    1964   Success and opportunity. New York:
                Free press.

Mortimer, J., Hall, R., &
Hill, R.

    1978   "Husbands' occupational attributes as
                constraints on wives' employment."
                Sociology of Work and Occupations, 5,
                285-313.

Ogden, R. W.

    1978   How to succeed in business and marriage.
                New York: AMACOM.

Oppenheimer, V. K.

1979   "Structural sources of economic pressure for wives to work: An analytical framework." Journal of Family History, 4, 177-197.

Papanek, H.

1973   "Men, women, and work: Reflections on the two-person career. The American Journal of Sociology, 78, 852-872.

Pleck, H. J.   "The work-family role system." Social Problems, 24, 417-418.

Portner, J.

1978   Impacts of work on the family. Minneapolis: Minnesota Council on Family Relations.

Powell, D. H., &
Driscoll, P. F.

1973   "Middle-class professionals face unemployment." Society, 10, 18-26.

Renshaw, J. R.

1976   "An exploration of the dynamics of the overlapping worlds of work and family." Family Process, 15, 143-165.

Rice, B.

1979   "Midlife encounters: The Menninger seminars for businessmen." Psychology Today, 12, 66-74, 95-99.

Scanzoni, J. H.

1970   Opportunity and the family. New York: Free Press.

Seidenberg, R.

1973   Corporate wives-corporate casualties? New York: AMACOM.

Tiger, L.

    1974   "Is this trip necessary? The heavy
                   human costs of moving executives around."
                   Fortune, September, pp. 139-141.

Vandervelde, M.

    1979   The changing life of the corporate wife.
                   New York: Jecox, 1979.

Young, M., &
Willmott, P.

    1973   The symmetrical family. New York:
                   Penguin.

*Patricia Voydanoff is Chairperson, Department of
 Family and Community Studies, Merrill-Palmer Institute,
 71 East Ferry, Detroit, MI 48202.

CHAPTER 15

DUAL-CAREER FAMILY STRESS AND COPING:
A LITERATURE REVIEW

Denise A. Skinner*

A significant influence on contemporary family living is the increasing rate of female participation in the labor force. Examination of Department of Labor statistics reveals that the married woman is the key source of this growth and helps explain the growing interest in dual-career families reflected in both the professional and popular literature. Although it is difficult to assess the number of married career women in the work force, it seems reasonable to assume that the percentage for this group is positively related to the general increase in labor force participation rates of women (Hopkins & White, 1978). As more and more women seek increased education and training, along with an increased demand for skilled labor and a greater awareness of sex-role equality, the dual-career life-style is likely to increase in prevalence and accepta-bility (Rapoport & Rapoport, 1976).

A significant feature of the dual-career lifestyle is that it produces considerable stress and strain. The often competing demands of the occupational struc-ture and those of a rich family life present a number of challenges for dual-career family members. Much of the literature implies that the stress is inherent in a dual-career lifestyle. However, some of the con-straints of the lifestyle might be explained by the fact that it is a relatively new and minority pattern. In coping with the pressures of this variant pattern, dual-career couples have been forced to come up with individual solutions as no institutionalized supports exist (Holmstrom, 1973).

The research on dual-career families has been primarily descriptive in nature and has focused on women. Rapoport and Rapoport, who coined the term "dual-career family" in 1969, were pioneers in the study of the impact of career and family on each other. Their research was followed shortly thereafter by oth-er definitive studies on the dual-career lifestyle (Epstein, 1971; Holmstrom, 1973; Garland, 1972; Poloma, 1972). More recent dual-career research has focused heavily on the stresses of the lifestyle and on the management of the strains by the participants (Rapoport & Rapoport, 1978).

The purpose of this chapter review is to delineate the sources of dual-career strain and summarize the coping patterns employed by dual-career couples in managing stress. Hopefully, this summary will benefit family practitioners as they assist individuals in making adaptive lifestyle choices as well as aid dual-career participants in effective stress-reduction and in developing coping strategies.

I. THE ETIOLOGY OF DUAL-CAREER STRESS

Rapoport and Rapoport (1978) in reviewing the 1960's studies of dual-career families have noted that the stresses of this pattern have been differently conceptualized by various researchers. "The concepts include dilemmas (such as) overload,...network, identity; conflicts between earlier and later norms..., barriers of domestic isolation, sex-role prejudices..., and problems such as the wife finding an appropriate job..." (p. 5).

Although there is a considerable degree of variation in dual-career stress, there are also common patterns. In the review that follows, an adaptation of the Rapoports' (1971) delination of strains confronting dual-career families will be used as an organizing framework in highlighting these common patterns reported in the literature. Although interactive and cyclical in nature, strains have been classified as primarily (a) internal: arising within the family; or (b) external: the result of conflict of the dual-career family and other societal structures (Bebbington, 1973).

Internal Strain

Overload issues. The problem of work and role overload is a common source of strain for dual-career families (Epstein, 1971; Garland, 1972; Heckman, Bryson, & Bryson, 1977; Holmstrom, 1973; Poloma, 1972; Rapoport & Rapoport, 1976; St. John-Parsons, 1978). When each individual is engaged in an active work role and active family roles, the total volume of activities is considerably increased over what a conventional family experiences (Portner, Note 1). In dual-career families this can result in overload, with household tasks generally handled as overtime.

The feelings of overload and the degree of strain experienced varied for couples in the Rapoports' study (1976). The Rapoports suggested that overload was affected by four conditions, which were, in part, self-imposed:

(a) the degree to which having children and a family life (as distinct from simply being married) was salient; (b) the degree to which the couple aspired to a high standard of domestic living, (c) the degree to which there was satisfactory reapportionment of tasks; and (d) the degree to which the social-psychlogical overload compounded the physical overloads (pp. 302-305).

There was a positive relationship between the conditions in items (a), (b), and (d) above, and the degree of strain experienced. Satisfactory reapportionment of tasks was a coping strategy that helped alleviate strain.

Identity issues. The identity dilemma for dual-career participants is the result of discontinuity between early gender-role socialization and current wishes or practices (Rapoport & Rapoport, 1976). The essence of masculinity in our culture is still centered on successful experiences in the work role, and femininity is still centered on successful experiences in the domestic scene (Heckman, Bryson, & Bryson, 1977; Holmstrom, 1973). The internalized "shoulds" regarding these traditional male and female roles conflict with the more androgynous roles attempted by many dual-career couples, resulting in tension and strain.

Bernard, (1974) focusing on professional women, observed that intrapersonal integration of work and domestic roles and the personality characteristics associated with each, does not constitute the "psychological work" of the career mother. Rather, the major difficulty, according to Bernard, is that the woman alone is the one who must achieve this identity integration.

Role-cycling issues. The dilemma of role-cycling, identified by Rapoport and Rapoport (1976), refers to attempts by the dual-career couple to mesh their different individual career cycles with the cycle of their family. Bebbington (1973) noted that role cycling, unlike other sources of strain, has a developmental pattern. Both employment and family careers have tran-

305

sition points at which there is a restructuring of roles which become sources of "normative" stress.

Dual-career couples attempt to avoid additional strain by staggering the career and family cycles such that transiton points are not occurring at the same time. Many couples establish themselves occupationally before having children for this reason (Bebbington, 1973); Holmstrom, 1973; Rapoport & Rapoport, 1976). Stress may also result when the developmental sequence of one spouse's career conflicts with that of the other (Bebbington, 1973). The structural and attitudinal barriers of the occupational world, yet to be discussed, further contribute to the difficulty in role-cycling for many dual-career couples.

Family characteristics. Holmstrom (1973) identified the isolation of the modern nuclear family as a barrier to having two careers in one family. The difficulty of childrearing apart from relatives or other such extended support systems is a source of strain.

The presence or absence of children as well as the stage of the family life cycle seems to affect the complexity of the dual career lifestyle (Holmstrom, 1973; Rapoport & Rapoport, 1976). Heckman, et al. (1977) found that it was the older professional couples and those who had not had children who saw the life-style as advantageous. The demands of childrearing, particularly the problems associated with finding satisfactory childcare arrangements, are a source of strain for younger dual-career couples, especially for the women (Bryson, Bryson, & Johnson, 1978; Gove & Geerken, 1977; Holmstrom, 1973; Orden & Bradburn, 1969; Rapoport & Rapoport, 1971; St. John-Parsons, 1978). In relation to this, a child-free lifestyle has been noted by Movius (1976) as a career-facilitating strategy for women.

External Strains

Normative issues. Despite changing social norms, the dual-career lifestyle still runs counter to traditional family norms of our culture. Rapoport & Rapoport (1976) have explained that although intellectually the dual-career pattern is approved, internalized values from early socialization are still strong and produce tension, anxiety, and guilt. Pivotal points such as career transitions or the birth of a child can activate these normative dilemmas.

One of the more frequently cited problems by dual-career professionals is the expectation on the part of others that the dual-career husband and wife behave in traditional male/female roles (Heckman, et al., 1977). This is consistent with the earlier findings of Epstein (1971) who indicated that dual-career individuals experienced guilt because they were not conforming to the socially approved work-family structure. Furthermore, the women often had to deal with the implied or overt social controls placed on them by their children according to Epstein's study.

Occupational structure. Holmstrom (1973, p. 517) has commented on the inflexibility of professions noting that "pressures for geographic mobility, the status inconsistencies of professional women because the professions are dominated by men, and the pressure for fulltime and continuous careers" are a source of strain for dual-career couples.

The demand for geographical mobility and its effect on dual-career couples noted earlier by Holmstrom (1973) was also examined by Duncan and Perrucci (1976). They found that the egalitarian orientation toward decision-making promoted in dual-career living was not carried out in job moves with the wives experiencing more of the stress. However, Wallston, Foster, and Berger (1978) using simulated job-seeking situations, found many professional couples attempting egalitarian or nontraditional job-seeking patterns. These authors have suggested that institutional constraints are in part responsible for highly traditional actual job decisions.

Finally, the demands of particular professions for single-minded continuous commitment, for other family members' needs to be subordinated to the job, and for a "support person" (typically the wife) to be available for entertaining, etc., are a source of stress for dual-career couples. The "two-person career" (Papanek, 1973) which depends heavily on an auxiliary support partner is incompatible with the dual-career orientation, according to Hunt and Hunt (1977). Handy (1978) in a study of executive men found that the dual-career relationship was infrequent and difficult when the husband was in such a "greedy occupation."

Social network dilemmas. Maintaining relationships outside the immediate family is a problem for dual-career members for a variety of reasons. The general dilemma exists because of the overload strain

discussed earlier, which creates limitations on the
availability of time to interact with friends and relatives (Portner, Note 1).

Rapoport and Rapoport (1976) found that the dual-
career couples whom they studied reported problems in
sustaining the kinds of interaction that their more
conventional relatives and friends wanted. Not only
was there less time for socializing, but, also, kin
were at times asked by the dual-career couples to help
out which sometimes produced tension. St. John-Parsons
(1978) reported that kin relationships deteriorated
when dual-career couples could not meet some of the
expected social obligations. The husbands in his study
experienced the greater loss as ties to their families
of orientation lessened.

The study of St. John-Parsons (1978) revealed that
none of the dual-career families maintained extensive
social relationships. According to the author, "a
salient reason for their social dilemma was their sense
of responsibility for and devotion to their children"
(p. 40).

II. IMPACT OF STRAIN

The sources of strain delineated above suggest
that dual-career families are vulnerable to a high
degree of stress. However, family stress literature
has indicated that the family's definition of the
situation is an important component influencing the
impact of various strains on the family (Burr, 1973).
Bebbington (1973) has differentiated between the following two kinds of stress which can co-exist or operate separately in a given lifestyle: "(a) that deriving
from an unsatisfactory resolution of conflict as between ideals and behavior and (b) that deriving from
intrinsic properties of the lifestyle, though ideals
and behaviors may be consistent" (p. 535). Bebbington
has suggested that dual-career participants do not
seem to find the principle of "stress minimization"
operative with regard to the second type of stress,
but rather, accept an orientation of "stress-optimi-
zation" in interpreting inherent lifestyle stresses.
Dual-career couples have accepted a high degree of
the second type of stress as their solution to the
dilemma of avoiding the discontinuity stress of the
first type, according to Bebbington. They come to
view their problems as having both positive as well
as negative components and of a more routine than unusual nature.

The cumulative effect of various strains arising from occupational and familial role transitions can be estimated as "transitional density" (Bain, 1978). Bain has hypothesized that the stress experienced and the coping ability of a family in a particular transition is proportional to the stress generated by the transitional density. Applied to dual-career families this idea is specifically related to the particular family characteristics and the multiple role cycling strains previously discussed. The degree of stress experienced from other sources of strain (e.g., overload) may be compounded for a given family by the strain of their family life cycle stage or the newness of the dual-career pattern for them.

Marital Relationship

A considerable portion of the dual career literature focuses on the marital adjustment, happiness, or satisfaction of dual-career couples implying that the stress inherent in the lifestyle has an impact on the marital relationship. In Orden and Bradburn's (1969) study of working wives and marital happiness, they found that a woman's choice of employment (vs. full-time homemaking) strained the marriage only when there were preschool children in the family. They concluded that the woman's decision to work is associated with a high balance between satisfactions and strains for both partners.

Bailyn (1970) found that an all-consuming attitude toward career was associated with lower marital satisfaction. Overinvolvement in one's career can result in strain on the marriage, according to Ridley (1973) who found marital adjustment highest when the husband was "medium" and the wife was "low" on job involvement. He concluded that tension in the marital relationship may occur when either partner becomes so highly involved in a job that family obligations are excluded. Occupational practices such as discriminatory sex-role attitudes can also heighten the stress in the dual-career marital relationship (Holmstrom, 1973; Rosen, Jerdee, & Prestwich, 1975). Finally, Richardson (1979) examined the hypothesis that marital stress would be attendant if working wives had higher occupational prestige than their husbands. He found no support for this hypothesis and suggested that its "mythic content" may be sustained, in part, because it is congruent with conventional sex-role orientations.

Rice (1979), focusing on personality patterns, noted the following psychological characteristics as typical of dual-career individuals:

A strong need for achievement, reliance on an extrinsic reward system (promotion, spouse recognition of efforts), hesitancy in making sustained interpersonal commitments, and vulnerability to self-esteem injury through dependency frustrations and fear of failure (p. 47).

The adaptive aspects of, for instance, high achievement may facilitate career advancement for both partners and contribute positively to marital adjustment, or high achievement needs may contribute to competitiveness in the pair.

Sex Differences

An overwhelming proportion of the literature reports that the impact of dual-career stress is felt most by women. Bernard (1974) has noted that a man can combine a professional career and parenting more easily than a woman can because less is expected of the man with regard to familial responsibilities.

Overload strain is a significant issue for dual-career women. Heckman et al. (1977), in assessing problem areas for dual-career couples, found that the women reported more problems in more areas than did men, and that many of the comments about problem areas by husbands were issues that had indirectly affected them because the issue had directly affected their wives. These researchers reported that several women in their study made significant concessions with regard to their careers because of family demands. They concluded that the continued existence of role conflict and overload strain are often at the expense of the woman's personal identity and career aspirations.

Occupationally, it has been the woman more often who takes the risks, sacrifices more, and compromises career ambitions in attempting to make the dual-career pattern operative (Epstein, 1971; Holmstrom, 1973; Poloma, 1972). Interestingly, however, some studies have reported that dual-career wives are more productive than other females in their respective professions (Bryson, Bryson, Licht, & Licht, 1976; Martin, Berry, & Jacobsen, 1975). One might conclude, as the Rapoports (1978) have done, that the wives were simultaneously exploited and facilitated.

Life for the dual-career male is not without its periods of stress, although the impact of various strains does not appear to be as significant as that reported for women. Garland (1972) reported that dual-career males felt strain in attempting to find free time, but overall, noted the advantages of the life-style. The findings of Burke and Weir (1976) do not provide as positive a report for dual-career men, however. While working wives were found to be more satisfied with life, marriage, and job than nonworking wives, husbands of working wives were less satisfied and performed less effectively than husbands of non-working wives. Burke and Weir indicated that the greater stress experienced by the dual-career husband may be due, in part, to him losing part of his "active support system" when the wife commits herself to a career outside the home, and also to his assuming roles (e.g. housekeeping) which have not been valued as high-ly in our culture.

Using more sophisticted methodology, Booth (1977) replicated the Burke and Weir study and reported dif-ferent conclusions. He found very little difference between working and nonworking wives, and reported that the wife's employment had little effect on the stress experienced by the husband. Furthermore, Booth con-cluded that the dual-career husband may be experiencing less stress than his conventional counterpart as the added income and personal fulfillment of the wife out-weigh temporary problems in adjusting to the lifestyle.

Children

Dual-career couples may increase the degree of strain they themselves experience in an attempt to pre-vent the lifestyle from creating strain for their chil-dren. As was noted earlier in the study by St. John-Parsons (1978), some of the social strains the couples experienced was due to their sense of responsibility to their children. There is no evidence to suggest that the dual-career lifestyle, in and of itself, is stressful for children. What may be more significant for the children is the degree of stress experienced by the parents which may indirectly affect the chil-dren. In her study of maternal employment Hoffman (1974) concluded that,

> ...the working mother who obtains satisfaction
> from her work, who has adequate arrangements so
> that her dual role does not involve undue strain,
> and who does not feel so guilty that she over-

311

compensates is likely to do quite well and under certain conditions, better than the nonworking mother (p. 142).

III. COPING STRATEGIES

Just as the type and degree of strain experienced varies for dual-career families, so do the strategies employed for managing the stress. As was mentioned earlier in this paper, Bebbington (1973) suggested that "stress optimization," the acknowledging of dual-career stress as inevitable and preferable to the stress of alternative lifestyules available, is an orientation of many dual-career couples. Defining their situation as such may serve as a resource in successful adaptation to the stress. Dual-career couples also employ stress-mitigating strategies. These coping behaviors are aimed at maintaining or strengthening the family system and at securing support from sources external to the family.

Coping Behavior Within the Family System

Poloma (1972) outlined four tension-management techniques used by the dual-career women in her study. They reduced dissonance by defining their dual-career patterns as favorable or advantageous to them and their families when compared to other alternatives available. For instance, the career mother noted that she was a happier mother and wife because she worked outside the home than she would be if she where a fulltime home-maker. Secondly, they established priorities among and withint their roles. The salient roles are familial ones and if a conflict situation occurs between family and career demands, the family needs come first. A third strategy employed was that of compartmentalizing work and family roles as much as possible. Leaving actual work and work-related problems at the office would be one way to segregate one's work and family roles. Finally, the women in Poloma's study managed strain by compromising career aspirations to meet other role demands.

Compromise is a common coping strategy noted in much of the dual-career literature as a way of reducing stress and making the lifestyle manageable. Women, in particular, compromise career goals if there are competing role demands (Bernard, 1974; Epstein, 1971; Heckman et al., 1977; Holmstrom, 1973). However, men in dual-careers make career sacrifices also, e.g., compromising advancement opportunities in an attempt to reduce role-conflict.

Prioritizing and compromising are coping strategies employed not only to deal with conflicts between roles but also in resolving competing demands within roles. Domestic overload, for instance, may be managed by deliberately lowering standards. One compromises ideal household standards because of constraints on time and energy in achieving them. Structurally, the domestic overload dilemma can also be managed within the family system by reorganizing who does what, with the husband and children taking on more of what traditionally has been the woman's responsibility. In these instances dual-career families are actively employing coping behaviors within the family aimed at strengthening its functioning and, thus, reducing the family's vulnerability to stress (McCubbin, 1979).

Some dual-career individuals take a more reactive orientation toward stress, and copy by attempting to manage and improve their behavior to better satisfy all of the lifestyle's demands. Holmstrom (1973) reported that the couples in her study adhered to organized schedules and that the women, in particular, were very conscious of how they allocated their time and effort. Flexibility and control over one's schedule are highly valued by career persons in attempting to meet overload and time pressures.

Finally, the presence of what Burke and Weir (1976) have labelled a helping component in the marital relationship can serve a stress-mitigating function within the dual-career family. Qualities such as open communication, empathy, emotional reassurance, support and sensitivity to other's feelings, characterize this therapeutic role; the presence of these qualities would serve to strengthen the relationship. Related to this, Rapoport and Rapoport (1978) reported that couples established "tension lines," points beyond which individuals feel they cannot be pushed except at risk to themselves or the relationship" (p. 6). Couples organized their family lives with sensitivity to these tension lines.

Coping Behaviors Involving External Support Systems

Dual-career couples also employ coping strategies aimed at securing support outside the family to help reduce stress. Holmstrom (1973) reported that couples were quite willing to use money to help resolve overload strain. Hiring help, especially for childcare, is a common expense in this lifestyle. Couples also buy time in various other ways such as hiring outside help to do domestic work and purchasing labor- and time-saving devices.

Outside support in terms of friendships were also important to the couples in the Rapoports' study (1976). The dual-career couples formed friendships on a couple basis, associating with other career couples. "Friendships, while gratifying, are also demanding, and in many of the couples there was a relatively explicit emphasis on the mutual service aspects of the relationship as well as the recreational aspect" (Rapoport, p. 316). Thus, establishing friendships with couples like themselves helped to validate the lifestyle for these dual-career couples and provided a reciprocal support structure.

The literature suggests that dual-career couples are increasingly interested in negotiating work arrangements which will reduce or remove some of this lifestyle's stress. Flexible scheduling, job sharing, and split-location employment are used by some dual-career couples as coping mechanisms to reduce the family's vulnerability to overload stress.

Finally, most of the researchers noted that achieving a balance between the disadvantages and advantages of the lifestyle was the overriding concern of dual-career couples. Although noting the numerous strains associated with the lifestyle, dual-career couples were equally aware of the gains--things like personal fulfillment, increased standard of living, pride in each other's accomplishments, etc. The goal for most dual-career couples, then, is to "...plan how to manage the meshing of their two lives so as to achieve an equitable balance of strains and gains" (Rapoport and Rapoport, 1976, p. 298).

IV. IMPLICATIONS FOR PRACTITIONERS

Increasingly, people are choosing dual-career living, a trend that will, no doubt, continue in the future. This has several implications for family life practitioners, particularly given the stress associated with the lifestyle. Certain changes seem necessary in facilitating dual-career living but these changes must occur by concerted efforts at many levels Rapoport and Rapoport (1976).

Individuals opting for the dual-career lifestyle, or any other family form for that matter, would benefit from knowledge of the issues central to that lifestyle's functioning. As Rapoport and Rapoport (1976) suggested "...the dissemination of a detailed knowledge of a range of lifestyles like the dual-career families will increase the potential for satisfactory choice of options in future" (p. 21). Such an education would enlarge traditional conceptions about men's and women's occupational and familial roles recognizing that different individuals would then have greater opportunities for making adaptive lifestyle choices.

Practitioners in marriage and family therapy may increasingly work with dual-career couples as their numbers increase and as the strains of the lifestyle remain. Rice (1979) has reported that competition, issues of power, and difficulty with the support structure are three common problem areas in dual-career marriages. He has suggested that "the guiding principle in therapy with dual-career couples is to help the partners achieve or restore a sense of equity in the marital relationship" (p. 103). Group-support sessions are suggested by Hopkins and White (1978) as a helpful therapeutic strategy with dual-career couples. Common-problem groups and groups of couples at differing life-cycle stages can provide a supportive structure for mutual sharing of concerns and coping skills. The goal of both preventive and remedial approaches should be to help couples assess their needs, increase interpersonal competencies, and deal constructively with the stress they experience (Rapoport & Rapoport, 1976).

Each family life professional has the opportunity to serve as a spokesperson for societal and institutional changes which would positively affect the functioning of dual-career families. Societal changes which would increase the quantity and quality of all kinds of services (educational, domestic, child-care, etc.) would strengthen the dual career lifestyle. Institutional changes which would increase the flexibility of the occupational structure would also aid significantly in reducing or eliminating some of the stress associated with the lifestyle. Flexible scheduling, increased availability of part-time employment, on-site day care facilities and maternity and paternity leaves are some of the occupational changes advocated to enable individuals to combine work and family roles with less strain. Assuming an advocacy role on behalf of the dual-career lifestyle involves initiating and supporting social policies which promote equity and pluralism (Rapoport & Rapoport, 1976). A society where these values prevail would enhance not only the dual-career lifestyle, but would serve to strengthen family life in general.

REFERENCE NOTE

1. Portner, J. Impact of work on the family. Minne-
    apolis: Minnesota Council on Family Relations,
    1219 University Avenue SE, 55414, 1978, 13-15.

                B I B L I O G R A P H Y

Bailyn, L.

    1970   "Career and family orientations of hus-
                bands and wives in relation to marital
                happiness." Human Relations, 23(2),
                97-113.

Bain, A.

    1978   "The capacity of families to cope with
                transitions: A theoretical essay. Human
                Relations, 31, 675-688.

Bebbington, A. C.

    1973   "The function of stress in the establish-
                ment of the dual-career family." Journal
                of Marriage and the Family, 35, 530-537.

Bernard, J.

    1973   The future of motherhood. New York:
                Penguin.

Bird, C.

    1979   The two-paycheck marriage. New York:
                Rawson, Wade.

Booth, A.

    1977   "A wife's employment and husband's stress:
                A replication and refutation." Journal
                of Marriage and the Family, 39, 645-50.

Bryson, R., Bryson, J.,
Licht, M., & Licht, B.

    1976   "The professional pair: Husband and wife
                psychologists." American Psychologist,
                31(1), 10-16.

Bryson, R., Bryson, J. B., &
Johnson, M. F.

1978   "Family size, satisfaction, and produc-
        tivity in dual-career couples." In
        J. B. Bryson, & R. Bryson (Eds.),
        Dual-career couples. New York: Human
        Sciences, 1978.

Burke, R. J., &
Weir, T.

1976   "Relationship of wives' employment
        status to husband, wife and pair satis-
        faction and performance." Journal of
        Marriage and the Family, 38, 279-287.

Burke, R. J., &
Weir, T.

1977   "Marital helping relationships: The
        moderators between stress and well-being."
        Journal of Psychology, 95, 121-130.

Burr, A.

1977   Theory construction and the sociology of
        the family. New York: Wiley.

Duncan, R. P., &
Perrucci, C.

1976   "Dual occupation families and migration."
        American Sociological Review, 41, 252-
        261.

Epstein, C. D.

1971   "Law partners and marital partners:
        Strains and solutions in the dual-career
        family enterprise." Human Relations,
        24, 549-563.

Fogarty, M. P., Rapoport, R., &
Rapoport, R. N.

1971   Sex, career and family. Beverly Hills:
        Sage.

Garland, N. T.

    1972   "The better half? The male in the dual profession family." In C. Safilios-Rothschild (Ed.), Toward a sociology of women. Lexington, MA: Xerox.

Gove, W. R., &
Geerken, M. R.

    1977   "The effect of children and employment on the mental health of married men and women." Social Forces, 56, 66-76.

Handy, C.

    1978   "Going against the grain: Working couples and greed occupations. In R. Rapoport & R. N. Rapoport (Eds.), Working couples. New York: Harper & Row.

Heckman, N. A., Bryson, R., &
Bryson, J.

    1977   "Problems of professional couples: A content analysis. Journal of Marriage and the Family. 39, 323-330.

Hoffman, L. W.

    1974   "Effects on child." In L. W. Hoffman & F. I. Nye (Eds.), Working mothers. San Francisco: Jossey-Bass.

Holmstrom, L. L

    1973   The two-career family. Cambridge, MA: Schenkman.

Hopkins, J., &
White, P.

    1978   "The dual-career couple: Constraints and supports." The Family Coordinator, 27, 253-259.

Martin, T. W., Berry, K. J., &
Jacobsen, R. B.

1975   "The impact of dual-career marriages
            on female professional careers: An
            empirical test of a Parsonian hypoth-
            esis." Journal of Marriage and the
            Family, 37, 734-742.

McCubbin, H.

1979   "Integrating coping behavior in family
            stress theory." Journal of Marriage
            and the Family, 41, 237-244.

Movius, M.

1976   "Voluntary childlessness--The ultimate
            liberation." The Family Coordinator,
            25, 57-62.

Orden, S. R., & Bradburn, N. M.

1969   "Working wives and marriage happiness."
            American Journal of Sociology, 74,
            382-407.

Papanek, H.

1973   "Men, women and work: Reflections of
            the two-person career." American
            Journal of Sociology, 78, 852-872.

Poloma, M. M.

1972   "Role conflict and the married pro-
            fessional woman." In C. Safilios-
            Rothschild (Ed.), Toward a sociology
            of women. Lexington, MA: Xerox.

Poloma, M. M., &
Garland, T.

1971   "The married professional woman: A
            study of the tolerance of domestication."
            Journal of Marriage and the Family,
            33, 531-540.

Rapoport, R., &
Rapoport, R. N.

1971   Dual-career families. Harmondsworth,
            England: Penguin.

Rapoport, R., &
Rapoport, R. N.

1976   Dual-career families reexamined. New
            York: Harper & Row.

Rapoport, R., &
Rapoport, R. N. (Eds.)

1978   Working couples. New York: Harper &
            Row.

Rapoport, R. N., &
Rapoport, R.

1978   "Dual-career families: Progress and
            prospects." Marriage and Family Review,
            1(5), 1-12.

Rice, D.

1979   Dual-career marriage: Conflict and
            treatment. New York: Free Press.

Richardson, J. G.

1979   "Wife occupational superiority and
            marital troubles: An examination of
            the hypothesis." Journal of Marriage
            and the Family, 41, 63-72.

Ridley, C. A.

1973   "Exploring the impact of work satis-
            faction and involvement on marital
            interaction when both partners are
            employed." Journal of Marriage and
            the Family, 35, 229-237.

Roland, A., &
Harris, B.

1979   Career and motherhood: Struggles for
            a new identity. New York: Human
            Sciences.

321

St. John-Parsons, D.

1978   "Continuous dual-career families: A
            case study." In J. B. Bryson & R.
            Bryson (Eds.), Dual-career couples.
            New York: Human Sciences.

Wallston, B. S., Foster, M. A., &
Berger, M.

1978   "I will follow him: Myth, reality,
            or forced choice--Job seeking experi-
            ences of dual-career couples. In
            J. B. Bryson & R. Bryson (Eds.),
            Dual-career couples. New York:
            Human Sciences.

*Denise A. Skinner is Assistant Professor, Department
of Human Development, Family Relations, and Community
Educational Services, University of Wisconsin-Stout,
Menomonie, WI.

COPING WITH FAMILY PROBLEMS AND CONFLICTS

Richard Nyberg* and
Douglas B. Gutknecht*

The family is in transition -- some would say, in trouble. Several chapters in this volume have addressed the fact that the ever increasing pace of change, both in contemporary lifestyles and societal values, has yielded significant and substantial alterations in the structure and functions of families. Many functions, traditionally within the scope of family responsibilities, are increasingly being adopted by the society at large. As society and the family changes so too does the character development of our young. In a very real sense, it is within the character structure and value development of the child that the family structure and its values are embodied and transmitted to a new generation. In short, as social values change so too will family values, which, in turn, impact on the character of the children. Family, self, and society are really three concentric circles through which contemporary culture can be viewed.

In viewing our cultures, several social critics have characterized our era as the "age of anxiety." Others might argue that the industrialized world has evolved from the age of anxiety to an age of depression. Regardless of whether we are in this or that "age," as measured by any popularly manifest psychiatric symptom, it is indisputable that ours can be seen as in an "age of coping." Even the most cursory review of the mental health and personal growth industries within our society bear witness to the fact that, in ever increasing numbers, we seek improved means of coping with the complexities of our world. The staggering proliferation of psychotherapeutic, and pseudo-therapeutic, "schools," the vast array of "how-to" literature in pop psychology, and the popularity of that endless series of workshops, and weekend encounters promising solutions to various expressions of dis-ease in this period of social transition, all reflect the eagerness -- or desperation -- people today feel in trying to cope with life.

Nowhere does this emphasis on coping find greater expression than in the context of the contemporary

323

family. The family of today is the place where many of the pressures of modern society are incubated and distilled. Today's family members, parents and children alike, are seeking survival skills for "making it" in an ever changing and uncertain world. Parents are tempted to begin earlier and earlier the process of preparing their young for coping in this turbulent and uncertain world. This situation is a dramatic contrast to the efforts made by parents to protect children from growing up that was commonplace 20 to 30 years ago.

Factors which have contributed to the destabilization of the family are complex and beyond the scope of these comments. Suffice it to note, however, that many of the factors which traditionally contributed to family stability have been significantly eroded over the past fifty years. Families today typically share those areas of work, religion, history, culture, and politics. Neither do they find legal sanctions, geographic, stability, or socially prescribed standards of labor as helpful in the stabilization of everyday living.

In chapters 16 and 17 the focus is upon brief, selected examples of therapy for families in trouble. The family therapy movement of the past thirty years might be characterized as a body of concepts and techniques in search of a theory. The authors of the articles offer some review of popular theories and also provide helpful guidance for the selection of a therapist.

In the midst of rapid social change there is a clear necessity to develop means by which individuals can first cope with their environment and secondly pursue personal actualization in the midst of it. Yet we are seeing increasing numbers of individuals who have grown weary of "coping" with life. Many of these pilgrims have spent a decade or two in pursuit of the promised personal fulfillment offered from a wide array of sources; only to find themselves at the end as confused as ever. Perhaps we are on the threshold of honestly exploring the difference between personal coping and social transformation and change, between the quest for personal mastery, to an appreciation of social responsibility and activism on behalf of supporting people who are exeriencing both stress and distress.

*Department of Social Relations, Chapman College,
 Orange, California.

CHAPTER 16

A FAMILY INTERVENTION: THREE PERSPECTIVES

James Buchholz* and
Richard Nyberg**

I.   INTRODUCTION

Family therapy as a distinct therapeutic model
found its genesis in the 1950's.   Since then, however, no single comprehensive theory of family therapy
has emerged.   Rather what we find today is a plethora
of therapy techniques for the family, each presuming
a certain conceptual framework.   Certainly implicit
theories provide the presuppositions for the varied
technical orientations, but as one commentator noted,
often, "...a therapist's theory was just a rationale
for his or her own clinical style" (Guerin, 1976:16).
Consequently, as yet no one has been successful in
unifying the many "schools", or "styles", which the
major clinicians practice; and which we therapists
emulate.

The purpose of this chapter is to comment on
three orientations to family therapy.   To facilitate
this goal we will offer a case presentation.   This
will provide the material for a discussion, and eventually a comparison, of how the three family therapists might proceed.   The three selected are Salvador
Minuchin, Virginia Satir, and Murray Bowen.   They were
done so because of the fact that all offer creative
and innovative insights to family therapy.   In addition, these particular ones were selected because
their intervention approaches to the family clearly
differ in emphasis--in what the process of family
therapy is.   Specifically, Minuchin places importance on individual, here and now, functioning within
a family structure; Satir because of her very practical approach to facilitating family communication
patterns; and Bowen because of the importance he
places on individual differentiation from one's family
through insight.   Therefore, it is to the task of
tracing Minuchin's participantobserver style, Satir's
empathetic-artistic style, and Bowen's didactic-coach
style, in the intervention with a family that the
following is dedicated.

II. A CASE STUDY EXAMPLE

The case study to be presented here will serve as the concrete foundation upon which all subsequent speculations will be founded. It concerns a family that one of the authors had seen in therapy. This is a white, upper-middle class, professional family, who live in a suburban community in New Jersey. The family consists of Mr. and Mrs. C., who have been married ten years, their nine year old son Michael, and their seven year old daughter Laura. This family came for counseling upon the recommendation of Michael's third grade teacher, who had subsequently referred Michael to the school's Child Study Team for a complete evaluation.

Michael, the identified patient, is a nine year old boy with a cherub-like face and blond hair. He wears heavy glasses and is of average height/weight for his age. When seen by the therapist he appeared neat and well cared for, and while his manner was somewhat abstracted, his appearance was not remarkable. Michael is an intelligent child, evidencing this through a WISC-R score of 121. This places him in the superior range of mental functioning. He also has an active and creative capacity for fantasy, which emerges in his prolific fabrications of comic strips, stories, drawings and the likes which he produces in spare moments.

Laura is a seven year old girl, currently in the second grade. She also, is an attractive child, with dishwater blond hair and a graceful, confident demeanor. She is a serious student who has always performed at the top of her class, even as early as kindergarten. She is Mrs. C's favorite child, as she characterizes Laura as "perfect", and Michael as "terrible". The worker sensed that behind Laura's school success and pseudo-adult style lies an anxious young girl; so driven by her need to gain approval through achievement that she finds it difficult to relax enough to simply be the child she is.

Both Mr. and Mrs. C are intelligent professional people. Mr. C is thirty-seven years old, and holds a Ph.D. in biochemistry. He is employed by a large chemical corporation, and functions at the executive/ professional level. Mrs. C., also thrity-seven, has earned a masters degree in biochemistry. Although she currently functions as a full-time homemaker, she is seeking a position as a university laboratory assistant. Both Mr. and Mrs. C appear to lack affective spontaneity, and outwardly disparage anything that is frivolous or non-scientific. Life, for them, is pursued with calculated logic and scientific objectivity.

The referral sent to the Child Study Team by Michael's teacher suggested that, although Mike is an intelligent boy who possesses the capacity to do work that is above grade level, he regularly gives the impression that he is a poor student. He forgets assignments, fails to do homework, etc., often claiming that he didn't understand the instructions given to the class. Hence, he gives the appearance of being "disorganized" and "irresponsible", unable to do classwork without intense personal instructions. Michael's teacher also noted that he sometimes seems oblivious to his surroundings, hiding underneath his desk or in the clothes closet. When confronted with his behavior Michael typically remains silent, or opens his mouth wide and bobs his head around. He has also been known to sing "nonsense songs" when asked questions concerning material being discussed with the rest of the class.

It was suggested that Michael doesn't relate well to other children in school. He appears socially inept, not knowing how to approach or play with others. He can usually be found reading or playing alone, but if he does interact with other children he often becomes excited and acts inappropriately. He might do this by leaving a game early, hitting his peers for reasons which aren't always obvious to the others, or change rules arbitrarily in games.

In the process of follow-up on the referral, the therapist observed Michael in his classroom setting and on the playground. These observations were in general agreement with the views presented by the teacher. Some of Michael's former teachers were contacted as well, and their statements concerning Michael's school behavior in the past were congruent with those presented in the referral. Some additional information gathered from these discussions suggested that Michael became easily frustrated when not immediately able to grasp concepts. He was said to have displayed a tendency to withdraw from reality into the fantasy world of his daydreams, and lacked any interest in forming relationships with peers; preferring

329

instead to play with machines like the tape recorder and other teaching devices.

Having received several different perspectives on Michael's behavior within the school setting, the therapist proceeded to arrange a meeting with the C. family; this in the hope of establishing a contact for some sort of counseling in the event that the pending medical examinations, and learning consultant's reports, proved negative. By the time that contact was made with Mr. and Mrs. C. they had already met with Michael's teacher. While Mrs. C. was anxious to speak with the worker, and hoped to get some recommendations on what might be done to help her son, Mr. C. expressed the feeling that Michael's problems were not so severe as to warrant counseling. He also deemed psychology worthless and unscientific, but agreed to meet with the worker once if it would serve to get his wife off his back. He made it clear, however, that he would not participate in or contribute to our discussion concerning Michael's behavior; and that he was certain that Michael would outgrow this "immaturity" as he grows older. The father further contended that he was much like Michael when he was a child, and, as anyone could readily see, he had obviously adjusted well, becoming a highly respected professional.

The initial meeting with the C. family was a tense affair. All members of the family appeared nervous and apprehensive. The chairs in the office were arranged in a circular manner with the worker flanked on either side by Mr. and Mrs. C., and Michael and Laura wedged between the parents. Laura sat near the mother, Michael next to the father. The following diagram illustrates the seating of the initial interview.

M

Mr. C.

L

Therapist

Mrs. C.

After some perfunctory opening remarks and a few comments designed to put the family at ease, the worker asked the general question of why each felt they were in to see him. The question was directed toward Mr. C. who remained aloof and silent. Mrs. C. acted as though the question was meant for her and

330

answered immediately. She said that they had come to discuss Michael's problem with school, and to see if anything could be done to help the situation.

Recognizing that Mrs. C. was presently acting as the spokesperson for the family, the worker made an attempt to elicit a response from Mr. C.. He asked Mr. C. what his opinion of the situation was. The father replied that he did not feel that Michael had any problems which the family couldn't work out themselves. These remarks made Mrs. C. agitated, and she proceeded to defend her point that indeed Michael did have problems. She began to relate these by noting that Michael was a "difficult" child. She claimed that as a baby he didn't seem "cuddly" like other babies she had held, but rather became stiff and tense when picked up. She also said that he always appeared overly sensitive to any sort of moderate stimulation, crying when brought into department stores because of the lights, music, and crowds, or screaming when he simply had an itch. She further spoke of his need to routinize activities, being obsessed with the desire to have his day run on a strict schedule, and of the pleasure that he finds in repetitive activities such as listening to the same records over and over again.

While Mrs. C. related the history of Michael's "problem," the worker asked others for their perceptions of what was being said. Mr. C. noted that he couldn't understand why everyone was making such a fuss over Michael, since, in his opinion, these activities were not at all strange; and that certainly Michael would outgrow them. Michael appeared detached throughout most of the discussion. He either remained silent or else suggested he didn't know the answers to queries directed to him. Laura said little when addressed by the worker, but responded actively when enlisted by her mother to share her perceptions of her brother. Here Laura noted that Michael was "odd" and that he remained as an outcast with most of their neighborhood peers. She agreed with Mrs. C.'s reports that Michael interprets other children's loud play as yelling at him, and either responds to it by withdrawal or fighting. Laura further related that the other children simply don't like Michael because he acts so strange.

At this point Mr. C. became angry and shouted at Laura for acting as though she was such a "goody-

goody." He suggested that all this talk was "foolish and illogical," and that he couldn't see where it could possibly lead. He moved to end the session at this point.

Subsequent sessions with Mrs. C. revealed certain information about her relationship with her husband, as well as some background information pertinent to our future discussion. Mrs. C. noted that her relationship with her husband had always been a "cool" one. She suggested that she decided to marry him because they were in the same field of study in graduate school, and that she felt that it was about time for her to get married. She claimed that there was never much emotional investment in their marriage, but rather that it was a bond of convenience more than anything else.

She noted that her pregnancy with Michael was unpleasant, and that when she learned that she was pregnant she felt angry and trapped; knowing that she would have to forego her career pursuits. She harbored feelings of resentment, also, throughout most of her pregnancy, finding herself jealous of her husband's career and depressed at the prospects of herself being simply a housewife. Mrs. C. claimed that near the end of her pregnancy she had "warmed up" considerably to the idea of having a child, but that once Michael was born these feelings quickly dissipated. This was largely due to the fact that Michael was a "fussy" and "troublesome" child, and that she felt inadequate at mothering him; often fearing that others would interpret Michael's behavior as an indication of her ineptness in being a mother.

Mrs. C. further related that beyond her general anger and anxiety at being a mother that she could expect little support from her husband in efforts to socialize and discipline the children. She views Mr. C. as an ineffectual husband and father; one who has saddled her with the entire responsibility for raising the children. She reports that Mr. C.'s contact with the children is only at his convenience.

These conversations with Mrs. C. also revealed that throughout the eight years since Laura's conception she and Mr. C. have had no sexual intercourse; and that Mr. C. has, on occasion, had extra marital affairs.

Finally, Mrs. C. spoke briefly of her own and her husband's family situations before their marriage. She noted that she had only one sibling, an older brother, who was not very intelligent and who was easily dominated by others--especially her parents. She characterized herself as the "smart responsible child" in the family. Her father, she said, was a "wild and angry man." He was prone to fits of violence, especially when drunk. Further, he had no respect for Mrs. C.'s mother, and evidenced this openly with his numerous extra-marital affairs. Mrs. C.'s mother enlisted her as a confidant, telling her what a poor husband she had and how lonely and upset she was. Mrs. C.'s father was very protective of his daughter, finding fault with all of her boyfriends. She claims that he would wrestle with the boyfriends to assert his own masculinity, and to show them that he was a better man than anyone his daughter would bring home. Once when he was drunk he became openly seductive towards Mrs. C. She was an early adolescent at the time, and was extremely frightened by his actions.

The picture that she presented of Mrs. C.'s family situation was quite different. He was the eldest child in a very large family. He has four younger brothers and three sisters. Mrs. C. claims that her husband's family was quite poor and lived in a rundown rural area. She noted that her husband was always ashamed of his family and had feelings of resentment at having to grow up in poverty. Reportedly, Mr. C. has always been a loner because of the embarrassment he felt at his family's economical situation; and to this day finds it hard to relate to people on a casual, friendly basis. She suggested that Mr. C. has come to face the world with a "chip on his shoulder" and maintains the attitude that he has to "get others before they get him." He reportedly has been able to channel this aggression into his career in becoming a "superprofessional," but has made many "enemies" along the way.

With this case material in mind, we can now turn our central task of speculating on how Salvador Minuchin, Virginia Satir, and Murry Bowen might intervene with the C. family.

III. THE MINUCHIN APPROACH

"I am myself plus my circumstances" (Minuchin,
1974:6) is a quote of Ortyga y Gasset which is of key
importance to Salvador Minuchin. He believes that
indeed "no man is an island." Rather that we all are
what we are, and who we are, in a psycho-social-bio
ecosystem. Further, it is one's immediate family that
provides the individual with a basis sense of self,
an identity. Consequently, since the family is the
"..matrix of identity.." (Minuchin, 1974:47) it is to
the family that Minuchin focuses his attention in
serving those in psychological, and often physical,
pain.

Structurally the family is viewed as a functional,
hydrolic system. This structure is "..an invisible
set of functional demands that organize the ways in
which the family members interact" (Minuchin, 1974:47).
The family is composed of "transactional patterns,"
the relatively stable ways in which members relate
to one another, as well as how they adapt to internal
and external forces which impinge on the system. According to Minuchin, each member within a family functions some role in the task of maintaining the system;
and that the vicissitudes of life, and the stages of
individual and family growth, require of the family
constantly new adaptive postures.

Within the nuclear family system are sub-systems.
Typically this would include the parental, spouse,
and sibling sub-systems. The role of each of these
is, hopefully, to coordinate their efforts in maintaining the whole system's functional integrity. Problems, both corporate and individual, arise when one of
the substysems fails to contribute adaptively to the
whole; when it abdicates on its functional responsibility. When this occurs, the entire family system is
thrown into disequilibrium, and consequently loses its
capacity to facilitate individual growth, and to make
adaptive responses to its internal and external environments. It is at this point in Minuchin's view
that individual pathology--symptomatic of familial dys-
function--emerges.

In viewing the C. family from Minuchin's perspective, we would see a family clearly in functional
distress. While Michael certainly is in pain, and
in need of corrective intervention, the pathological
seed is not to be found in his personality. Rather,

334

since "..children function as conflict-detouring mechanisms" (Minuchin, 1974:8), Michael's are but an expression of a system in distress--a system of family pathology. Consequently, according to Minuchin, the goal of intervention with this family would be to relieve Michael's symptomatic behavior by first assessing where it fits into the family system--how it functions in the family--and secondly, by conceiving of a plan to correct the system. The goal then is to promote a more adaptive family, one without the need for Michael's symptoms.

In pursuing this end, Minuchin finds it incumbent on the therapist to "join" the family: to "... become an actor in the family drama" (Minuchin, 1974: 60). By joining the family the therapist psychologically enters the family so as to experience firsthand its dynamics. From this vantage point Minuchin would make his assessment, and, as a functional member, (albeit more objective than the others) would seek to restructure the family so that it will be more corporately and individually adaptive.

In this process a family map is of paramount importance. "A family map is an organizational scheme" (Minuchin, 1974:90) which charts the family's predominant transactional patterns, as well as their subsystems. In turning to the C. family, a family map would appear as follows:

			Minuchin's (1974:53)
FATHER	MOTHER		key:
		LAURA	Clear Boundaries------
			Diffused " ......
			(emmeshed)
	MICHAEL		Rigid Boundaries_____
			(disengaged)
			Affiliation ******
			Overinvolvement ******
			Conflict
			Coalition __ __
			Detouring

Here we find graphic expression of the family dynamics. The father is psychologically seen as outside the family. This is depicted by a rigid boundary. The mother and sister are in an alliance; one which not only short-circuits the functional parent, spouse and sibling sub-systems, but also undercuts each's

335

individual autonomy through the overinvolved enmeshed relationship between mother and her responsible
"tattle-tale" daughter. The map further portrays
Michael's place as the symptom bearer of the family
system. He is seen to function not only as to divert
the spouse system from their own conflicts, but also
provides a focus to justify mother's overinvolvement
with the daughter; an alliance which serves to satisfy
emotional needs of the mother left frustrated through
her marriage.

According to Minuchin, Michael's symptomatic role
in this family is critical. Since the entire system
proved unable to respond creatively to the internal
requirements of the executive function, it became
rigid in the transactional pattern illustrated above.
It is therefore crucial for its current homeostatis,
albeit a maladaptive homeostais, that Michael remains
symptomatic. For without Michael's problems the
parents would no longer be diverted from the family's
fundamental problem, viz, a malfunctioning executive/
spouse sub-system. In short, the parents, so as to
rigidly maintain the sad status quo, need a troubled
child.

The family map is the product of the therapist's
assessment of the family. To Minuchin it results from
the therapist's skillful joining with each member of
the family, and with each sub-system. This is a critical point. The therapist must join with all aspects
of the family so as to: 1) arrive at an accurate
diagnosis/assessment; 2) broaden the problem focus to
the entire family; and 3) lay the ground-plan for the
task of restructuring the family system--all without
provoking unyielding family resistances.

In Minuchin's view, the ideal resolution to the
C. family's problem would look something like this:

```
        HUSBAND       WIFE
        ----------------------

        FATHER        MOTHER
        ----------------------

        CHILD         CHILD
```

Here the spouse, parent, and sibling sub-systems would
be free to function adaptively and homeostatically;
flexible to internal and external contingencies, with

a clear operational hierarchy, and a functional distribution of tasks. However, Minuchin believes that no system can tolerate too great a disruption at one time. Consequently, his intervention would aim at maintaining the system to a degree, while gradually restructuring it towards the goal; this "...in such a way that they are not threatened by major dislocation" (Minuchin, 1974:119).

In hazarding successive approximations, eventually transforming the family into acting in functional transactional patterns, Minuchin first joins the family. With the C. family this would require the immediate enlistment of the father, the one most resistant to change. Given this man's technical propensity Minuchin might appeal to Mr. C.'s scientific penchant by claiming that "...as a therapist I am at times more artistic than scientific, and I'll need your scientific skills in helping me make your son happier." This might enlist the "outside" father by: 1) placing him in the appropriate, socially accepted, executive function in the family; 2) defuse the father's defensive negative attitudes towards psychotherapy; and 3) manipulate him publicly into active and cooperative participation in the therapeutic process.

In effect, in joining with the family members Minuchin believes that "I turn other family members into my co-therapists" (Minuchin, 1974:121). Once the most resistant member is enlisted into the process, by hook or crook obviously. Minuchin would then turn to the subtle task of restructuring.

Rather than attacking the marital dysfunction head on, it seems likely that Minuchin would work towards disengaging the mother-daughter coalition. By pointing out that the daughter works too hard at being responsible (all the while affirming how fortunate the parents are to have such a responsible child), as well as entering into more playful activities, Minuchin would begin to open a "back door" to the central family problem. If the girl is encouraged by the parents to spend less time in the system, the system will begin to lose its homeostasis. Presumably, the mother will then begin to feel her pain more; which, in turn, might make her more amenable to dealing with her husband. In essence, Minuchin's maneuver to place himself between the mother and daughter, promoting each's autonomy, is aimed at having repercussions throughout the entire system. And, to Minuchin, it is as the system loses its balance that it is most vulnerable to therapeutic change.

In restructuring the family Minuchin might employ a variety of techniques. With the aim of restructuring the mother--daughter boundary, we saw hom Minuchin might have intervened. This intervention might, in turn, begin to re-form appropriate boundaries throughout the system.

Secondly, because action precedes insight in Minuchin's view, the therapist would want to manipulate the physical space in the sessions. This would be aimed as having the family act out boundaries which the therapist wants them to move towards. One way this could be achieved with the C. family would be to change the seating arrangement. As noted in the previous seating arrangement diagram, during the initial interview the family's dynamic boundaries, their transactional patterns, were embodied in their selection of seats. By trading seats with the mother to the folowing:

M

Mr. C.   L

Mrs. C.   T

the therapist would be actualizing boundaries during the session which he hopes to eventually see in the new family structure.

In addition to the in-session tasks which stimulate the formation of new boundaries (e.g., asking the parents to decide on ways that Laura might be encouraged to play more), Minuchin utilizes homework assignments. In this way he holds that the clients are "...in effect taking the therapist home with them" (Munichin, 1974:6). With the C. family Minuchin might have the parents agree to get together at a certain time, and for a specified period, each evening to discuss how they might encourage their daughter to be more playful/spontaneous (each quality, of course, precisely what the spouse sub-system needs). In addition, the father might be assigned the task of spending forty-five minutes each night alone with Michael for the explicit purpose of reading his science fiction comics to his son. (Mr. C. has an exhaustive collection of comics which serve as a refuge from family interaction.) To facilitate this, (actually to paint the father into a corner) Minuchin might

explain that, since the child has such a good and
creative ability to entertain fantasies (the paradoxical view of one of the presenting symptoms), and
since the father is both a respected scientist and
lover of good comics, that each would really enjoy the
task.

In this final regard Minuchin would be utilizing
the symptom in service to the restructuring process.
This would be achieved by: 1) capitalizing on both
the father's and son's defensive adaptive maneuvers;
that is to say, employing the existing systemic resources, maladaptive as they are, in service to the
restructuring tasks; 2) return the father to the
father--son relationship; and 3) begin the process
of redefining the child's symptoms, i.e., from the
family's perception of fantasy as part of Michael's
pathology to one of his strenghs.

According to Minuchin, the role of the family
therapist is to "...manipulate the family system
towards planned change" (Minuchin, 1974:140). To
accomplish this he has to firstly know the family
structure, their boundaries, and their transactional
patterns. In addition, the family therapist must
know how the presenting problem serves the family
system. With this in mind the therapist then "...
becomes an actor in the family play" (Minuchin, 1974:
138), joining sub-systems, entering alliances, with
individuals, disrupting transactional patterns, and
manipulating the entire system. In short, just about
anything which promotes the system's movement towards
greater adaptability and functionality. All of this,
of course, must proceed while satisfying the "first
rule" of family therapy, i.e., "...to leave the family
willing to come again for the next session" (Minuchin,
1974:212).

IV. THE SATIR APPROACH

At this point, the family presented in our case
study will be examined from the perspective offered
by Virginia Satir in her theory of family therapy.
In order to better understand how this particular mode
of family treatment would apply to the case at hand,
a brief overview of several of Satir's most basic concepts will be offered, as they appear embodied in her
goals for treatment. Secondly, in assessing the case
study, our focus will be upon pertinent issues from
Satir's theory of family interaction. Specifically,

this will include: 1) the notion of self-esteem and how this plays an important role in the selection of a spouse; 2) environmental or societal stresses affecting the family that seeks out therapeutic help; and 3) the process of triangling that often causes children to be pulled into their parent's distressed marital relationship.

It has been suggested that the most basic element in Satir's theory, and hence, the major treatment goal, is that of "maturation" (Foley, 1974:94). Satir writes that maturation is the most important concept in therapy, because it is the touchstone for all the rest (Satir, 1967:91). What she means when speaking of maturation, is that state of functioning when one is fully in charge of oneself and one's actions, and is able to make choices and decisions based on an accurate perception of oneself, others, and the context in which one finds oneself. The mature person can acknowledge the choices and decisions that they make as their own, and accepts responsibility for their outcome (Satir, 1967:91).

Although this might appear to be a rather broad and idealistic treatment goal, one must remember that it remains the hub around which all secondary treatment goals are constructed. That is, there are several intermediate steps which must be implemented and fit together in order to arrive at the overarching goal of maturation. One of these secondary goals is that of developing the ability to manifest oneself clearly through communication. Satir suggests that people must be able to communicate clearly if they care to give and receive information that accurately conveys what is being thought or felt (Satir, 1967:64). She claims that the meaning of words is often unclear, hence it is important for open dialogue to take place between people in order that they might clarify and qualify what they mean. Satir is quick to note, however, that communication is more than simply a verbal process. One communicates on at least two levels: 1) the denotative level, and 2) the metacommunative or non-verbal level (Satir, 1967:76). Unless one is sending clear messages on both levels, misunderstandings resulting in stress may occur.

Implicit within the concept of communication for Satir is her emphasis on expression of feelings. Foley suggests that the focal point on which Satir's communication theory revolves is the emotional or feeling level of this process (Foley, 1974:93). He notes that Satir attempts, from the beginning of treatment, to engage the family in therapy by responding to their "pain." Faulty patterns of communication can evolve from many sources, but ultimately one must get beyond the pain and anger that one feels at not being understood before one can deal with any of the other issues. Hence, expression of feelings is a necessary correlate to open communication.

Another important component necessary for helping a person toward mature functioning is a sense of differentiation of self from significant others, and an acceptance of differences in those who are important to us. This concept of differentiation is intimately related to Satir's notion of self-esteem. That is, if a person has a low sense of self-esteem he will be crippled in the areas of individuality and autonomy (Satir, 1967:8). Satir believes that people with low self-esteem attract one another in the world of social and sexual relationships. Each entertains the fantasy that the other will take care of them and provide them with that which is lacking in their life. Once these such persons become married, however, this illusion is quickly dispelled. The spouses soon realize that they are called upon to give as well as to receive in this relationship (Satir, 1967:11). Each partner experiences the other as being "different" from what they had expected and needed in a marital relationship, and any hope of somehow merging with their mate and having all of their deficiencies eliminated is shattered. Hence, work toward differentiation of self, as outlined by Satir, must necessarily entail work toward developing greater self-esteem.

As Satir proceeds with her elucidations on the couples' sense of frustration, and their unrealistic expectations in terms of marital needs, i.e., they gradually awaken to the fact that he/she does not exist primarily to meet the needs of the other, the logical outcome points toward a stress situation. Each member of the marital dyad, upon finding that their needs will not be met automatically, finds it difficult or impossible to negotiate clearly for what they desire or to effect any sort of compromise. They will often move, at this point, to "triangle" one of their children into their relationship. This is done by the parents, in an attempt to have their needs met through this child, and also to express their aggression indirectly toward one another as well (Satir,

1972:58-59). This development brings us full circle, back to the need for effective patterns of communication, a means to adequately express one's feelings and a persistence in working toward becoming a mature and fully functioning person.

Having outlined some of the major theoretical foundations of Satir's concept of family therapy, we can now turn to our case study to explore how this mode of treatment could be implemented in practice. When attempting to encapsulate Satir's style of initiating treatment with families in distress, two variables stand out immediately. These are: 1) her attempt to "join" the family in a relaxed, non-threatening manner, and 2) her willingness to direct questions to all members of the family in a low-keyed, probing way, geared toward allowing everyone to express where the "pain" in their family resides for them. Using these guidelines from the beginning, Satir might have made her first contact with Mr. and Mrs. C. by telephone. Here she would attempt to present herself as a warm and understanding person, one who is interested in what they have to say. To Mr. C.'s initial resistance, Satir might have replied that she could understand how he might feel confused over many of the issues that both the school and Mrs. C. were raising, and that she would hope that he might come to the first session to express his bewilderment.

The initial interview with the family would involve an assessment of what each member hopes or expects to get from treatment. During the first interview, it is also imperative that the therapist bring the family to the point of recognizing how they experience the pain of their dysfunctional family system. This can be done by merely asking each family member to discuss when they first noticed the symptom or what has been done to relieve it (Satir, 1967:110). In the case of the C. family, this direct tack might not be effective. In this situation Satir might observe the family interaction surrounding the question of Michael's symptom. She might point up that this whole question must be a very painful one for everyone. She would suggest that Mr. and Mrs. C. must feel the tension that comes between them as a result of this situation. She could also note that Laura must feel torn as well, since she receives mixed messages from both parents concerning how she should react toward Michael's behavior. Finally, Satir might note that Michael must feel very confused about this whole matter, wondering if, in the end, he is alright or not.

If Satir can get all members of the family to feel the pain that the "family symptom" causes each of them individually, she can key into their probable puzzlement over why the symptom exists and what they can do about it (Satir, 1967:110-111). Here she would suggest that everyone finds it hard to understand why their family hurts so badly. She would point out that often we do everything that we know, and yet things remain the same. Satir makes these sort of comments in an effort to decrease the threat of blame and to accentuate the idea of good intensions exercise to no avail (Satir, 1967:110). If she senses that the family is actively experiencing the pain and confusion that is a result of their collective dysfunctioning, Satir moves to gain information by means of the family chronology.

The taking of the family chronology serves a myriad of purposes. First, it provides the therapist with a wealth of information concerning the family process and its evolution from the time when Mr. and Mrs. C. were first dating to its present status. Secondly, it serves to take the focus off Michael as the "identified patient," and shows everyone that the family has a history where they all experienced happier moments (Satir, 1967:113). Finally, the family chronology will serve to point up the "different-ness" in each member of the family. Satir writes that, "Different-ness is a loaded idea in dysfunciontal families" (Satir, 1967:123). She would want to continually note how Mr. and Mrs. C. are, indeed, different from one another in many ways, just as their parents were different, and that the ways in which they have been handling their different-ness may be unsuitable for them.

Hence, through taking this family chronology, Satir would quickly learn that both Mr. and Mrs. C. entered their marriage with a low sense of self-esteem. Mr. C. may have hoped that his wife would provide the nurturance and acceptance that he had never received as a child. Mrs. C. may have felt that her husband would be a strong figure upon whom she could depend for support and approval. Once married, their illusions were shattered and the sense of disappointment set in. To complicate matters, Michael was conceived early in their marriage. This

343

put added stress on their relationship, in that they now had to carry what Satir characterizes as, "the extra load" of parenting (Satir, 1967:26). Hence, a disillusioned Mrs. C. was left with no opportunity to gain the approval she required through the outlet of a career. A frightened Mr. C. faced the prospect of becoming a father, and being required to give his child love and support, while he, himself, remained frustrated in his attempt to secure the reassurance he needed.

It would soon become apparent to Satir that this family is showing the signs indicated in the postulate that, "a pained marital relationship tends to produce dysfunctional parenting (Satir, 1967:2). Mr. and Mrs. C. undoubtedly learned to communicate their feelings of anger and disappointment toward one another through their first child. Mrs. C. covertly communicates the message that if Michael has problems, it is because Mr. C. is an ineffectual father, unable to lend their son the support and approval he requires to be a "normal" child. Mr. C., in his denial of Michael's "problems," is suggesting that Mrs. C. is an over-demanding mother, unable to love her child for what he is. Both parents need to have Michael exhibit problem behavior in order that this subtle power struggle might continue. Hence, the "rules" that this family operates within are uncovered by means of the family chronology and observation of family interaction.

Satir would then want to intervene in this faulty network of communication by attempting to have the family clarify what they mean when they communicate and verbalize how they feel about the messages being sent. She would do this first, by creating a setting in which all could take the risk of looking clearly and objectively at themselves and their actions (Satir, 1967:160). This is facilitated by the active participation and direction offered by the therapist in the counseling sessions. Satir would undoubtedly ask family members to continually repeat or restate their messages if they are unclear so that nothing is left to the imagination. She would also want to ask for continual feedback regarding how family members feel about issues being discussed, and to point up non-verbal inconsistencies that go with verbal messages. Finally, she might use some direct confrontation when she felt that the family was ready for it.

344

Direct confrontation might come in the form of suggestions that Mrs. C. is acting very much like her own mother when she shuts Mr. C. out of her life and aligns herself with her daughter. It might also be noted that Mr. C. has never really learned to trust his wife enough to ask for the affection that he so desperately desires. The consequences of these actions are a storing up of hatred and resentment that ultimately emerges through their child's symptomatic behavior.

It would be of great importance to the therapeutic process that the C. family actively practice clear and direct patterns of communication both in therapy sessions and at home. To enable this to take place, Satir might assign homework tasks in the form of games that the family could play together. Several of these games, outlined in her book, Peoplemaking, are designed specifically for this sort of task. If the C. family would pursue at a more open stance on communication and expression of feelings, they would be taking their first steps toward the ultimate goal of family maturation.

V. THE BOWEN APPROACH

The final portion of this paper will deal with Murray Bowen's view of family therapy as it applies to our case study. For Bowen, the family is an emotional system made up from a variety of emotional subsystems. Bowen would suggest that the "nuclear family" is really non-existent. Rather, what is generally referred to as the nuclear family is but a tip expression of a multigenerational entity. However alienated the nuclear family is from its family of origin, be it geographical, psychological, or cultural, Bowen holds that individuals within any particular family system are influenced significantly by their ancestry.

As Bowen translates this into family assessments, he seeks to investigate as far back into its antecedent history as possible. To Bowen, there is a "... remarkable consistency of family functioning through the generations" (Bowen, 1976:86). Since he believes that family members are "replicas of the past," Bowen explores emotional systems and styles of family relations, which were valued, taught, and passed on through the generations, and the current family style of relating serving as its legacy.

In scrutinizing the influence which the family of origin has on any family problem, Bowen is particularly interested in the "levels of differentiation" of the various members. For both past and present family members, Bowen attempts to answer the query, "How successful was each individual in differentiation from their family of origin?" For while Bowen believes that the family is essential in providing the nurturing context for developing individuals, that is the matrix of pre-adult development, the family can also impede this process of individuation. To best grasp this we must briefly explore Bowen's notion of "differentiation and indifferentiation."

In Bowen's view, every individual functions at some level of differentiation from his or her family of origin. In a somewhat arbitrary fashion, Bowen postulates a differentiation scale from 0 through 100, with the least differentiated the former, the greatest the latter. Within this scheme the average adult functions somewhere around the 45-55 range, the superior in the 60's. What this means is that the greater one's differentiation rating, the greater one's emotional and physical independence from one's family. The less one's differentiation, the greater one's immersion in the family. In short, the more differentiated, the greater the individual's ability to function autonomously, discover self, and respond to the environment. The less one's differentiation from their family, the less one's autonomy and the greater one's bondage to feelings -- reacting to the environment. Hence, "a poorly differentiated person ..." to Bowen "...is trapped within a feeling world" (Bowen, 1976:67).

With these assumptions, Bowen concludes that it is from the family that individuals receive their basic differentiation rating -- the "real self." To Bowen the "real" or "solid" self says, "This is who I am, and what I believe, what I stand for, and I will do or will not do in a given situation" (Bowen, 1976:68). The basic differentiation rating is the legacy of one's family system. Furthermore, Bowen goes on to suggest that certain offspring will tend to be less differentiated than their parents; and so on until, as "...we follow the most impaired child through successive generations, we will see one line of descendants producing individuals with lower and lower differentiation" (Bowen, 1976:86). To Bowen, it is the schizophrenic that is the natural outcome of this downward spiral.

346

Certain individuals tend to be less differentiated than their parents because they are "triangled" into the emotion system. Triangles are the cornerstone to Bowen's theory. They are the, "basic building blocks of any emotional system" (Bowen, 1976:76). A triangle exists when a dyadic relationship, faced with stress, enlists a third to provide it stability; the price of which is some form of family symptom. In short, when a marital couple is in conflict and seems unable to cope with it, they will "triangle" a child to discharge the anxiety generated by their seemingly unresolvable discord. It will be this triangled person who will tend to bear the family symptom, and be a less differentiated self than the parents.

Just why a certain child is selected by the parents to be triangled is a complex matter in Bowen's writings. It may have to do with the parental sibling positions, triangled emotional systems brought into the marriage which predate the birth of children or outside stress factors. Whatever the reason, it is certain that triangles will appear in any emotional system, and that they have the capacity to interlock and draw in others again, when stress becomes unbearable.

Finally, as we found with the family therapists previously noted, Bowen views the family as the locus of treatment. It is the family unit which precipitates most of the psychological complaints that bring people into treatment. Even though one member may come with a particular symptom, the dynamic roots of this problem are to be located in the family's emotional system. In short, a symptom is conceived by Bowen as the negative side of a family triangle. Consequently, it is the therapist's task to analyze the family's emotional system, perceive its triangles and initiate the process of "de-triangling" individuals from their enmeshed family system. Hence the goal is, "to restore love and togetherness in the family" (Bowen, 1972:161), and to "...help individual family members to a higher level of differentiation" (Foley, 1974:116).

With these comments in mind we will now turn to the C. family in an attempt to examine Murray Bowen's approach to family treatment as it pertains to this particular case. Although it is certain that Bowen recognizes the family as the locus of treatment, unlike the previous theorists we have discussed, he does not always require that all family members participate in the therapy process. He notes that, "My optimum approach to any family problem, whether marital conflict, dysfunction in a spouse, or dysfunction in a child, is to start with the husband and wife together ...but this optimum is not always possible..., hence some 30 to 40 percent of family hours are spent with one family member, mostly for situations in which one spouse is antagonistsic or poorly motivated" (Bowen, 1976:185). Keeping in mind Bowen's adage that, "a theoretical system that thinks in terms of family and works toward improving the family system is family psychotherapy" (Bowen, 1976:169). We can recognize that this is a valid position in the realm of family treatment.

Concurrent with Bowen's view of family psychotherapy is the fact that nowhere in his published literature does he openly discuss dealing with resistant clients. Rather, he appears to presuppose a highly intelligent, motivated, and wealthy clientele; for his therapeutic intervention process is often quite time consuming and rigorous. In this sense, Bowen would undoubtedly have dealth exclusively with Mrs. C. in this particular case, keeping the emphasis and focus clearly on family patterns of interaction. Since Bowen believes that, "The mechanisms that operate outside the nuclear family ego mass are important in determining the course and process within the nuclear family" (Bowsen, 1976:178), he might engage Mrs. C. in treatment by suggesting that before Michael can begin to be understood and changed, she herself would need to assess how the patterns of relating which she has learned from her family of origin contribute to Michael's behavioral symptoms.

If Mrs. C. would agree to pursue treatment with Bowen, her first task would be to compile a detailed, "chronological review of symptom development, with specific dates and circumstances at the time of each symptom eruption, because many symptomatic eruptions can be timed exactly with other events in the nuclear and extended family fields" (Bowen, 1976:181). For this she would have to go back to her family of origin and do some interviewing to secure the required information. Once she had completed this task, which could take from three weeks to several months, Bowen would take on his "coach" role. Here, he would examine the material, pointing out triangles and enmeshed relationships, and ask for feedback from Mrs. C. in order to establish the validity of his assumptions. The intent at this point is to afford some insight into the process that holds Mrs. C. captive to her current manner of relating to others.

Once insight is established, Mrs. C. would be further "coached" in the task of "detriangling" herself from her family of origin. Bowen would undoubtedly point up the fact that Mrs. C. was triangled into a relationship with her mother and father which served to dissipate the stress that occurred between them in their marriage. He might suggest that this very same process is mirrored in her own nuclear family. There, Laura serves as her confidant and source of gratification, while her husband, like her own father, remains detached, only to be reached through their mutual involvement with Michael, who like her brother, needs to be taken care of. In order to break up this insidious network of interlocking triangles, Mrs. C. would need to go back to her parents to work toward getting them to relate to her on an individual level, rather than as a means of reducing anxiety between themselves.

Hence, under the guise of friendly visits home, Mrs. C. would be put to the task of: 1) meeting alone with each of her parents in the hope of getting them to recognize and relate to her as an individual rather than a stopgap for their own marital stress, and 2) attempting to facilitate direct discussion between her mother and father, while she, herself, remains detriangled. Although this appears to be a fairly straight-forward task, it will be no mean feat to accomplish a breakthrough in well established coping patterns. Mrs. C. will undoubtedly need to visit her parents numerous times over the course of at least one or two years, writing countless letters and visiting her equally triangled brother. If after all of this work and constant coaching from Bowen, Mrs. C. is able to detriangle herself from her parents, a radical change should be seen in her extended and nuclear families.

The most obvious result of this process would be a freer, more differentiated Mrs. C. She would have the capacity now to "respond" to her parents and brother rather than "reacting" at the smallest indication of stress. Secondly, Mrs. C.'s parents would become more capable of dealing directly with

349

one another, and perhaps would no longer require
Mrs. C.'s brother to act as the oaf who constantly
requires direction. Finally, Mrs. C. should be prepared, at this point, to enter her own nuclear family
with renewed freedom and flexibility. She has acquired a myriad of detriangling techniques that she
should now to able to use with her husband and children.

If this is beginning to sound like a smooth and
predictable process, a false image is being perpe-
trated. Bowen will be quick to point out that in this
work toward differentiation, some family members may
become worse off for the process. That is, if Mrs.
C., while becoming increasingly independent, begins to
be perceived as threatening by her husband, he might
cause a stress situation in their marriage which could
occasion Michael's symptoms to become exaggerated.
The ultimate goal, of course, is to, "help family
members become systems experts who know the family
system so well that the family could readjust itself
without the help of an outside expert, if an when the
family is stressed again" (Bowen, 1971:168). This
could only become possible if Mrs. C. would ultimately detriangle herself from her dysfunctional marital and family relationships, and allow everyone to
experience the benefits of this freedom.

Naturally, it is hoped that somewhere along the
way Mr. C. will feel the need to be "coached" toward
differentiation himself. If this could happen, then
ultimately, the C. family would be relating on a
healthy, detriangled level of functioning. Hence,
Michael would no longer be required to exhibit pathological seeming behavior and Laura would be free to
act like the child that she is. It is, however, a
long process that requires much hard work, motivation,
and financial resources.

VI. INTEGRATION OF THE THREE APPROACHES

In light of the foregoing, it is clear that there
is a basic theoretical unanimity among the three
theorists surveyeds, including the assumptions that:
1) individual maladaptation is causally related to
family dynamics, and 2) the family is the locus of
treatment. However, as evidenced by the above discussion, techniques or styles of intervention based
on these premises are somewhat disparate. To date we
are aware of no empirical evaluative studies endors-

ing one style above the other, consequently, when selecting a treatment of choice, one must take into consideration the idiosyncratic nature of the family dynamics as well as the idiosyncratic disposition of the therapist.

With this in mind, in attempting to select the ideal treatment of choice for the C. family, we would suspect that each of the three reviewed modes of family intervention would have their own shortcomings. With regard to Satir's interventive style, we feel that, given Mr. C.'s proclivity toward one-dimensional communication, and ostensible denial of the illogical or feeling level of communication, that his resistance would be massive against any change on this level. His style of communication is simply too entrenched in his personality and emotional needs, hence it seems highly improbable that this person would agree to participate in any form of communication exercises. Consequently, unless the Satirian therapist is inordinately skilled at evoking more effective levels of communication from this family, then this approach would appear to be contraindicated.

Bowen's interventive approach, on the other hand, might prove fruitful if: 1) Mrs. C. is willing to invest the time required for this form of family therapy, 2) financial and emotional resources are readily available, and 3) Mrs. C. could place a moratorium on her current marital unhappiness and the immediate family dysfunction so as to pursue the multigenerational insight oriented requirements for Bowen's intervention. However, recognizing that Mrs. C.'s general level of differentiation and ego functioning to be at the lower end of Bowen's scales, it is doubtful that she would be equiped to maintain the rigorous investment required here.

Although there are also shortcomings involved with Minuchin's approach, including the important question as to whether he could, indeed, enlist Mr. C. as a "co-therapist," these authors find his approach to be the treatment of choice with this case. Reasons for this decision would include: 1) the use of the current family system, including symptoms as a fulcrum for change, 2) Minuchin's willingness to appear "foolish" so as to enlist the father in the therapeutic effort, 3) his use of hidden agendas to subtly manipulate (restructure) the family system, 4) his emphasis on problem solving and immediate reduction of "pain" in the family, and 5) his ability to "join" a less than functional family system to act himself as the needed executive function until the parents can actively accept the role themselves.

Family therapy, as a unified theoretical system, is yet to be realized. Movement in this direction will entail intense and long term empirical evaluation. Until that time, however, the authors feel comfortable with the fact of varying, ununified treatment styles, as these allow for an individualized approach to particular family dysfunctions. To this point, there is enough diversity in styles to encompass most family and therapist idiosyncracies.

BIBLIOGRAPHY

Bowen, M.

    1972   "Toward the differentiation of a self in one's own family." In Framo, J. (ed.), Family Interaction: A Dialogue Between Family Researchers and Family Therapists. New York: Springer Press.

    1971   "The use of family theory in clinical practice." In Haley, J. (ed.), Changing Families. New York: Greene and Stratton.

    1976   "Theory and practice of psychotherapy." In Guerin, P. (ed.), Family Therapy, Theory and Practice. New York: Garden Press Inc.

Foley, V.

    1974   An Introduction to Family Therapy. New York: Greene and Stratton.

Guerin, P. (ed.)

    1976   Family Therapy, Theory and Practice. New York: Garden Press Inc.

Minuchin, S.

    1974   Families and Family Therapy. Cambridge Massachusetts: Harvard University Press.

Satir, V.

    1967   Conjoint Family Therapy. Palo Alto, California: Science and Behavior Books.

    1972   Peoplemaking. Palo Alto, California: Science and Behavior Books.

*James Buchholz, 410 N. Dryden, Arlington Heights, Illinois.

**Richard Nyberg, 15 Sheridan, Irvine, California.

CHAPTER 17

SEEKING FAMILY THERAPY: THE PROCESS
OF ASKING FOR HELP

Jane Totman*

I. INTRODUCTION

People purportedly seek out counselors of whatever persuasion because they are faced with a problem
they want help with or they wish to change themselves
and/or at least to explore their options to change.
Many counselors make these assumptions except in some
very obvious situations. It is the purpose of this
chapter to examine the notion that clients or patients
wish help to change and to suggest what other purposes
and motivations might be involved in one or more contacts with a counselor.

II. INTAKES

The first phenomenon worth noting is the failure
rate of first appointments--"intakes"--of most counseling agencies. The nationwide estimate is over 30%.
This event is commonly attributed to various factors:
fear that getting counseling or therapy means the
person is crazy, ambivalent about seeking help, the
refusal of one of the parties involved to cooperate,
a wish to take care of one's own problems, the perceived negative attitudes of the person answering the
agency phone, the resolution or elimination of the
presenting problem, etc. Perhaps it would be useful
to add another dimension--the fact that the person
calling has taken some specific action designed to
add another alternative to his/her repetoire of problem-solving behaviors. It is easy to underestimate
the power of the simple act of a phone call to arrange
a vent to a profssional person whose role it is to
make things better or at least more understandable.
Consider the impact on a marital partner or a recal-
citrant child of the statement, "I've made an appoint-
ment to see a counselor." The entire troublesome
situation may take on new dimensions, behaviors and
attitudes of family members may change, the problem
may be upgraded to crisis status, or downgraded. Even
an individual wrestling with personal dilemmas may,
with one phone call, feel less alone and have a sense

of some one out there who is willing to help--if it becomes really necessary.

III. ONE CONDITION OF PROBATION IS . . .

Many therapists and counselors are cynical about the interest and motivation of those clients who have been ordered by a judge and probation officer to obtain psychological aid or go to jail. Most probationers (parolees or persons on "dimension" programs) will choose counseling over incarceration. This is one obvious group of clients whose purpose in requesting assistance for alleged emotional disorders may be problematic. Interestingly, some of these customers do get involved in the therapeutic endeavor, particularly when other family members are also included. It is frequently the spouse or the children, along with the probation officer, of course, who support a real effort on the part of the offender to be different--meaning mostly less difficult and burdensome to the family and the community. If the law violator is able to go beyond the initial goal and become a positive and contributory member of society, all the more cause for celebration. It is still prudent, however, to wonder about the incentive of the sentenced counselor.

IV. MARITAL COUNSELING

Many couples seek professional help with marriage or living together problems. Everyone tells them to go see a clergyman, lawyer, physician, their parents, or to use newspaper or T.V. advice-givers. Any experienced marriage counselor will tell you that in the majority of cases, appearing in their offices, the ball game is already over. Typically, one of the partners has already made the decision to leave and the remaining member doesn't want him/her to go. Why come in at all if, in fact, in one person's mind the end is at hand and there is no turning back. The reasons are familiar--guilt over leaving a not-so-bad person with whom one has shared part of his/her life (often parenting children together) for another one, internal and external pressure to try to resolve problems by submitting to this one last ministration-- the "I-tried-everything-but-nothing--not even counseling--helped" rationalization, fear that the deserted or about-to-be deserted partner will make good on self-destructive threats which will tend to make one's

356

life very complicated and unpleasant and will spoil
the new relationship, the state has a law that says
reconciliation efforts must be made before a divorce
can be granted, etc. The major purpose, then, for
appearing at the counselors office is not to resolve
or lessen the difficulties of the marital situation so
it can continue in a better, happier fashion--or even
to resign oneself to an unhappy but more palatable
home life. A typical example are Harry and Sophie,
married 20 plus years, who are purportedly seeking
counseling because Sophie wants a "trial separation."
Harry doesn't. When asked why, Sophie, with Harry
present, complains that he has always been mean with
the children (all but one are adults now), he takes
her for granted, he drinks too much, is not very clean
and neat, is careless about his appearance, and she
needs a rest from him after all these years. When
Harry becomes more thoughtful of her and the children,
cuts down on his drinking, and improves his appearance, interestingly, Sophie still wants a separation.
Her family tells her she's crazy. Harry is bewildered
and depressed and wants to stay married. He doesn't
feel life would be much without Sophie. Sophie, of
course, has a boyfriend she would like to get to know
better.

The reasons on the leaver's part are to obtain
the official sanction to depart more or less grace-
fully and in a socially acceptable way, and to leave
the partner behind (also any offspring) in sympathetic and, hopefully, competent hands. The leavee
(left), on the other hand, wishes to enlist the counselor as an ally at the outset in his/her fight to
maintain an unbroken married (or otherwise committed)
state. If the counselor does not come down clearly on
the non-separation side of the issue, it is common for
the leavee client to either question the capability
and morality of the therapist or to switch to another
one. If the leavee finds him or herself without a
companion after a few weeks, he/she may stay with
the counselor because he/she feels lost, scared, depressed, and crazy--and this nonfamily trained person
at least is familiar with the situation and seems to
care. Besides, who wants to try to deal with the
sympathetic and unsympathetic relatives and childrens'
questions and usually disruptive behavior alone?

V. PARENT-CHILD CONFLICT

In contrast to the marital scenario, parents and minor children come to the counselor's office not just because of internal discomfort but because someone else is complaining about the kid's behavior or attitude. These someone elses may include the police, the school, the probation department, neighbors, relatives, or a combination of the above. Parents usually feel their expectations for their children are relatively fair and just and are angry, dismayed, and embarrassed when the kid doesn't do what they're supposed to. Most parents have been sufficiently exposed to mental health doctrine (dogma?) to believe they are to blame, at least in part, for whatever sorry state of affairs exists. Johnnie won't go to school, Julie uses drugs, George is rude, defiant, and impossible to live with, Helen is promiscuous, Billy fights with other kids on the playground, Allen peeped up a little girl's dress, Mary refuses to talk to her teacher or any member of her family, Harold's only friends are hoods, etc.

Parents really do want some relief from whatever the painful script is--but how they want it done is for the therapist to tell them that they are right and the kid is wrong. Then the counselor is supposed to fix up the kid. The son or daughter from his/her perspective would like some affirmation from a powerful adult that his behavior and attitude are acceptable or at least understandable because there is actually nothing very wrong with them or because his inept parents caused him to act that way due to their almost complete incompetence or meanness. The youth then wishes the professional to see the rightness of his ways and then to set his parents straight. In the child's view, these usually should take the forms on the parents' part of increased permissiveness, fewer rules, more freedom, little disapproval, and absolutely no threats of further drastic action.

Again, the counselor may well find the true intention of the call at the office door is not a call for validation by each of the waning factions. Other motives may also be discerned. Some parents want approval to be very angry and to do something awful to their errant son or daughter--like hit them, send them to reform school, farm them out to relatives or strangers, etc. Some parents have given up and want the authorization (formal o.k.) to throw in the towel.

Some kids enjoy talking and being with their counselors in order to underline their ability to get along well with most adults, especially those who do not have characteristics similar to their parents. "You're the problem, Mom and Dad!"

It is an error to assume that these motives for entering family counseling are to be regarded only as therapeutic puzzles to be solved by the counselor. They certainly may be--but they may also be phenomena in and of themselves, serving their own purposes within the family group.

VI. RESEARCH AND IMPLICATIONS

Researchers in outcome studies of individuals, couples, and families who have received professional counseling are sometimes perplexed by the honorable ratings given by "drop-outs" clients or the unfavorable assessments of persons perceived by their therapists as having benefitted from their experience. One possible partial answer might be that the client/patient and the counselor are not really pursuing the same objectives. The next obvious question might be--Is that o.k. or is it bad? Should counselors close their doors to applicants who really don't have problem resolution clearly in mind? Should we be about trying to identify more carefully what is really going on in this special kind of encounter between human beings? Have our research instruments reflected only our own wishful perspective without attending to the other realities of the therapeutic process? Counselors have their set of institutional expectations, behaviors, goals, projected outcomes, etc. for their therapeutic organizations. Our clients may have quite another set--and it may be as utilitarian and meaningful as the professionals think theirs is.

359

B I B L I O G R A P H Y

Allen, George

1977   Understanding Psychotherapy.
            Champaign, Illinois, Research Press.

Cross, James

1979   "Can Casework Be Rational." Points
            & Viewpoints Section, Social Work,
            Vol. 24, No. 3, May, pp. 245-249.

Fischer, Joel

1973   "Is Casework Effective?, A Review."
            Social Work, Vol. 18, No. 1, January,
            pp. 5-20.

1976   The Effectiveness of Social Casework.
            C. C. Thomas.

Reid, William &
Ann Skyne

1969   Brief and Extended Casework. New York:
            Columbia University Press.

Wood, Katherine

1978   "Casework Effectiveness: A New Look
            at the Research Evidence." Social Work,
            Vol. 23, No. 6, November, pp. 437-458.

*Associate Professor of Social Work, Department of
Social Science, California State Polytechnic University, Pomona.

Appendix

Discussion, Debate and Review Questions – Douglas B. Gutknecht
and Barbara L. West

Introduction to Section I

1. Discuss your view of the two positions suggesting that the modern family is either collapsing or merely going through normal changes and transitions.

2. Define marriage and the family. Can we ever create a universal definition? Discuss any problems that arise when trying to develop a universal definition of marriage and the family.

3. List some new or emerging roles in the modern family. How are family roles changing? How do roles influence good family interaction and communication? Can rigid role expectations and behavior actually detract from positive family life (communication, decision making, sexuality, shared parenting, etc)?

4. Why is it important to understand social, cultural and personal values when trying to understand the relationship of family, self and society?

5. Define the key components of any healthy family system (e.g., rules, patterns, values, assumptions, expectations, boundaries, type of feedback mechanisms)?

6. Compare open and closed family systems. How do boundaries relate to either system?

7. Discuss how you would apply a family system perspective to a problem like alcoholism, anorexia, etc.?

8. Compare family systems theory with exchange and conflict theories.

9. Which family management skills are most important in your view?

10. Define family prevention and wellness. Distinguish primary, secondary and teritiary prevention strategies. Why is it important to begin teaching a positive view of healthy family functioning early in life?

11. Compare the various positions for promoting family wellness. Develop your own definitions.

12. Why have we focused so much on family crisis, problems, and difficulties? How can we better educate families about strengths, problem solving strategies and the develoment of positive and healthy life skills?

13. Why does the modern family have to understand the larger political and social context in which it is situated?

Chapter 1. Marriage: The Dream and The Reality

1. What socialization processes do little boys and girls go through which make them susceptible to the idea of marriage as a dream and a reality? How do men's and women's dreams of marriage differ? Is the gap between dreams and reality greater for the woman's marriage and the man's marriage?

2. Beside the fact that a husband in such a marriage needs to learn to give reciprocally and the wife needs to expect, request and demand equality, what about society's view of children, house and chores that makes it a stepdown position rather than a proud profession?

3. If you were the therapist how would you support the wife's feelings without injuring the husband's?

Chapter 2. The Growth Perspective of Interpersonal Relationships: a New Vista

1. Do you agree, with the author that you are an artist of your own creation? Discuss.

2. The author said that, "we need to get away from the concept of exclusively long term relationships". How would that work with families raising children?

3. Have you heard of the human potentiality hypothesis before? If so, where and what are your opinions of it? If not, what is your opinion after reading this chapter?

362

Chapter 3. <u>Individual and Family Well-being Over the Life Course:</u>
<u>Private and Public Dimensions</u>

Introduction:

1. If you were to draw your life course today, which paths
   would you include, noting importance by size of the path;
   the family path could be a bridge to the educational path,
   which leads to a career path or the career path could lead
   to the educational path then permitting entrance to the
   family path. Use colored ink or any materials to draw the
   various dimensions of your life course.

Well-Being Defined:

2. In what ways can family life enhance well-being and in what
   ways can it interfere with an individual member's well-
   being? How can we better reconcile individual and family
   well-being.

3. Reflecting back on a transitional time in your own life,
   which demanded a developmental change (for example,
   starting school for the first time, leaving home to go to
   college, recognizing an unfulfilling career path and
   returning to school, etc.) what factors aided a sense of
   well-being and what made you able to adapt to the changing
   social demands? Did you experience much role conflict and
   strain?

4. Can you support the statement that "without public support,
   any private energy or initiative families may muster will
   soon be drained away and the rhetoric of a private
   sanctuary will become instead a living nightmare"? Give
   reasons for your answer.

5. How are adults able to make social commitments, like "til
   death do us part", when in fact they are in constant
   motion, "as selves in process"?

6. List all those activities, encounters, and interactions
   that give you a flow of energy and those that leave you
   exhausted, unmotivated, procrastinating? Give examples.

7. Define education -- work -- retirement lockstep. Do you
   think that well-being is facilitated by the recognition
   that people are no longer expected to be in a lockstep
   today? Why is it important to overcome a one-dimensional
   life plan and to learn techniques, and strategies for over-

coming stress, overload and role strain? Give examples for your point of view.

8.   Create brainstorm groups of four or five students per group and spend five minutes listing creative ideas for promoting individual well-being. Each person must keep their own list. Now synthesize and combine the best ideas under general headings like leisure, good friendships, (10 minutes). Now brainstorm creative ideas for promoting family well-being (5 minute). Synthesize and combine the best ideas under general headings like communication (15 minutes). Now discuss how you can reconcile problems or contradictions between the two lists (5 minutes). Prepare a group statement addressing the issue of how to promote individual and family well-being. Have each group discuss their list with the entire class (15 minutes). Each student can write an essay due the next class period addressing the difficulties, contradictions and problems of reconciling individual and family goals, behaviors, pursuits, values and happiness, etc. Focus also on both both short-term and long-term goals and values.

Chapter 4.   Education for Choice: Implications of Alternatives in Lifestyles for Family Life Education.

1.   What effect do you think having decided to marry or not marry would have on one as s/he dated? Does deciding to not marry make one predominately aware of flaws, while someone who decided to marry is more prone to be blind to the lover's faults?

2.   What concerns might a step-family have that a traditional nuclear family would not?

3.   Do you think that every couple should enter marriage with a contract stating expectations and promises? What would you include in such a contract?

4.   Why do you think that there has been more of an attitude change in "removing sex-role stereotyping and achieving more sharing of child-rearing and household responsibility" than in actual practice?

5.   Do you think that there are viable alternatives to married couples not being sexually exclusive to one another?

6.   Discuss similarities between heterosexual and homosexual relationships.

364

7. Do you think that everyone, at some time in their life, should live alone? Why?

8. At what age should individuals take a course in family life education?

Chapter 5. Viewing of Love and Sexuality Today and Tomorrow

1. Research and discuss the debate regarding the assertion that sexuality is more social than biological.

2. Explore the proposition that "masturbation is unhealthy".

3. Discuss whether it is necessary to have love with sex. Is it more appropriate for sexual lovers to become friends (platonic love) or is it easier for platonic lovers (friends) to become sexual (erotic) lovers?

4. Why is societies' pre-occupation of romantic love increasing?

5. List the ingredients essential for building mature love.

6. Discuss which of the sexual myths listed in the text are the most detrimental to good sexual relationships.

7. Discuss the following sexual dysfunctions (impotence, premature ejaculation, orgasmic dysfunction). Why are sexual dysfunctions increasing in modern society?

8. Discuss why teenagers make excuses about the dangers of possible pregnancy.

9. Discuss the various contraceptive techniques and their effectiveness.

10. Discuss the pros and cons regarding abortion.

11. Do you believe that sterilization is a viable birth control technique? Discuss.

12. Is sex education the responsibility of the school, the family or both? Discuss.

13. Develop a total sex education program.

Chapter Six. Sex and Gender Roles: Toward Equality

1. Define and discuss the difference between gender and sex roles. Does masculinity and feminity relate to gender identity or sex roles?

2. Research and discuss the latest evidence regarding the relative importance of the two cluster of influences, nature-gender identity versus nurture-sex roles, social environment. What position does your text support on this issue?

3. Discuss the practice of often beginning sex-role typing and socialization from the first encounter with the baby in the delivery room.

4. Is it healthy for full adult development of either sex to make play and leisure activities correspond to sex role stereotypes and expectations? Discuss.

5. Review the following models of sex role development: (1) social-learning; (2) cognitive-development.

6. Describe and discuss Margaret Mead's study of sex roles in three primitive cultures. What are the implications for contemporary socialization practices?

7. Examine the sex role stereotypes presented by Chafetz in her research done in mid 1970s. Do you think these same stereotypes exist today? Are new stereotypes emerging? Which stereotypes for each sex no longer exist in your view.

8. Examine several children's textbooks, adult books, television programs, romance novels, advertisements, commercial films or other entertainment media for current sex role stereotypes. What is causing the stereotypes to change?

9. Discuss how sex role stereotypes and learned sex role behaviors can limit friendship between the opposite or same sex pairs.

10. Discuss androgyny as a lifestyle option. Can men and women reduce sex role stereotypes and behavior without thinking they need to be the same? Is equality confused with sameness in many arguments regarding the need to change our rigid views about sex related limitations or potentials?

11. Discuss the women's liberation movement and its effect upon sex role expectations, actual behavior and the social organization of work and family life.

12. Discuss the need for a more active men's liberation movement. What could such a group hope to accomplish?

Chapter 7. Processes Surrounding the Decision to Remain Permanently Voluntarily Childless.

1. Often it has been stated that couples who choose not to have children are "selfish". Do couples who choose to have children ever have "selfish" motives for having them? Discuss.

2. The author of the article stated that "voluntarily childless couples constitute an estimated 5% of the population". Do you think that, that statistic would increase appreciatively if people who planned not to get married, because they did not want to have children, were included? Also, how would the statistic increase if we included the involuntary childless (i.e., those who want children but are unable to give birth.

3. Do you think society makes motherhood look unrealistically appealing?

4. Do you believe that those couples who choose to be childless are "mavericks"?

5. Do you think that childless couples have a more "glamourous" lifestyle?

6. How has your decision making process developed or changed in deciding to be a parent or not? Did this article cause you to examine your decisions?

7. What other reasons, than stated in the article, do you think some couples would give for remaining voluntarily childless?

Chapter 8. The One-Child Family: A New Life-Style

1. Prior to reading this chapter, what were your thoughts about one-child families?

2. Are you of a one-child family and/or have you know such families? If so, have the experiences been similar to those described?

3. Prior to research work on one-child families, why do you think it was assumed that such families were selfish, that the children were at a disadvantage?

4. Discuss the advantages and disadvantages of one-child families.

Chapter 9.   Fact and Fiction in Modern Divorce: Dimensions and Issues

1. What do divorce statistics actually reveal? Can you give cases that used statistics to prove a point which really could not be derived from the statistics presented.

2. If you were the judge, what grounds for divorce would you consider admissible?

3. Do you feel that custody issues still portray children as possessions?

4. How responsible do you feel our society should be in encouraging divorcing parents to not divorce their children, to respect our children's right to know and spend time with both parents?

5. Discuss motives for concealing one's child from the other biological parent and how society can help to remove these motives which often lead to child stealing.

Chapter 10. Alcohol Abuse and Family Structure

1. Why do you think some children of alcoholics become problem children and troubled adults while others appear to develop normally?

2. The article clearly addressed seven stages wives of male alcoholics go through. Why have we ignored the co-alcoholic spouse for such a long time?

3. What role should society play in protecting children of alcoholics?

4. Do the problems of alcohol abuse and dependency resemble other types of addictions, abuses, and dependencies (like drugs, eating disorders, etc.)? Discuss.

5. Why do we need to treat the problem of alcohol abuse as a problem of the entire family?

Chapter 11. Media and the Family

1. What are the possible positive or negative effects on children of regular viewing adult TV programs?

2. Does television depict our culture or does the viewer try to depict the media?

3. Do you agree with Marc's assessment of how sitcoms have become a dominant force in our society?

4. Do you feel that TV is focusing excessively on some vague middle America by gearing programs to the lowest content level possible? Discuss. Do you feel that the true potential for television lies ahead, why?

5. What factors would you consider in trying to prove the effect of television viewing on academic achievement?

6. Do you think that there is a particular profile of a child who watches a lot of television? How does it differ from a child who watches little television?

7. Do you think there is a correlation between viewing violence and aggresive behavior? Why?

8. Some theorists feel that there are people who purposely drink alcohol so they can act aggressively and blame alcohol consumption. Would this also apply to those who watch violent television programs? Why?

9. Discuss strategies for family media management.

10. If more families took a more active role in media management, would programming change? In what ways?

11. What kind of programs provoke discussion among your family and friends? Have you purposely selected programs to enhance a particular interest or course of study?

12. How can families be encouraged to more actively use the television media?

Chapter 12. Home Computers and the Family

1. The author stated "that males in our society are socialized to be competitive may also explain why the predominate sex of the video arcade player is male". Discuss. What other means can you give?

2. What are some positive and negative considerations for a student who is no longer in a formal classroom environment, receiving education via computer in one's own home?

3. If you own a home computer, how has it affected your household (interaction between _____, siblings, leisure activities, school work, sense of well-being)?

4. Do you think computers can ease some of the pressures caused by the breakdown of the family as the author suggested?

5. What pressures might the computer put on the family to cause problems?

6. Observe families with home computers. Discuss the idea that the greatest change in our lives brought about by computers in rethinking what it means to think, to feel, and to be human.

Chapter 13. The Family and the Firm: A Coevolutionary Perspective

1. Discuss the ways in which a family's purpose, organizational system and culture can effect a family firm.

2. How would you imagine decisions would be made by a firm which is operated by a husband and wife who have:

    a symmetrical marital relationship
    a complementary marital relationship
    a reciprocal marital relationship

Which one would you like to be employed by, why?

3. The chapter pointed out that "For the family involved with a firm, the business may be experienced as a shadowy but none-theless potent third party to their family life". Would that not be true of any profession or important job chosen to support the family? Why?

4. How might the critical family transition periods affect a family run business?

5. What influences can a family firm have on the family's home life?

6. Information and awareness were given as two guidelines to help prevent serious problems. What other guidelines would you offer?

Chapter 14. Work Roles as Stressors in Corporate Families

1. If the hypotheses that "men with middle-level incomes and occupational status may be best able to combine work and family roles whereas those at the lower end have too few economic resources and those at the upper end have diffi-culty performing family roles" is true, which occupations would you recommend to a man who wants to successfully combine work and family? What occupations would you point out as possibly causing conflicts?

2. Why have managerial careers stressed the development of the "head" at the expense of the "heart"?

3. If you were employed by a large corporation to set up pro-grams to ease the strain of transfers for their employees and their families, what would you initiate? Be as specific as possible.

4. Can you make comparisons of the "role of the corporate wife" with another chapter in this book entitled "Marriage: The Dream and The Reality"?

5. What kind of supportive strategies would you consider impor-tant for corporate families? How might organizations interested in employee relations, human resources, and the quality make life develop better strategies and programs for supporting the integration of work and home?

371

Chapter 15.   Dual-Career Family Stress and Coping: A Literature
Review

1. Were you surprised that Richardson found no support for the
"hypothesis that marital stress would be attendant if
working wives had higher occupational prestige than their
husbands"? With wives having to make more career compromises, having more responsibility for the children and household tasks, how can they be known as the "weaker sex", the
"second sex" the sex not even considered equal to man?

2. Should career women have to compromise as much as they do?
How might the art of negotiation with their mates, employers
and significant others be more helpful?

3. One of Poloma's tension management techniques "was that of
compartmentalizing work and family roles as much as
possible". The example given was in leaving work related
problems at work. What about home related problems?
Shouldn't employers offer an avenue to get assistance?

4. Rice was quoted as saying "the guiding principle in therapy
with dual-career couples is to help the partners achieve or
restore a sense of equity in the marital relationship".
What guidelines would you give to help facilitate that with
society a it is? Do we need to change societies expectations about sex roles and work demands along with individual
family member expectations?

Chapter 16. A Family Intervention: Three Perspectives

1. Which therapist - Minuchin, Satir, or Bowen - would you
refer the C. family to? Why?

2. Discuss the strengths and weaknesses of each of the therapeutic approaches.

3. If you were to take from the three approaches to formulate
your own approach, what would you especially adopt and what
would you stay away from?

4. How do you envision the C. family after the therapeutic relationship is ended?

5. Compare: Each approach to the ideas of conflict, systems,
and exchange theory raised in the introduction to Section I.

Chapter 17.   Seeking The Process of Asking for Help

1.   Discuss how a counselor, about to see a client who had a choice of receiving psychological help instead of going to jail, might begin a therapeutic relationship.

2.   The chapter stated that "any experienced marriage counselor will tell you that in the majority of cases, appearing in their offices, the ball game is already over." Discuss what you think about that statement.

3.   Do you believe that parents are to blame for their youngster's misbehavior?

4.   Is the counselor's role to take the side of the right person, be it the parent or the child?